The Art of the Real

Muriel Spark's Novels

Joseph Hynes

Rutherford • Madison • Teaneck
Fairleigh Dickinson University Press
London and Toronto: Associated University Presses

Associated University Presses
440 Forsgate Drive
Cranbury, NJ 08512

Associated University Presses
25 Sicilian Avenue
London WC1A 2QH, England

Associated University Presses
2133 Royal Windsor Drive
Unit 1
Mississauga, Ontario
Canada L5J 1K5

The paper used in this publication meets the requirements
of the American National Standard for Permanence of Paper
for Printed Library Materials Z39.48-1984.

Library of Congress Cataloging-in-Publication Data

Hynes, Joseph, 1927–
    The art of the real.

    Bibliography: p.
    Includes index.
    1. Spark, Muriel—Criticism and interpretation.
I. Title.
PR6037.P29Z69   1988   823'.914   86-46329
ISBN 0–8386–3314–5 (alk. paper)

PRINTED IN THE UNITED STATES OF AMERICA

For Mary, who has had her own questions about reality in these book-years; and for Tom, Mary, and Martin, whose presence has helped with the answers.

Contents

Acknowledgments

This study would never have been conceived had I not become frustrated over the years with the discrepancy between varied bases for the welcome reception usually given to Muriel Spark's novels and my growing conviction that, despite critical enthusiasm, most of the appreciation has tended to miss what seems to me the thematic core of her works. The words chosen as epigraph for my Introduction may seem presumptuous: many others have, after all, paid serious attention to Muriel Spark. Nevertheless, I have experienced the need to spell out at some length what others have variously observed and what I have worked out with my students. Much of what follows originated in graduate classes at the University of Oregon, and I thank my students for their challenges, questions, critical insights, and patience over the years. I am also grateful to the University of Oregon's Office of Research for the Faculty Summer Research Award that assisted me in this project, to Maurice Legris for sharing his ideas on Muriel Spark, and to Patricia Merivale and Mas'ud Zavarzadeh for encouragement when it was needed. Lori Wilkerson, Joann Brady, and Donna Holleran have stoically and kindly (at least in my presence) typed the manuscript. For their professionalism, my thanks. My friends and colleagues Danna Schaeffer and Donald Taylor have labored long and hard to improve the manuscript—indeed Donald Taylor has read some parts as many as three times and has enriched my understanding of Defoe as well. The book would perhaps be better had I listened to my advisers more often. I am grateful to them both, as to Walter Cummins of the Fairleigh Dickinson University Press and Julien Yoseloff, Beth Gianfagna, and Lauren Lepow of the Associated University Presses, all of whom have provided painful and therapeutic reminders of the stylistic differences between me and Muriel Spark. My deepest thanks go to my wife and children, to whom this book is dedicated. Their collective understanding, long-suffering, and sense of humor have lofted and deflated me at appropriate times.

I wish to make further acknowledgments to the following:

To Muriel Spark and to Harold Ober Associates, Inc., of New York, for permission to quote from British, Canadian, and United States editions of Muriel Spark's novels. Specific publishers and dates are provided at the beginning of my Select Bibliography. Beyond my debts to Macmillan and the Bodley Head Press in London, and to Lippincott, Knopf, Viking, Coward, McCann &

Geoghegan, and G. P. Putnam's Sons in New York, I am indebted to Harper and Row, New York, for permission to quote from *The Prime of Miss Jean Brodie.*

To A. P. Watt Ltd, London, and Macmillan, New York, for permission to quote two stanzas from "Nineteen Hundred and Nineteen" and four lines from "The Tower," in *The Collected Poems of W. B. Yeats,* copyright 1928 and 1956 by Michael B. Yeats and Georgie Yeats.

To Faber and Faber, London, and Random House, New York, for permission to quote four lines from "Lay Your Sleeping Head, My Love," and two lines from "In Memory of W. B. Yeats," in W. H. Auden's *Collected Poems.*

The Art of the Real

Introduction

"But he takes my work so seriously," said
Charmian. "Nobody ever wrote of it like that."
                                                —*Memento Mori*

Over the past twenty years, in my efforts to work out the complexities of Muriel
Spark's novels with my students, I have found us tending to slide unconsciously
either into a sort of frolicking, uncritical, appreciative laughter, or into a rather
solemn sobriety. I am convinced that criticism must take into account what in
Spark prompts both of these moods and any moods falling between them, that
criticism must strive to do justice to any and all evoked moods. The present
study attempts this precarious task. Muriel Spark is one of the wittiest and one of
the most serious of writers. My aim is to get at the textual causes of the broad
spectrum of critical responses that her work arouses and to articulate my own
mediating response.

Although Spark began publishing novels in 1957, these have elicited relatively little serious, sustained criticism. Her friend Derek Stanford compiled a
reminiscence (1963) almost before Spark's novel-writing career got under way.
Since then, in Great Britain, Peter Kemp has written a fine introductory
discussion of Spark's frame of mind and her preoccupations. Anyone addicted to
Spark is indebted to Kemp's pioneer performance. Allan Massie has written a
second thematic introduction, somewhat briefer than Kemp's. The best book to
date is Ruth Whittaker's *Faith and Fiction of Muriel Spark*. My work clearly
overlaps hers. The principal difference, apart from the present more detailed and
expansive readings of the novels, is that where Whittaker is inclined to separate
"sacred" from "secular," and otherwise to dichotomize, I find and stress paradoxical merger. Britain has also given us the critical essays of Frank Kermode, David
Lodge, Malcolm Bradbury, and Alan Kennedy. In the United States, on the
other hand, the most durable work has been Karl Malkoff's pamphlet, a section
of Francis Russell Hart's book, and John Updike's *New Yorker* reviews. Much
other criticism has appeared, of course, as the following pages and the Select
Bibliography will make abundantly evident. But I note these particular critics to
stress how few have paid any prolonged heed to the novels, as well as to
acknowledge indebtedness and to intimate something of my different critical
direction.

13

This difference requires brief discussion. The present study is not a survey of all of Muriel Spark's writing or even a biographical-chronological view of her work or her development. Kemp has already provided such a general introduction—a chronological survey to 1974. Nor does my book attempt to work from or to establish particular current theories of literature. Rather, this study is a conceptual reading of Spark's seventeen novels that is designed to enable details of particular texts to make their greatest sense and fullest impact. I believe that such an aim can be achieved when we realize the interplay within the books of Spark's theistic awareness and her artistic techniques.

My premise is that our seemingly contradictory critical responses—say, laughter and shock and reflectiveness—make sense together only when we see what Spark takes to be real and how she makes use of both traditional and unique fictional methods in order to convey her sense of that reality. While I have something to say about each of the seventeen novels, I have adjusted the length and placement of my treatments in accordance with my particular conceptual approach and my sense of how this approach can best be presented and urged. Longer or shorter treatment of a particular text is, therefore, no indication of the value I place on it: sequence and length of discussion simply indicate my judgment of how each text can best make its point and mine. Thus, for example, *Robinson*, which is neither so well known nor so successful as other Spark books, and which is not her first published novel, is treated first because it provides a most useful and convenient means of presenting the basic premises of my book. Similarly, earlier and later books—such as *Memento Mori* and *The Abbess of Crewe*, or *The Comforters* and *Not to Disturb*—are consistently read together in chapters 2 through 4 because my conceptual focus, not the sequence of publication or of Spark's development, is the basis of organization.

So much, in general, for what I have attempted and not attempted. My four chapters may be summarized briefly. In the first chapter, *Robinson* serves to distinguish Spark's view of reality from the conventional notion of realism. While it may seem that no such distinction need be made at this stage of fictional and theoretical evolution, my experience not only in the classroom but among colleagues in residence and in attendance at professional conferences indicates firmly otherwise. The French postmodernist critics may have landed and may have made some inroads into our academies, but readers still expect what *looks* realistic to *be* realistic.

The two sections of the second chapter apply the opening chapter's principles to seven novels: *The Bachelors, The Ballad of Peckham Rye, The Mandelbaum Gate, The Girls of Slender Means, The Prime of Miss Jean Brodie, The Driver's Seat,* and *The Hothouse by the East River.* I have chosen to discuss these books in this order for the purpose of moving from comedy to tragedy and beyond tragedy: the progress is from genre to genre. Moreover, this progress and this grouping are meant to clarify the structures of the seven books and to demonstrate the abiding necessity of their ambivalences. These seven books arranged along this particular generic continuum can show, as analysis of authorial development could not, that comic structure is compatible with increasingly stark attitudes, and also that comic structure is illuminated by contemplation of tragedy and of purgatorial transition.

The third chapter moves from structure to texture—to the extent that one may presume to separate the two for purposes of analyzing and then reuniting them—and to some particularly witty or funny characteristics to be admired within (and of course because of) the ever-serious structures examined earlier. Again, I consider both earlier and later books for the purpose of demonstrating paradoxical sameness abiding with textural variation.

The final chapter concentrates on particular aesthetic ramifications of those authorial habits embodied in the genres, structures, and textures explicated in the first three chapters. By building to this deliberately aesthetic pitch, and by again juxtaposing analyses of early and late works, I hope to achieve a sort of circular epiphany—to establish that the conscious theistic-aesthetic impetus, design, and effect of *The Comforters, The Public Image, Not to Disturb,* and *Loitering with Intent* manifest Spark's imagination from first to last, from surface to depth, in life as in art.

I wish to gain more and better readers for Spark, in the academy and outside. In my view, Spark's books work to change modern mental habits—not merely to upset categories treasured by literary critics. This study will have succeeded if the reader comes to share my conviction that the wonder and pleasure of Spark's fiction reside largely in its luring passive readers into becoming active—indeed, conscious—creators. The economy and force with which Spark accomplishes this metamorphosis make nonsense of the complaint that she ought to be writing longer books with sympathetic characters in them. As always, a reader's job is to find out what kind of book an author writes (a task that I by no means underestimate), and then to enter into *that* kind of book. If we have the initial grace to grant Spark her own vision, her art can radically reshape our own visions. An author can hardly be asked to offer more pleasure or to be more serious.

Trick or Truth? Reality in *Robinson*

Reading Muriel Spark's fiction requires first of all—like the reading of anyone else's work—coming to terms with a version of reality. And grasping this author's version of reality means not *primarily* telephoning her or writing her a letter of inquiry, nor does it mean testing her books against what we have understandably come to regard as *the* standards for fiction; rather, we have to see what demands are placed upon us by the pages she has written. Although this is precisely what we have rightly to do in reading any fiction, Spark gives readers trouble in my opinion because we are so accustomed to look for the kind of book given us as "novel" for two hundred years that we tend, when we see that Spark is up to something else, to accuse her of failing to meet some implicit set of supposedly absolute standards. The standards are, with copious variations, approximately those that we have established for *the* novel as it has made itself felt since at least the time of Defoe. We tend to forget that every work of fiction cooperates with its readers to set out its own criteria for success or failure, regardless of how similar those criteria may be to criteria learned from and assigned to other books. I should therefore like to establish some few general distinctions at the outset.

My experience is that reviewers and readers in general—including students and faculties of literature—look for something called a novel to be written in prose and to do certain things: to specify a social setting; to establish the emotional condition of one or more characters as that condition relates to the social setting; to make readers feel that characters' involvement and development and outcome are convincing and probable, given the environment and the kinds of characters therein; to move us to feel something about characters and setting, by virtue of their interrelationship; to make us infer that the feelings and ideas evoked are worth evoking and best able to be evoked by this particular fiction. We believe, I think, that these ends cannot be gained unless we are given adequate character-background and character-sounding, together with considerably detailed social setting. We then tend to judge a work successful when "I could almost reach out and touch that house" (furniture, clothing, fog, skin, etc.), or when "you wouldn't believe how real that person seemed," or when "it was all so vivid that I didn't want the book to end; those people were my friends," or when "I cried at their getting married" ("I wanted to call him/her up"), or when "anyone is a better human being for reading such a book," or when "it just shows you what kind of world we live in and what it does to people who try to be good." Such clichés suggest that responses to realistic conventions tend to fall into certain patterns, although the patterns are hardly confined to these stereotypical remarks.

I am not attacking realistic fiction or the kinds of responses it properly triggers. But such fiction and the traditional responses to it are only *one* convention included in the range of things fictional, and fictions can be read only when we know what conventions they do and do not fit, despite their individual uniqueness. Thus, for example, *Robinson Crusoe* and *The Rise of Silas Lapham*, however different, may (must) be read as members of the same realistic fictional tradition. Muriel Spark's *Robinson*, on the other hand, besides being itself, both depends upon our conditioning within the realistic tradition and compels us to make an understanding of that tradition the basis for our perception of how the book departs from the tradition's ground rules. This distinction is elementary but nonetheless fatally ignored explicitly or implicitly by numerous serious readers. And it can lead us to other basic truths that are routinely and unaccountably ignored.

This may be the place to indicate that I am *not* suggesting that all readers look for fiction to be realistic in the nineteenth-century sense to which I here refer. On the contrary, it is obvious that our world is filled with such deliberately nonrealistic fiction as fantasy, science fiction, space fiction, supermarket romance, the *nouveau roman*, and any amount of so-called postmodernist experimentation. At the same time, however, critical commentary shows that many readers like or dislike Spark's novels while missing what she means to do—and that the basis for confusion may well be her *seeming* to promise orthodox realism without delivering what we have come to expect of realistic writers.

For one thing, the fictional convention of realism is commonly confused with reality. By reality I mean absolutely anything and everything that can objectively and/or subjectively be thought or known or imagined to exist, whether past, present, or future, in the mind or outside the mind. Thus we speak of the real (past) existence of Napoleon outside anyone's mind as well as within; we may speak of the real potentiality of someone's giving birth to twins; we may speak of the real economic depression or of a real hallucination or dream or fantasy. Reality is infinite, whatever one's share of that infinitude may be. The real is not temporally or spatially limited, although we tend—necessarily and inevitably— to impose temporal and spatial limitations upon it. Whatever can be not only seen, felt, heard, smelled, or tasted, but also written, said, imagined, known, supposed, dreamed, thought, believed, remembered, fantasized, or desired, must—in my use of the term reality (the real; what is or exists)—be said to be real to at least one capacity of at least one person. No consensus is required; one person's sanity (view of the real) may well be reported as insanity, but the report is a measure of the reporters' limits rather than of reality's scope. Thus, reality is simply all: whatever has been, is, will be, could be; all actual or potential *experiences* of the foregoing; all efforts to *externalize* or concretize or convey or express such actual or potential experiences—all such are included (as how not?) in this term that by definition cannot exclude anything.

On the other hand, realism—interchangeable with literary realism for present purposes only—means in my usage a set of presuppositions, so traditional as hardly to be noticed as a particular set of prejudices, according to which author and reader tacitly agree that what count as real are certain combinations of sensory, mental, social, and ethical impressions or reactions. Author and reader tacitly agree that the writing presents a real or true notion when the reader comes to respond in ways suggested by the quoted clichés. A book is regarded as at least partly successful if readers believe that characters like these are vivid or familiar enough to be instinctively spoken of as persons; if the social milieu and the descriptions of places, garb, shapes, textures, shades, and aura are careful enough to be thought actual; and if the characters' predicaments, developments, reactions, and outcomes are judged to be convincingly possible—even when, in fact, not precisely tallying with what the reader has experienced. Readers implicitly ask and answer certain kinds of questions. "Do you believe in these characters?" "Do you care about these people (characters and people here considered interchangeable)?" "Are you moved?" "In what ways?" "Are you convinced by the society and the social truth of the book?" "What do you think of a world in which such people can come to such ends, whether through force or by choice?" "Is the particular milieu responsible or have we here a comment on the human condition?" "Does morality here become religious?" Thus the emphasis is on an understanding between author and reader that realism means whatever "most people" would accept as the way settings look and systems function, the way people interact when depicted as of certain temperament and training and when they are placed in situations with people trained and disposed in certain other ways. When we are convinced and accordingly moved, we judge the book successful; when we are unconvinced and thus unmoved, or when we resist being moved as we suppose we are intended to be moved, we judge the book to be other than successful. The test seems to be whether the author has given us what "most people know" to be the "real world of real people." Thus, while my idea of reality is all-encompassing and necessarily requires no agreement—in fact precludes agreement so long as no two of us perceive alike—my view of realism is of a single, very well established convention that is rooted in the implicit need for agreement between author and reader. This taking realism for reality, while it constitutes a tribute to the powerful influence of the realistic tradition, accounts for much confusion and many missed signals; for hilarious, infuriating, frustrating, pathetic misreadings.

A related problem arises from the use of the word *fiction*. Here again a distinction may be useful. Confusion arises because people often assign a sort of second-class status to the word *fiction*, taking for granted that the word is opposed to "fact" or "truth" or, again, "reality." Thus many have said that they have no time for fiction and have little enough time for the real world of grown-ups where mature and responsible people must confront the problems of earning a living, raising a family, meeting a payroll, coping with foreign policy, exposing corruption in high places, and so on. Fiction for such persons is unserious stuff reserved for relaxation and escape from the problems of the "real world." Oddly enough, these critics of "escapism" often hold to the convention of fictional realism. Such readers embody a contradiction between the views that the best fiction is true to life and that fiction is time out from life. (Here I pass over those who elect to read junk because they *want* to escape from a hard life. I wonder only about those who want things both ways.)

My view, on the other hand, like that of current metafictionists, is that fiction may be thought of as anything made out of a desire to convey experience. In such a view, the facts of experience cannot be duplicated or literally rendered, and anything said, filmed, painted, written, sculpted, or otherwise rendered (by conscious artistry or otherwise) is therefore necessarily a fiction, a "thing made" to effect the illusion of an inevitably personal and irrecoverable experience. Inner cannot become outer, and so everyone "makes things"—everyone fictionizes—in the effort to externalize experience. In this reading, clearly "illusion" is not a dirty word or some sort of second-class human phenomenon, nor is it something we can or should do without because we prefer truth or reality. To be human is to live other than alone. To be several or social is to have to communicate, to get out what we have experienced. To get things out is to have to make. To make is to fictionize, and that in turn means to create illusions. If we're human we "make" illusions.[1]

In recapitulation, then, two mistakes in reading are unfortunately frequent. Some readers denigrate fiction as if they were somehow above committing it. Some, whether or not they think poorly of the fictive, believe prose fiction, realistic fiction, legitimate fiction, serious fiction, and good fiction to be synonymous terms. It follows from such assumptions that fiction which accords with realistic conventions but finally departs from realism is likely to encounter incomprehension. The instinctively applied rules of the realistic game will not help us understand and evaluate pseudorealists.[2]

To come back to particular cases, let us clarify generalities by looking at the instances, mentioned earlier, of two realistic books and one not so realistic. *Robinson Crusoe* and *The Rise of Silas Lapham* plainly belong to the realistic tradition for a number of reasons. They are concerned with making the psychological development of their characters look like something we can accept as credibly allied to our own motives and the behavior in an acquisitive, entrepreneurial society. Also, the books go into very great detail to establish solid-seeming settings—whether city or island, office or cave—so that we will more readily lend belief to what goes on in such places and to the characters whom we suppose solidly occupying such sites. It is indeed crucial to the enterprises of Defoe and Howells that we be induced to think of places, clothing, tools, money, food, furniture, and all other trappings of what we take as life—to think of these as so solidly *there* that we minimize, ignore, or even fail to notice the question of probability. Are Silas's rise and demise too gradual or too fast or too manipulated from outside the illusory terms established by the novel? Is it altogether probable for sole survivor Crusoe and a warehouse of supplies to be washed ashore together? Similarly, it is part of the realist's procedure to make us think and talk of people and persons rather than of characters. Plot, character, setting, progress, outcome, theme, are designed to make us think this illusion no illusion at all, but "the real thing," "true to life." And all of this is, again, perfectly proper—up to the point where we think it the only fiction possible.

On the other hand we must think of a fiction like Spark's *Robinson* quite differently—and properly, not mistakenly or weakly so. Very likely *Robinson* would be impossible without *Crusoe* as ancestor. I mean this not only in the sense that *Robinson Crusoe* is the archetypal British representative of realistic novels, but also in the sense that a familiarity (which is likely) with this famous fictional character and his memorable career will compel us to play off Spark's fiction against Defoe's. Doubtless, Spark would communicate even with some who had not heard of the earlier novel; but that so many will have an idea of what to think of Defoe's book gives Spark the kind of advantage accessible to Tom Stoppard, whose *Rosencrantz and Guildenstern Are Dead* is virtually assured of an audience with some knowledge of *Hamlet*. Indeed, Spark derives much of her effect from forcing us to dredge up, on the one hand, all the realistic props, framework, usual ways of regarding and responding to characters in their socio-moral milieu (i.e., all the ingredients opposed to science fiction, Harlequin Romance, futuristic allegory, etc.), and then to realize, on the other hand, that we must integrate all of *that* reader's furniture with material in unique ways quite foreign to realism. We have to figure what the foreign element is, how to reconcile it with the familiarly realistic, and what effects are achieved by putting together apparently separate styles. Let us first look at some similarities that induce us to align the two books.

Defoe and Spark both write first-person narratives. Defoe's Crusoe survives shipwreck; Spark's January Marlow survives an airplane crash. In each case what we read is a postrescue narrative derived from a journal kept while the writer awaited rescue from isolation and return to British society; and in each case that narrative includes patches of the journal from which the eventual narrative (the autobiographical fiction given us as novel) has been selected and shaped. Each narrator (Crusoe in his Caribbean kingdom and January on the Atlantic island called, after its resident-owner, Robinson) shows us in the first person much about himself or herself—and inevitably much about the world from which he or she has come. *That* becomes *this*; past seems to be present. For, as might be expected (cf. *Lord Jim, Heart of Darkness, Pincher Martin, Lord of the Flies, The*

Admirable Crichton, Gulliver's Travels, Swept Away, etc.), each of these narratives is a coming to terms, after the fact, with what that stranded status signified to the narrator and with what isolation taught that narrator about the traditional problems of self and society, the one and the many. Each author has given us a central figure who needed to get away to comparative solitude and a radically un-British milieu in order to learn who she or he is. Thus the similarities of hardship and remoteness, the need to learn how to manage on a fairly primitive level, and so on—all such bases of comparison may be interesting on a superficial level. But interest picks up and the contrast begins to generate significance when we see not so much what Spark borrowed from Defoe and other authors who have stranded characters, but what kinds of imagination the characters manifest. What they do *not* learn about themselves and the world characterizes them as fully as does that which they *have* learned. By finding out who these first-person protagonists are and how each of them defines the relationship with others (society, the cosmos), we also find out what each of them takes to be *real.* And to find out what is real to a first-person narrator is to confront what each book presents as reality.

Let us begin with the older book.[3] Crusoe is writing an autobiography, chronologically arranged, late in his career, and featuring at its core his renowned twenty-eight-year stay on a Caribbean island. More specifically, in the Modern Library edition, the first fifty pages are given to the old survivor's account of some preliminary bouts with adversity in his youth, the next two hundred and fifty to his adventures on the island, and the final forty to his returning, resettling, and writing his autobiography in the present. Clearly, the bulk of his life and of his writing energy is given to making something of his singular isolated situation. What has been variously noted for two hundred and sixty years is that all his endeavors circle back to exemplify what his father told him in his childhood (virtually the only familial heritage in a lifetime of solitariness): to avoid griefs of high station and low, one should strive for the middle or upper-middle. Defoe has arranged for Crusoe to have only limited chances for viable aspirations to worldly lavishness, so that compared to the orphaned, penurious misery of most of his brief prestranded existence, almost anything is an improvement, an advancing to some relatively middle station.

When we have seen that extremes are ruled out for Crusoe by birth, economic class, and acts of God, we learn that his survival is to be a struggle between a minimal wretched existence and relative comfort, an advertisement for what we are implicitly asked to think the middle way, the fairly comfortable way. That middle way amounts to the illusion of testing eighteenth-century British imperialistic-mercantile values—an illusion beneath which we can see that the lot is simply accepted not only unquestioningly, but enthusiastically. In both journal and major narrative (that is, in both past and present) Crusoe asks himself questions about his proper relationship to Friday in particular, but also to the other natives of the islands and to the European sailors encountered on his island

and elsewhere, as well as to Providence—and time after time his questioning turns out to be comfortable for him and to show us that his seeming solitude in no way deprives him of support from values of the British Empire surrounding and forming him. For example, he simply accepts Friday's loyal, undying servility and instinctively takes charge of their relationship. And although he initially shuns killing any of the native clan opposed to Friday's (since he feels their wars to be their own national affair and since, monstrously benighted though they are, they have done him no harm), he soon changes his mind. He sees that consistency in the situation demands that he do what he thinks proper for others to do (he *is* their leader, after all), but that he ought to leave the really dirty slaughtering and mopping up to others (black and white, but not British). Or again, the accident of his salvaging a Bible occasions his *sortes Virgilianae* experiments with Scripture, all of which reinforce his ideas and precede successes of various kinds—with the result that he instinctively rejects what he supposes to be Catholicism's hierarchically arranged superstitions and embraces his native Puritan individualism. This scriptural support for his pragmatic successes contributes to his return home (not to Catholic Portugal) as an archetypal Puritan, a British merchant of considerable means. If in fact he had had other glands and a heterosexual society in which to operate he might have been another Moll Flanders. The point, however, is that Robinson Crusoe turns out to have left home only to show us that his values and his island domain are emblems of omnipresent empire: white (in this instance, Protestant) capitalism justifying its exploits by accepting responsibility for enlightening and enriching the undercultivated. Moreover, following his dark night of the soul and his affecting embrace of Christianity, his difficulties are principally those of raw survival. Assuredly he suffers fear and trembling, but when he does in fact survive, his conclusion—grateful indeed—is that Providence approves. As the sun sets on the life he writes for us, perhaps the most prominent fact of his character is not that he embodies precisely what his father advised him to become (he *is* his father), but that he questions his achievement no more than he questioned his striving. And this assurance is the measure of his moral imagination.

Crusoe is remembered, to be sure, for ingenuity. For instance, even when he has no training in particular modes of husbandry or carpentry, he nonetheless knows how to go about teaching himself the rudiments of these and other skills. He then sets about schooling himself with all the aplomb demonstrated in his later assumption of command over all others in his neighborhood: he is equally confident in his approach to things and to people. It is of course no mean trick to manage raw survival and simultaneously to learn several trades and the art of governance. But this trick is also one that he pulls off because, luckily, he has certain advantages unavailable to many a shipwrecked man and, more importantly for present purposes, because neither he nor anyone else in the book ever has occasion to examine the values on which he instinctively models his little empire.

None of this emphasis on Crusoe's limited human horizon is intended to slight him, his virtues, or his creator. The point is only to make plain that Defoe's brand of literary realism is confined in the main to (1) the believable illusion of tangible food, seed, clothing, dry goods, weapons and shot, candles and Bible, tools, seasonal temperatures, etc., and (2) the illusorily recognizable, readily unexamined social, religious, moral, economic, and political values of Defoe's eighteenth century (rather than of Crusoe's seventeenth century). These are such as show that, despite the genuineness of his religious conversion, Crusoe is interesting on the level of physical adventure and the application of given values to his personal situation. Crusoe is a self-made engineer or technologist; he is not a thinker or one who questions received ideas. Accordingly, the book's view of the *real*, of *reality*, comes through in one character's outlasting adversity to return to a home that he left only in the most literal physical sense. He goes away to make himself into one of "them." We learn how he became religiously and economically like the rest rather than what he found out about them or himself by asking questions arising because of distance from "them." The irony perennially persists: Defoe's mythmaking genius unobtrusively lays bare the materialistic roots of modern Western civilization through Crusoe's providential grasp of craft and technique.

Muriel Spark's January Marlow is similar, but very different. In *Robinson* (1958),[4] aside from the superficial difference that January is one woman with three men and a boy, whereas Crusoe, when not alone, is essentially the male master of a male servant, we note that Robinson, like Prospero and unlike Crusoe, positively relishes privacy and has bought this remote Atlantic island (amusingly resupplied at intervals with canned goods) precisely to avoid contact with the human race (always excepting the boy, Miguel, who, like Miranda but unlike Friday and Caliban, must soon be schooled in his guardian's history). Moreover, January's first name signifies one of her prominent characteristics— the ability to look in more than one direction: to see double, as it were. Her last name inevitably evokes Conrad's narrator, always seeking and always learning that the need to seek is for the imaginative person as inevitable as the failure to find. This is not of course to suggest that January is identical with Marlow of *Heart of Darkness* or *Lord Jim*, but only to intimate, as Spark does, that her character, like Conrad's, sees complexities, brick walls, unresolvable mysteries. Moreover, although January spends only three months (in 1954) on Robinson, her subsequent narrative, with its journal patches and its filling in of her preisland past, provides all the evidence we need of the value of her experience and of changes arising therefrom, just as Crusoe's narrative convinces us that twenty-eight years or three weeks or any other amount of time would still serve only to reinforce the basically changeless character of the narrator.[5] We learn how he remains intrinsically unchanged by half a lifetime, and we learn how isolation and the following effort of narration compel her to face herself with insight and to appreciate more profoundly the risky freedom attendant upon the realization of human fallibility and myopia.

Oxymoronic coexistence of dual vision and myopia is indeed strikingly characteristic of January's narrative, *Robinson*. Spark has set up the island situation so that her narrator, a widowed mother of an adolescent son, is confronted with two men who occasion her making and unmaking comparisons between them and her two brothers-in-law; with a young boy who looks like her son, Brian; and with the title-figure—who is, among other things, also a single parent. Robinson contrasts with January in many ways and also causes her to think of parallels with her brothers-in-law. Additionally, Robinson summons up, in his similarities to Crusoe and his opposition to January, a psychological set that enables Spark to show something indirectly about ways of being Catholic (amidst ways of being islanded). In fact, where Defoe's Crusoe constructs a replica of home abroad, Spark's January, on this man-shaped island, discovers a habit of seeing that neither here nor there is anyone ever anything *but* an island, *and* that both here and there one's isolation is social. Crusoe is an excellent example of the able-seaman, no-nonsense type that did at least as much as Etonian fields to sustain the empire. He is commendably businesslike, lacking in perspective on himself, certainly sincere, thoroughly humorless. January is serious enough, humorous, bitchy, vain, compassionate and selfish, petty and thoughtful, accustomed to consider complexities actual and potential. She has the kind of moral imagination the lack of which is Crusoe's strength—so her imagination opens her to risks unknown to Crusoe.

Her narrative bears out her habit of seeing more than singly and of following up the significance of so seeing. Almost as soon as she recovers from the airplane crash that only she, Tom Wells, and Jimmie Waterford survive, she is given a notebook by their host and rescuer, Miles Mary Robinson, and advised to keep a journal, taking exceptional care to stick rigorously to "facts." At once the reader, like January, is alerted to an implied contrast, and from the beginning of her journal-writing she distinguishes between "fact" and conjecture or supposition—and continues to do so as she writes her narrative for us. Thus, on the surface of both journal and narrative, she would appear to be of a piece with Crusoe: solid, opposed to make-believe, dedicated to getting things straight. And indeed she is so dedicated. Her narrative fully substantiates her genuine effort to honor the wisdom of Robinson's advice (even as Crusoe diligently follows his father's advice). At the same time, however, the reader watches signs of her awareness that among the most important facts is mystery—undeniably real events, occurrences, experiences, none of which can be explained or understood.

A minor case in point is, for example, her periodic noting of likenesses between Jimmie or Tom or Robinson, on the one hand, and Ian Brodie or Curly

Lonsdale (husbands respectively of her older and younger sisters, Agnes and Julia), on the other hand. Her narrative records her journal's citing such a similarity at a particular moment and its citing another and seemingly contradictory similarity, or even a retraction, at another moment. The reader infers that a common fact of anyone's real experience is that of impressionistic insight. That it all may dissolve the next day does not undercut the point's truth. The impressionistic flash was a fact of the journal-writer's moment and may become once again a fact of the reader's moment, whether that reader be the author-narrator or the audience represented by us. Where Defoe arranges matters so that Crusoe will be enabled to work them out according to his lights, Spark arranges things so that January's working them out or at any rate facing them must always lead her to an impasse of unknowability so vast and commonplace as to be manageable just *because* it is the first and last, the most prominent and obvious, and thus the most natural and normal fact of life.

This being the case for the two books, what we predictably find in Defoe's book is a sincerely convinced protagonist-narrator whose view of isolation remains *psychologically* unchanged for a lifetime despite that religious change called conversion: he is isolated when cut off from God and other people, rescued from isolation when restored to God and others, especially to other British people. Spark, on the contrary, shows such a notion to be untenable, given a certain quality of imagination. *Robinson* testifies to the meaning and validity of Robinson's slogan, *Nunquam minus solus quam cum solus:* never less alone than when alone. These words are funny as applied to Robinson's impatient sense of his visitors' extended intrusion into his privacy, but hardly funny in their ironic reference to human inclusion in all that is. In other words, this narrative starts where Crusoe's begins and ends, and it then builds upon paradox in such a way as to demonstrate the meaning and truth of Robinson's slogan. Hence, again, the usefulness of a Janus-like narrator.

For instance, January understands the difference between Catholicism on the one hand and any given Catholic's express ideas and practice of it; yet she loses her head and this distinction in facing Robinson's attitude toward the place of, say, Mary and the rosary in Catholicism. She can be appalled to the point of violating charity, given Robinson's superstitious anti-Marianism—but she records with cool objectivity her own Catholic belief on the one hand and her pagan yearning toward the moon on the other. (These two religious pulls are differently portrayed in *The Takeover.*) Looking one way, again, she knows, as we and Crusoe know, that rational existence requires hypotheses; looking (eventually) the other way, she is reminded of the obvious truth that it is easy and often disastrously mistaken or immoral to act as if hypotheses were facts. One *must* suppose in order to work things out rationally, but suppositions may very well turn out to be explicably or inexplicably thwarted. Again, January's hasty fear and wishful thinking lead her to accuse Tom Wells of murdering Robinson (she has built a journal-kept case for that hypothesis because she wants to believe

this explanation of Robinson's disappearance and because she finds it convenient
to support her quite credible dislike for Tom Wells). But her narrative subsequently shows Robinson to be alive and thus validates Jimmie Waterford's
consistent refusal to accuse anyone of a "murder" that has not been shown to be a
fact. Moreover, as January inevitably notes parallels and analogues between
"larger" and "smaller" worlds, she writes that she has much in common with
Robinson in that she too needs others in some sense, but wants them on her own
terms. All this, of course, she says *after* the facts of disappearance, hypothesis,
reappearance, and her return to England. Like any first-person narrator, however, she sets it all out early (pp. 39–40) to create the illusion that reading-time
is happening-time; that what happened long enough ago to have been set down
in the journal for narrative re-creation in the fiction-making present is something as new and fresh to the narrator as to the reader.

The disappearance of Robinson occasions in little the essential Defoe-Spark
contrast with which I am dealing. When Robinson turns up missing, January
becomes Sherlock Holmes. She follows blood trails, examines landscape, seals
up the gunroom, checks Robinson's desk for clues, goes through various per-
mutations in her journal asking herself how she might reasonably expect this or
that person (including herself) to act if one or a pair were involved in murdering
Robinson, and otherwise behaves—like Crusoe in discovering a footprint or a
dying campfire—as if effects of this kind must be traceable to causes of that kind.
Crusoe is right, given his book. January is wrong, not for proceeding rationally
and deductively, but because she is the central imaginative character of Spark's
very different kind of fiction, wherein the humanly explicable and inexplicable
must be balanced. Such balancing is this kind of book's norm. Spark regularly
insists that one's best hypotheses may or may not be right, regardless of one's
intelligence or of one's need to form hypotheses in order even to fail reasonably.
Moreover, outcomes have a way of standing inexplicably alone or of being
explainable on grounds other than those one had supposed, and thus of leaving
one short of any leverage for contending that one had figured things out.[6]

What January's experiences come to, as she remembers and narratively fash-
ions them for us, is the paradoxical play among several *facts*. Effects are by
definition caused. Humans (not only Crusoe) are happily equipped to seek out
causes. Depending upon the fiction that one imaginatively stars in and thus
attempts to reproduce, by first-person illusion, for others, one will be more
restricted or less restricted in one's conviction that one will find those causes. As
a corollary, it would seem to follow that Crusoe's character is inherently protected from a certain kind of disillusionment: since he does not ask beyond the
level of what he regards as the satisfactorily answered, he can suffer losses of some
sorts, yes, but he is constitutionally incapable of, say, spiritual despair. Food,
clothing, and shelter, together with pragmatic imperial principles providentially
supported, give him reason to live. Beyond the tangible he is virtually restricted
to reminding himself reasonably and regularly that Providence is doing right by

him. And since he has all he seems to need, he finds this confidence readily
borne out. Defoe has created Crusoe incapable of making skeptical—potentially
cynical—moral-economic observations with respect to his own psychology, or of
seeing any trouble in reconciling causes or reasons on the literarily realistic level
with their counterparts on the tragically or the comically metaphysical level. On
the other hand, when you know both that you have to keep trying to know *and*
that often you cannot know, you can simultaneously decline pursuit of the
unknowable and settle for the limited results of your own best nonpresumptuous
seeking. This psychology describes of course January's conscious limits and her
temptations to exceed them.

Like Conrad's Marlow, January is called upon to find things out. Sometimes
she does so with such success that she forgets her limitations and substitutes the
label "fact" for the label "hypothesis." For example, in the beginning of her stay,
her journal, and her narrative, she several times turns out, Crusoe-like, to track
intelligently and to have been on the right trail. Because she assumes that she is
right, however, she begins to think well of her skill as a detective, and to behave
as if all mystery were to be solved by ratiocination. And here is the source of her
trouble: on the one hand she acts as if her best thinking were guaranteed to
discover answers; on the other hand she knows perfectly well both the value of
analogies and parallel-drawing, and the danger of basing arguments upon them.

As I have said, her impressions of her various acquaintances must not be
extended to imply that because this manner looks like that one, two persons are
substantially alike. In fact the isolated manner of any *one* character is no
evidence of what he or she is like. We can see, in Tom Wells's assuring January
that of course Robinson and Jimmie are homosexuals, the potential for characterizing these two; but to her credit January both weighs this as a plausible
reading of Robinson and refuses to type Robinson without some real evidence.
In fact we never know the truth of Robinson's or Jimmie's sexuality, whereas Tom
Wells's circling about January casts doubt on his motives for trying to make her
think the other men homosexual. Again, given her Catholicism, she quite
consistently rejects Robinson's anti-Marianism and his wish to keep January's
rosary from Miguel, because according to her lights these fears are signs of
superstition in Robinson, ex-Catholic, ex-seminarian. She realizes at the same
time, however, that Robinson looks upon the veneration of Mary and the use of
the rosary as themselves superstitious, and that she and Robinson can talk with
some little understanding because their beliefs are in a sense mirror opposites.
Tom Wells's presence in the book, indeed, serves to contrast familiar belief in the
efficacy of charms, of "luck," to the narrating character's belief that luck is
nonexistent; that our not knowing how and why things occur affects not a bit
their being caused. There's a reason, necessarily, in January's Christian view; but
that reason is no more the tangible rosary or the statue of Mary than it is the
lucky charms or horoscopes in Wells's salvage. Nor is there basis for thinking we
will find out reasons. She sees this and remains a coolly orthodox Catholic.

Wells either sees nothing at all except profit in selling "luck" or else believes exclusively in his pagan charms. Robinson rejects both sides of the debate and tries to keep himself and Miguel from being involved.

So long as January adheres to Crusoe's practice and to Robinson's advice—so long as she sticks to the demonstrable, provable—she is quite successful. But of course the narrative is designed to show us one who does not persist in her adherence to this sort of "fact." Robinson says, "Man proposes and God disposes." January accepts this adage and still loses control—out of fear and a bit of pride in her ability to reason things out—when Robinson vanishes.

At the disappearance, January's narrative tells us, she felt a kind of anguish of rationality: "I could not put out of my mind the blood. . . . I had the rare and distressing experience of becoming objectively conscious of my rational mind in action, separate from all others, as one might see the open workings of a clock. This only happens to me when faced with a group of facts which hurt my reasoning powers—as one becomes highly conscious of a limb when it is damaged" (p. 106). Her trouble is that since one element of her situation has changed everything else comes to look different as well. She even increases her suspicion of Jimmie because he feels sorrow and a failure of nerve rather than her need to accuse someone of murder.

Interestingly, she tells us in her narrative that she came to think of Robinson, his career, and his supposed fate in genuinely mythic terms: "In thinking of Robinson, I had to perform an act of imaginative distortion in that I could not think of him as a part of the present tense, a human creature who has been born into a particular age and at a particular point of developed doctrine—I vaguely thought of him as having no proper station in life like the rest of us. . . . he took on the heroic character of a pagan pre-Christian victim of expiation" (p. 132). This tendency to mythologize (a tendency later stressed often, as in *The Public Image*, *The Abbess of Crewe*, *The Takeover*, *The Only Problem*) is fed by her recollection of Robinson's having several times told the survivors, concerning the island, "The history is obscure." Thus everything she does between Robinson's disappearance and return is an attempt to see him either mythically, as tied universally to pagan gods, or historically, by way of his library and other effects among the recoverable, detectable signs surrounding his absence. To make either history or myth can be truth-directed fictionizing, of course; and January's is this kind (whereas Tom Wells's "story" given to a Sunday paper after their rescue is fiction-making as lie). As she writes, January is conscious of what she was doing at the time. Clearly, she is like Crusoe in having to work things out for herself much of the time—and unlike Crusoe in seeing, imagining, thinking of a great many possible connections to wonder about. The reason for this difference, again, is that his belief in Providence admirably conforms to his imperial ventures, whereas her religious belief obviously includes Providence but accentuates rather than allays her awareness of complexities that her best efforts are unable to meld.[7]

And indeed, while it is perfectly reasonable in retrospect for Robinson later to say, of several frightening or sordid occurrences during his absence, that "it was only to be expected," we who know about January's efforts to stick to the facts, and about her reasons for thinking Robinson cruel to leave his guests to snap at one another, observe the difference between the perpetrator of the disappearance and the ones suffering its consequences. Robinson seems to be playing God to January's Job, a choice of role-playing that a believer—even more than an unbeliever or a doubter—is not likely to let him get away with. It is (for a believer) one thing for the Creator of the universe to have a master reason for events' occurring as and when we temporal creatures choose for them to occur; it is quite another for humans to assume something like the same divine prerogatives. It is fine to be able to quote this or that Christian saying from one's reference library of Church Fathers and Christian mystics, but absurd to do so as if from on high. That man proposes and God disposes means that no human has any business crossing the line between the two clauses; and January thinks Robinson ought to be conscious of this distinction and to realize that she would be aware of it.

In any case, because of the range of January's imagination, she is seemingly inconsistent or self-contradictory, and of course her narrative shows her ignoring her own apparent good advice, wavering between vindictiveness and small-mindedness on the one hand and tolerance and charity on the other. The reader cannot fully pin her down. Her narrative, in turn, derived from her own attempt to figure herself out, in the journal and later, shows her conscious of an inability to achieve this. But the narrative also shows (1) the impossibility of ever figuring out oneself or anyone else, and (2) the perfect rightness of accepting this impossibility while reconciling it with the fullest intellectual and imaginative curiosity. Herein lies perhaps the key distinction between Crusoe and January: because he thinks, unquestioningly, in such a way that (1) above would make no sense if brought to his attention, it must follow that (2) above could not occur to him. She, on the contrary, gives us a thorough awareness of how mistaken is anyone's assumption that thinking or wishing will make it so (or will make it to have been so). We are therefore convinced of the usualness of passing through whole periods of time and experience acutely conscious of paying attention and thinking hard, and then of waking to find that whatever happened it must have been other than we had supposed. In January's case the awareness has a Christian dimension psychologically larger than Crusoe's awareness of Providence. Thus she says, to conclude her narrative, that "all things are possible" (p. 176), as Christ said (Matthew 19:26). But even without the Christian emphasis, the book addresses itself to anyone whose imagination can take (can help to make) its point. By lumping together, for instance, such possible dangers as fire, murder, traffic accident, and mortal sin (p. 39), the narrator suggests her kind of imagination—her version of what is real. And this is more than a religious matter.[8]

Early on, for example, making a distinction between ways of thinking about *place*, she remarks that she and her sisters lived in Chelsea, Chiswick, and Wimbledon. "We soon found the only common ground between us [to be] our childhood" (p. 16). At book's end, she reinforces this notion upon reading that the physical island is sinking. "In a sense I had already come to think of the island as a place of the mind."

> It is now, indeed, an apocryphal island. It may be a trick of the mind to sink one's past fear and exasperation in the waters of memory; it may be a truth of the mind.
> From time to time since I read this news I have pictured Robinson wearily moving his possessions on to some boat bound for some other isolation. . . .
> And now, perhaps it is because the island is passing out of sight that it rises so high in my thoughts. Even while the journal brings before me the events of which I have written, they are transformed, there is undoubtedly a sea-change, so that the island resembles a locality of childhood, both dangerous and lyrical. I have impressions of the island of which I have not told you, and could not entirely if I had a hundred tongues—the mustard field staring at me with its yellow eye, the blue and green lake seeing in me a hard turquoise stone, the goat's blood observing me red, guilty, all red. And sometimes when I am walking down the King's Road or sipping my espresso in the morning . . . and chance to remember the island, immediately all things are possible. (Pp. 175–76)

Obviously, Crusoe's psychology separates here from there, this place from that, this time from that, thinking and remembering and wishing from their objects, one's *locus* from oneself, one's youth from one's later years, one person from others, the experiencer from the experience. And Crusoe assumes that what has been experienced can be conveyed in words to others. That is, as we have seen, his idea of the way it is. January's idea, as this passage insists and implies, does not so much reject his as it engulfs and, at least secularly, converts it. She knows, as well as Crusoe knows, about time and place, subject and object, the ages of man, differences between history and myth, and so on. But she insists upon the simultaneity of all such abstractions and phenomena. She thereby recognizes what Crusoe sees as distinct about them, but she also acknowledges the partial truth, the lie, ingenuously rendered, which must be experienced by anyone whose imagination—capacity for the real—exceeds Crusoe's. For Crusoe, as in common parlance, childhood ends, we reach maturity, and we can capture these stages in writing. For January, as for Proust, childhood will endure for as long as she retains the capacity to recall visiting her mature sisters (whether or not she should ever again physically do so) and for as long as she can go on imaginatively recombining all prior and later experience into an increasingly complex version of reality. This reality is by no means dependent upon her for its existence, but it sometimes tends to look solipsistic because one's own means of *expressing*—of fictionizing—the real are inherently no one else's. Thus January's way of writing is to build paradoxes; but even she cannot find words to merge the elements of her paradoxes. And this normal human incapacity is a measure of the inadequacy of words or any other medium to become more than a medium, more than an illusion of an experience, more than a re-presentation posing as a presentation. January, taking up where Crusoe stops, and refusing to ignore or slight his assumptions, writes a narrative illusion that in a sense does nothing *but* make such distinctions even though she may seem to be telling a story (like Crusoe's) about her stay on an island.

Crusoe says, in effect, "This is my life." January allows us to infer that *Robinson* is autobiography, to be sure, but her book demands that we separate her source experiences from her writings about them, while we acknowledge also that reality for January now includes what she has narratively made of her prenarrative version of reality. She of course knows and all but says this; Crusoe (whose book—like January's, in a curious sense—is named for its author) doubtless supposes that his book is himself, all there is to be said or known about him by anyone—and who could know more than he does, after all? The answer is plainly that we readers cannot help knowing more about him than he knows, partly because we have access to such a counter-narrator as January Marlow. To the extent that he thinks his prose is his life or captures his life or changes "about" into "is," he lacks distance from himself and his writing enterprise. January, meanwhile, knows that experience is of the mind; that while illusion must remain illusion, the only way to get any real intimacy into it or closeness to it—for writer as for reader—is to get away from it. Thus her book's central implicit paradox is that geographical isolation occasions psychological isolation from the usual notions of herself and her relations with others and so enables her to start herself over, so to speak, and to become more intimately attuned in her imagination to what she had supposed to be real. As a corollary, her solitary confinement expands that view of the real, colors and solidifies it, but does so in large part by revealing to her how much always has been and likely will remain unknown. To understand that and to be reconciled to it, as to a vast and comforting fact, is some measure of January's difference from Crusoe. For Crusoe, the mind is what comes to terms with experience—both secular and sacred—and figures how to convey it; for January the mind keeps on reexperiencing *and* copes with the difficulties of establishing something *like* intelligibly arranged pieces of an ever-expanding, ever-renewing reality. Crusoe wants to tell the truth, to get it right, to find the words that will dump his experience into our laps. January is writing in this same realistic literary tradition to the extent that she wants us to take her initially as we are accustomed to take Crusoe and hundreds of narrators in this tradition; but we fail her and her endeavors if we stop there. For she goes on from realism to show how romantic psychology and Christian belief transcend Christian realism alone.

Perhaps it is as writers after all that Crusoe and January—Christian realist and Christian romantic—can be best distinguished. For him the problem of writing is implicitly that of dissolving the wall between life and book so that the wall will vanish between book-as-writer and the reader: if writer = book and book = reader, then writer = reader and all's one for that realistic enterprise. For January, communication to herself and to us is no less important than it is to Crusoe, but just as certain for her are the porous but permanent walls between her experience and her understanding of it, between her partially understood experience and the conveying of it, between the thing produced and the reader's experience of it, and thus between the original experience and any reader's internalizing—or critical externalizing—of it. Even if some reader were to empathize completely with the writer, no words or other media exist by means of which the two could make the identification known to each other or to a third party. Thus for January expression of whatever kind is fiction, and it does only confusing harm automatically to label fiction as *lie* or *nonfact*, when the only relevant question to be asked of that fiction which in the nature of things cannot *be* what it is *about* is this: how successful is it as illusion? The core of the trouble seems to be that to talk and act this way is to try balancing (1) the knowledge that representations are needed and are necessarily not the reality they fictionize and (2) the knowledge that the fiction achieved becomes added to and a transformer of that reality previously unreproducible—and becomes this new and real entity for producer and receiver alike, since both are receivers of the achieved fiction.[9] Both (1) and (2) are *facts*, as Robinson and January might agree, but not Crusoe's kind. For him the task is to tell the truth; for her the fictions with which we are blessedly stuck become themselves facts of life, of reality. As I say, the psychology, the aesthetic, is more nearly romantic than realistic or classic: Crusoe separates object from subject, where January merges them cyclically and organically.

Robinson is in fact stitched with varied alliances between the skills of detection and those of communicating (or preventing communication): not very surprisingly the two kinds of skill become entangled and confused. That mystery of coexistence means that loose ends are "only to be expected." Instances of differently motivated attempts to get a "story" straight occur frequently. We note that January never finds out how Jimmie and Robinson are related, or anything at all about Jimmie's history and the reason for his wonderful Dutch-Jacobean idiom. We have previously noted January's consciousness of the history-mythology split and have seen her own participation in that split. Moreover, as she talks to herself in the journal she is in fact inventing the past—tracing the facts, or reconstructing the past, as a detective (like Philip Marlowe) might say. Finally, in this regard, we might note that Tom Wells's purple account of their adventure is another of his efforts toward fiction-as-lie. Here Miguel's definition of a lie works: "When you say something is different from what you think it is"

(p. 146). And we understand that while it is impossible to separate fiction from untruth, it is useful and necessary to separate fiction as illusion in the service of what the fictioneer has really experienced, from fiction as illusion designed to falsify experience.

January is, then, unlike Crusoe, a self-conscious writer. She talks of forgetting and of then being returned to the past (very much like Proust's Marcel): "Some word or thing, almost like a sacramental, touches my memory, and then the past comes walking over me as we say an angel is walking over our grave, and I stand in the past as in the beam of a searchlight" (p. 8). Here, interestingly, as on the last page of the book, she interchanges perceiver and perceived—the past finds her and enlightens her. And along these same lines she rationalizes her displeasure with Robinson's failure to grow his own food: "It was not simply that it offended some instinct for economy and reproduction. It was more; it offended my aesthetic sense. If you choose the sort of life which has no conventional pattern you have to try to make an art of it, or it is a mess" (p. 85). Of course she elsewhere concedes that Robinson's life has *his* pattern, so that this judgment is unfair. But its point remains: she is conscious of the need to shape, to make, to fictionize.

In summary, *Robinson Crusoe* accommodates religion and economics on grounds of archetypal realistic fiction, understood as I have described it at the beginning of this chapter. *Fiction,* seen from Defoe's and the reader's stance, accordingly means that which has been made up; whereas, seen from the first-person narrator's stance, fiction is true, factual, honest conveying of experience.[10] On the other hand, *Robinson* seems to be realism where it in fact combines realism with romantic psychology in aid of a larger reality. It is of course fiction, but different from Defoe's in that Spark, January, and the reader share the basic assumption that although the fiction need not tell lies in the sense of deliberately deceiving, and is real in that it enters organically into the mind-workings of its writers and readers, it can never be other than an illusion of that which it appears to be conveying. Such, for Spark, is the nature of things. Distortion is inevitable, given the human, islanded condition. No less natural and good is the attempt to break out of isolated experience and to carry messages to oneself and others. What is evil is deliberately to cause distortions (to lie, as Wells does) rather than strive to dispel natural distortion. The main point, however, is that to be human is to make fictions, so that to comment upon fiction-making is inevitably to comment upon the human condition rather than to comment upon a comparatively frivolous activity in which we engage when we can afford to relax from seriousness and fact.

This chapter has tried to show Muriel Spark's penchant for loose ends and unresolved mysteries not only as consistent with her view of reality, but also as fictional sign of that reality. In the next chapter I will explore seven other Spark novels by way of examining indirectly why she is frequently charged with arbitrariness and irresponsibility—and by way of demonstrating, as directly as is possible for the fiction that is criticism, the maladroitness of such charges when one attends carefully to Spark's generic structuring of the dimensions of reality. For while her books are filled with unexpectedness, incompleteness, and puzzles, she never takes loose ends lightly.

Reality's Generic and Structural Range

God knows how many charlatans have preyed upon their fellows with whispers or shouts and tried seducing them with William Blake's splendid poetry:

> To see a World in a Grain of Sand
> And a Heaven in a Wild Flower
> Hold Infinity in the palm of your hand
> And Eternity in an hour.

However great the number of such frauds, however, that number in no way detracts from the power and scope of those words. Muriel Spark's reality principle, we may now state, is summed up in Blake's language, and her books in a sense bear out that principle. Whatever *uses* may be made of Blake, we can see in the words his attempt to hold onto everything at once, imaginatively. This, again, is what we were saying about Spark in her differences from Defoe. She, like Blake, not only resists discarding the literary realist's idea of what *is*, but she in fact works—again like Blake—to achieve a noncondescending dual view of literary *realism's* reality (sand, flower, hand, hour) *and* her own (in this case Christian) romantic's reality (sand, flower, hand, hour, all contained *within* world, heaven, infinity, eternity). Indeed, it is her successful merging of the two realms that generally and particularly accounts for her humor, her eccentricities, her character-conflicts and character-confusions, her kinds of dramatic confrontation, and a certain inconclusiveness in her books' conclusions. In this section of chapter 2 I wish to examine these and allied traits of Spark's novels, with an eye to their functions in demonstrating her sensibility and in embodying her art. As may be supposed, in the discussion as in the reading of an author's "sensibility" and of her "art," an overlap to the point of indistinguishableness will sometimes be inevitable, just as "form" and "content" are necessary but finally indistinguishable terms. Nonetheless, we must use such clumsy terms to come to grips with Spark's individuality.

At the heart of Muriel Spark's integrated, double-realmed vision is an acute awareness that convincing readers of this view of reality will be difficult. Moreover, we can hardly fail to note that the psychology is colored to some extent in many of Spark's books by the religious consciousness of the central figure or of the narrator. That religious psychology, furthermore, even when it is not that of a character who has been converted to Catholicism, comes at us narratively in such a way as to compel us to see how Catholicism traditionally makes certain religiopsychological distinctions. Thus, whether the dual view comes at us from a character who can offer us pre- and postconversion attitudes, or whether similar distinctions are made by the narrator, we invariably confront and must deal seriously with Spark's organic duality. Specifically, January Marlow of *Robinson* (Spark's early first-person novel) is, as we have seen, a convert to Catholicism. The same is true of Caroline Rose of *The Comforters*, Jean Taylor of *Memento Mori*, Sandy Stranger of *The Prime of Miss Jean Brodie*, Nicholas Farringdon of *The Girls of Slender Means* (a rare male convert), and Barbara Vaughan of *The Mandelbaum Gate*. Ronald Bridges of *The Bachelors* is a lifelong Catholic with, nevertheless, a convert's double view. Dougal Douglas of *The Ballad of Peckham Rye* is nondenominational in every way but is also the occasion for many characters and the narrator to cogitate and comment theistically. *The Abbess of Crewe* plainly offers central opportunity for religious reflection. The characters of *The Hothouse by the East River* are both a-religious and intricately involved in the theology of purgatory, as we shall see. Finally, while the characters of Spark's seven most recent novels never behave other than secularly, they are narratively imagined in contexts situationally compatible with the psychology prevalent in all Spark novels. In short, concern with organic duality consistently inspires Muriel Spark.

These remarks are not in the least intended to suggest that only Catholics can read Spark adequately or that anyone's approach to Spark's novels must place primary emphasis upon religion. My point is that some initial emphasis upon the valence of religion in the books will be useful to any reader, because some understanding of this point will bear upon the sort of psychology encountered. Indeed, I find it impossible to read Spark without some elementary attention to Catholicism's role in her writing; religion is for her not a narrowing parochial concern but rather a means of dealing with what I have called her reality principle—her concept of all that is. Her psychology is, then, religious, but that observation should alert us to concrete-abstract vastness rather than confine us to any notion of religion as parochial pettifoggery. For Spark, as she has said, religious commitment has meant formal confirmation of a basically religious, previously unnamed, psychology.[1] The reader's task is, accordingly, to see how the novels operate psychologically and in the process to comprehend the appropriateness of the word "Catholic" in describing how the fiction works. I suggest that one way to read her books and to remake the distinction between her and Defoe is to see that implicitly she pushes us to reverse the modern world's usual rendering of "Catholic" and "catholic." That is, where speakers are customarily quick to say "with a small *c*, of course," and thereby to insist that they mean bigness rather than smallness, Spark's books implicitly and regularly suggest the reverse idea of smallness and bigness, of container and contained. For Muriel Spark, as we stressed in contrasting *Robinson* to *Robinson Crusoe*, reality is everything and includes that portion emphasized by literary realism. In the same way, "Catholic" is an adjective redundantly but properly attached to reality, so that "catholic" by implication modifies the literary realist's precinct—the area in which he attempts illusions to make his writing real. Uppercase "Catholic" means, then, for Spark, in the first instance, not the description of Roman Catholics' institutional behavior but a virtually tautological modifier of reality—of everything that *is*. This reversal of modern values, this reversion to the logic of capital and small letters, is very seldom a specified issue in the novels; nonetheless, I believe it is the basis of what occupies narrator and characters alike, although Spark's genius is partially apparent in the skill with which she shows her characters usually (but by no means always) to be unaware that this issue—psychologically, not religiously speaking—is what separates them. This split between reality-seers and realists is sometimes nearly tragic, sometimes very funny, but ubiquitous in Spark's work.

For example, Spark's novels are regularly concerned, centrally or otherwise, with investigation—with attempts to find out what happened, who did precisely what, when events occurred, how they occurred, what the results of their occurrence may be, and why the events took place (including the question of human motives). We have seen how, in *Robinson*, January Marlow and her fellow islanders are caught up, consciously and unconsciously, in processes of search and investigation, and how the results of that searching may hardly be considered satisfactory or indeed other than failing so long as we and they adhere to the customary assumptions of ratiocinative procedure. But this same theme pervades Spark's other work as well. In *The Comforters*, for instance, Caroline Rose often hears a typewriter and then hears concerted voices speaking words that we will be reading, or reiterating dialogue or narrative that we have just read. At times what is reiterated records something of which Caroline is aware as in the past for her; at times it foretells her future; and at times it is information—concerning other characters—that she would have no realistically conceived means of knowing about. Laurence Manders, who loves Caroline, is among those who think that anyone who hears her own and others' dialogue repeated or careers renarrated, or who feels compelled to behave so as to defeat the voices of prophecy, or who is inadvertently attuned to the narrative reports of others' lives, is mentally ill and desperately in need of psychiatric help. Caroline, ever reasonable, does not at all rule out this reading of her case but of course cannot get him to sympathize with the additional possibility that she is in touch with reality whether or not she is ill. She, like Laurence, is afraid for her sanity and joins with him in looking into adjoining rooms and apartments for typewriters. These are not to be found. She then even goes along with Laurence's instructions that as soon as voices interrupt her sleep or her waking thoughts she leap up and switch on a tape recorder in the hope of catching these voices. This rational if silly procedure she also follows to its soundless conclusion. At this point Laurence gives up the search and assumes that Caroline is mad in some degree; and at this point of course Caroline, who after all knows the sounds of a typewriter and of voices when she hears them, faces the disconcerting need to switch from reading realism to reading the larger reality. Such varying views of what *is* lead to predictable results, in this case nearly disastrous as well as humorous—for predictability is measured ratiocinatively and is thus suited to Laurence's efforts in detecting his aged grandmother's smuggling activities, rather than to his pursuit of Caroline's experience.

Or again, in *Memento Mori* (1959), various characters (all of them aged) receive telephone calls and hear different voices say the words, "Remember you must die." The characters may then be arranged on a spectrum according to whether at one extreme they take the words as threat and try therefore to hasten police detection of the caller, or at the other extreme they disregard the matter of the caller and the possibility of threat and attend instead to the exhortation itself. The first extreme is that of the realistically inclined, those who, hearing something they regard as dangerous or unpleasant, take the only precautions they know of in order to safeguard those things which alone they regard as real— their physical existence and the property that extends it. The second extreme is that of those who, when all the phone tracing and Scotland Yard-work prove unavailing, look again at the words to discover that they are not so much a threat as a reminder useless to ignore and beneficial to recall. Once again, the point is that the second will likely entail inclusion of the first kind of awareness, whereas settling voluntarily or otherwise for the first will signify incomprehension and necessary exclusion of the second. Along this spectrum Spark places a number of familiar sorts of investigation that find these old people variously prying into one another's lives and keeping files on what they've been up to in private for perhaps eighty years. But these delights serve to remind us of the straddling task that Spark sees human life to be: one leg must be rooted in the mundane realm, the other leg in the extramundane, the whole person properly attentive to both realms. Moreover, to demonstrate that this awareness is universal rather than confined to the Christian sensibility of Jean Taylor at the fuller end of the spectrum, Spark arranges for Inspector Mortimer of Scotland Yard to abandon the phone-tracing process as futile and beside the point, to observe that really we ought to spend more of our life thinking about our death, and to announce secularly in a way that cuts religiously as well that "if you look for one thing . . . you frequently find another" (p. 210).[2] The book makes his words mean that investigation begun in the lesser realm can lead to discovery in the larger realm. What one discovers in this larger realm may indeed be evidence of greater mystery, but such discovery is more, not less, human in Spark's novels.[3]

"Human" is, in fact, another word that, like "catholic" and "realistic," is nearly always used to convey synonymity with "bigger," "wider," "more serious," "better," "more valuable," at least in modern parlance. As may be supposed, Spark's books implicitly challenge and deny this usage on grounds already discussed—that to regard such meaning as definitive inverts reality and stunts human experience. Thus, for example, in *The Bachelors* (1960), another novel concerned with investigation and its fruits, Ronald Bridges at one point explodes significantly: "Don't ask me . . . how I feel about things as a Catholic. To me, being Catholic is part of my human existence. I don't feel one way as a human being and another *as a Catholic*" (p. 82).[4] That is, he rightly thinks his questioner is implying that being "a Catholic" entails having a view less than "catholic," whereas Ronald, by using the nonarticled expression "being Catholic," and by attaching that condition to being human, plays up the universal, not the parochial, dimensions of his religious allegiance.[5]

Ronald's is more than a random outburst: it is tied to the main action of *The Bachelors*, a novel built specifically around investigation of the unknown and culminating in a trial that predictably tests more than judge and jury see. On the one hand is Ronald Bridges, bachelor, Catholic, "first-rate epileptic," professional graphologist (pp. 14, 15). On the other hand is Patrick Seton, bachelor, professional spiritualist and "first-rate medium," server of sentences for forgery and "fraudulent conversion" of funds (p. 26). These two extremes meet when Ronald is retained by the prosecution as a professional handwriting expert to determine that a certain letter ostensibly showing Seton innocent of fraudulent conversion is in fact a forgery written by Seton himself. This final action is, however, mere setting for a match-up particularized throughout the novel. Values, motives, psychological and philosophical attitudes are set out by the narrator and sometimes overtly suggested by Ronald, too, although not by Patrick. Incidentally, a distinction is made between brain and mind, one doctor assuring Ronald that epilepsy will affect only the brain. Also, the book sets up a difference between, on the one hand, Ronald's natural epileptic seizures and his ironic view of his conscious self as a "truth machine," and, on the other hand, Patrick's medicinally induced epileptic seizures and his using them to advertise his fame as medium—as a result of which fame he is able to prey upon gullible women sexually and financially.

Each man is a realist in Defoe's sense and lives in the familiar world. Ronald is reconciled to his being adjudged physically unfit for the priesthood and breaks off an affair with a woman he loves, for fear that he will marry her and be strapped with one who, because she loves him, will smother him with pity and protective possessiveness. He is apparently reconciled to celibacy and what must be called his vocation as an epileptic: indeed, as we shall see, we are aware of him as a kind of priest despite his being rejected by the seminary, although he never consciously thinks of himself in this way and seems not to attract attention as a notably pious person. Patrick, on the other hand, manifests his realistic attitude in his thoroughly selfish blend of pragmatic scheming and adolescent, self-excusing sentimentality. Patrick is, in short, realistic in a fairly readily recognizable sense: "realism" for him means doing what one must in order to survive comfortably and means as well finding the right excuses for doing to that end what might otherwise be regarded (even by oneself) as immoral.

As I say, the book is ostensibly plotted so as to resolve this question: what role will Ronald's expert testimony play in bringing the jury to decide that Patrick Seton is either innocent or guilty of forgery and fraudulent conversion? But obviously Spark is concerned to have us latch onto this matter so that she may show us both that we may not neglect the mundane meanings of mystery, detection, investigation, and, more urgently, that mundane meanings may or may not bear upon questions of investigation, detection, solving of encompassing mystery.[6] That is, the third-person stance of *The Bachelors* enables its courtroom contestants and participants to learn but additionally allows us readers to discover the differences made by what the characters cannot know. In this way the point of view reinforces Spark's reality principle. The novel emphasizes the truth that, while clearing up mystery in the realistic realm may in fact see justice done, or some truth supported, finding such answers invariably has its way of somehow intensifying one's awareness of one's larger ignorance and immersion in ever-greater mystery. This two-realmed distinction is established even on the courtroom level, when we come to realize that, despite Seton's conviction for what we know him to have done, the jury could not have known as much as we readers know, and that in fact all we can say of their verdict is that somehow they did what we can firmly call justice and the right thing, even though what they would seem to have relied upon as hard evidence came down to rival graphologists' readings necessarily unresolved. Indeed, who can say what reasons they might specify in support of their decision? Thus, even on the realistic level, less is resolved than a verdict seems to nail down.

That the trial of Patrick Seton may be seen doubly is stressed by the attitude of Alice Dawes, who carries his child and expects to marry Patrick when he is free to marry her. We readers know that Patrick is not married and therefore cannot divorce anyone in order to marry Alice, to whom he intends not to be tied, especially since she has declined abortion. We know, too, that if the verdict is favorable to Patrick he will take Alice on a vacation to Austria and will there kill her. We know, further, that Alice's friend Elsie doubts that Patrick is married and that he will ever marry Alice—and she tells Alice as much. None of this advice and conjecture based on probability, however, and nothing said at the trial about Patrick's conduct can sway Alice. She insists, stupidly but genuinely, that she regards the trial as "a test of God" (p. 189), and in fact when the jury convicts Patrick, Alice "clutch[es] her stomach" and says, "I don't believe in God" (p. 218). Just as Mortimer and Jean Taylor try to distinguish between the telephone caller and the meaning of the message, so Spark sets out here a distinction between the doing of justice on the courtroom level and that event's mysterious connection to the saving of the lives of Alice and her unborn child—

although of course Spark's narrator impersonally makes this point against the irony that Alice emotionally severs any such connection.

The reader doesn't have to reach the conclusion that God exists when he sees the trial ending one way for the culprit and another way for the woman who loves him, but Spark's arousing our interest in courtroom drama has lured us in far enough so that we have at least to deal somehow with Alice's way of concluding upon the trial's outcome. We know that things have come out right, justly, and the terms of the trial leave us not only free but, I think, disposed to infer a causal link between the realms of courtroom realism and larger reality. To make this inference by no means entails understanding or penetrating the mysteriousness of that causality, of course; but convincing us of that mystery is no small part of Spark's point in developing her fiction to reach a conclusion which opens upon the increasingly inconclusive. Spark succeeds here, in my opinion, largely because she presents characters who take for granted as not raising the need for further inquiry what happens on the realistic level, while she forces readers to see what must be regarded as humanly inexplicable in the context of extrarealistic reality, and to experience discomfort in trying to dismiss double awareness on the grounds that it is after all rooted in accident or authorial whimsy. Spark adroitly puts the reader consciously or unconsciously addicted to realism in the position of having to say certain things. "Patrick is guilty. Patrick is justly found guilty and sentenced. I don't know what persuaded the jury; it was luck or an accident or some reason I can't pin down, but there must be an explanation. Further, Alice's 'atheistic' reading of the trial has to be placed against the fact that justice was done here for no evident reason, and against the more sizeable fact that I think there's a reason for everything: effects have causes whether or not I call some effects accidents. Negatively, I must conclude that the prevailing of justice in this case at least precludes anyone's reasonably using this trial to endorse Alice's conclusion." If such a sequence of remarks is likely, it may serve to expand upon my contention that conclusions are deliberately inconclusive in Spark's fictions—which is another way of saying that she wishes to block the realists' interpreting her in their accustomed manner. To puzzle the realists *and* to be taken seriously by them is tantamount to effecting that sense of open-endedness or inconclusiveness which I have been suggesting here. Perhaps the realists will not say yes; but if honesty compels them not to say no, Spark will have succeeded in conveying with some measure of forcefulness *her* view of the real.

The investigational motif on which *The Bachelors* depends is enforced variously. Ronald and Patrick, for instance, are contrasted in several ways, and indeed each of these characters is himself two-sided, with the result that the trial judge's incidental remark, "There has been a great deal of mystification in this case" (p. 211), makes more sense than he knows. Again, as we proceed from smaller to larger and more important instances of comparison and contrast, the point to keep in mind is that Spark persists in her effort to make the realist feel at home in her fiction even as she artfully contrives to elicit his admission that his premises are questionable. What the comparison between the two characters provides is, of course, not only much of the plot, but also Spark's conviction of the difficulty of arriving at finished evaluations of human acts. What these characters see is not all we get, but Spark's further point is that narrative omniscience is itself an illusion.

Much about Patrick Seton is obvious. He is emotionally retarded, having retained only such memories as give him warmth and rationalize his behavior. This condition is manifest in Patrick's introspections as paraphrased by the narrator and in his conduct. Patrick feels close to his late mother, seeks the strong Detective-Inspector Fergusson as a father figure promising punishment and security, and convinces himself that women who sleep with him (thereby taking from him) implicitly contract to give him what he requires—including, besides sexual solace very closely allied with mother-love, money and, in Alice's case, the sacrifice of life itself. He relishes Yeats's early poems; similarly, he likes J. M. Barrie's *Mary Rose* when he reads it but is disturbed when he sees live men and women acting it in the theater; he finds "a lot of nasty stuff in life," and "is upset by all the disgusting details" of sexual relations—details that interfere with "dreams," "ecstasies," "transports" (pp. 159–60). Fidelity to these "dreams" requires, indeed, frequent violation of "man-made laws and dogmas." He takes his adolescent needs as implicit moral rights to what he seeks. He is a crook—a forger and fraudulent converter, a liar, a misuser of affections, a cynical opportunist and moral shark, a violator of persons and their trust. He has reversed customary notions of give and take as the terms are used in moral economy. In fact, given so much obviousness of character, we are left with very little to justify calling Patrick at all complex or opaque. Qualification of his crookedness is perhaps slight but appears real enough in that doubts about fullness of responsibility and assertions about his credentials as medium demand that we see something unknowable about even this plainest and most patently reprehensible character. Being "a first-rate medium" means in this case, certainly, being morally fraudulent; but not even the narrator, apparently, is willing to assert of Seton that his depths or maybe even his potential for good can be plumbed. Even Patrick Seton may be seen doubly, as known and unknown.

Ronald Bridges, on the other hand, is both more nearly central to this third-person narrative and more unknowable in proportion to our great familiarity with him. While epilepsy retards him in that it prevents his either becoming a priest or marrying (for different reasons), it does not block his intellectual, emotional, spiritual, and psychological development: unlike Patrick, he has grown up, whatever his limitations. He has learned to control his life, including his seizures, and to settle for the possible without indulging in self-pity; in fact, he even acts as a sort of confessor in that a number of persons seek his advice—despite (or because of) his unobtrusive practice of Catholicism and his quiet, undemonstrative manner. Also unlike Patrick, he has no wish to be possessed or coddled or pitied and indeed thinks of his single state as a vocation. He is, he says, "a *confirmed* bachelor"—a pun referring to the sacrament of confirmation, as the novel elsewhere drops such religiosecular puns as "fraudulent conversion" and "the falling sickness" or "sacred disease" or "evil spirit," three terms for epilepsy that also convey universal notions suggested by the Fall, by the *felix culpa*, by Original Sin. Ronald moreover trains his memory for sharp accuracy rather than for Patrick's preferred impressionistic blur and careful imprecision. Ronald does want to know the truth and he never ceases to exercise reason and common sense in looking for it. At the same time, while his seizures find him simply blacked out and totally unaware, his lucid moments frequently disclose him to be a seer or even a prophet, much like Caroline Rose of *The Comforters* but on a more modest if equally uninduced scale—whereas Patrick, whatever his genuine "medium-ship" may include, induces apparent seizures at séance-time and seems in every way grubbily earthbound at other times. Again, where Patrick seeks out the dark and guardedly averts his eyes from anything that may disturb his fantasies, Ronald sets himself to live with facts however cold. So cold are they—so forbidding is human behavior, including his own—that, while he does not despair, he does adopt the stoically pessimistic attitude that one had better expect the worst of life if one would avoid broken expectations and needless pain, and he prays for grace to reconcile this joylessness with his Christianity (pp. 102–3). Patrick is for the most part dull and ordinary in his cagey waking moments, while in trances he tries to read the other world; Ronald limits himself to reason and scientifically inferred conclusions in his practice of graphology and his reaching of conclusions in general, while in his seizures he is virtually nonexistent and certainly unconscious: if Ronald is a seer when he's *not* in seizure, he cannot help this any more than he can help being epileptic. Such faculties are mysterious, as is the genuineness of Patrick's mediumship.

Ronald's two-sidedness is more complicatedly developed than Patrick's and is related to his Caroline-like capacity as visionary. A single section of the novel (pp. 111–16) will indicate what I mean. In a moment of singular depression Ronald is attempting "to ward off the disgust, despair and brainburning" but nonetheless feels himself "suddenly surrounded by a company of ridiculous demons." These demons are in fact most of his friends and himself, toward all of whom Ronald feels acute lack of charity, and all of whose most detestable and intimate secrets Ronald's imagination intuits even as he finds himself disgusting in his epilepsy. Events elsewhere in the novel indicate that he is not inventing these various instances of behavior (adultery, legal misuse of funds, blackmail, etc.) but is indeed mysteriously seeing into the lives and motives of others. He resists this demonic vision into private lives, prays for grace, and forces himself to see these people with charity; to see the sufferings they endure and the good they do. Spark's achievement in such a deliberately double episode is not to allow the second kind of intuition to deny or retract the first, but to balance the two, truthfully, and thereby restore the mysteriousness of any human being rather than to let vile evil or soupy sentimentality alone dominate and falsify. Thus the temptation that Ronald resists here is not only that of thinking ill of others, but that of hubristically supposing that his vision is all that can be seen or known: the sin of judging the human person's complexity, something that must remain unknown despite juries' verdicts and our common need to act as if we understood enough to act. What we get, then, is an insistence upon restoring the balance, even as we see Ronald's remarkable faculty—source of grief as well as occasion to seek grace—for double viewing. And of course this faculty is yet another indirect comment upon the need, as Spark sees it, to become whole by living partly in the realistic social realm and completely both there and beyond (in the world but not of it). This process is difficult, a fact manifested by Ronald's vomiting and experiencing a particularly untreatable seizure. When he wakes, however, he knows in his prideless exhaustion that he has won this round, and he decides to go to confession—"to receive, in absolution, a friendly gesture of recognition from the maker of heaven and earth, vigilant manipulator of the falling sickness." In this manner Spark rounds out the doubleness of the section with the familiar awareness that, regardless of social pressures, solitary Jacob-like ordeals, and the necessity to choose, events occur or are in some way determined according to purposes unknown to us but mysteriously real.

Shortly after this episode, after we have seen Seton's duality and Ronald's, Spark sets up two consecutive passages by means of which she extends and complicates our sense of her point. In the first passage (pp. 157–62), wherein we learn much of what I have already explained of Patrick's character, Patrick's thoughts are paraphrased by the narrator as Patrick observes the pregnant, loyal Alice, glimpses fearfully the prospect of being tried and convicted, and firmly returns to *his* version of the real. "I have loved her, I still love her," he is said to be thinking. "I don't take anything from Alice. I give. And I will release her spirit from her gross body. . . . a man has to protect his bread and butter, and Alice has agreed to die, though not in so many words." He then settles more comfortably into the plan to kill her. "She is mine, I haven't taken a penny from this one. I can do what pleases me. I love this one. She has agreed to trust." He is pleased to think of Alice "free from her heavy body, beyond good and evil," and comforts himself with the reflection that they have "a pact. . . . She has agreed to believe in me." In this passage what stands out is the contrast between—on the one hand—Patrick's repeated insistence upon his deep love for Alice even as she is excluded from his thinking and from the reasons compelling it and—on the other hand—the psychological use of what he calls love to support, even to fuel, his determination to murder her. The point here is that reality for Patrick is solipsistically conceived in a manner that assigns intentions to others but requires absolute airtight privacy. Most of us would consider Patrick insane in some measure; but regardless of our limited realistic views, he is giving us, through the narrator, one version of one kind of reality.

Immediately following a break in the page at the end of Patrick's self-convincing unchallengeable introspection on love, Spark counters Patrick's thoughts by means of the sole encounter between Alice's friend Elsie Forrest, who has stolen from Ronald's lodgings the letter that he was to examine for the prosecution, and Ronald himself, who has come to ask her to return it (pp. 162–71). Ronald tells Elsie that perhaps he can use copies in his testimony but that he would like the original in order to keep his responsible position as a reliable expert witness who can be trusted to retain evidence entrusted to him. He says he is here at her flat not to bribe her, but only to ask a favor. When she says no and he unprotestingly prepares to leave, she says she will give him the letter if he will spend the night with her. He declines.

> "Why, tell me why? Is there something wrong with me?"
> . . . .
> "I'm a stranger. That's why I can't sleep with you."
> "Am I a stranger?"
> "Yes," Ronald said.
> "You're only playing for time," she said. "I'm well aware you're trying to handle me. It's the letter you're after. Take all and give nothing."
> "I thought we were having an interesting conversation, mutually appreciated as between strangers," Ronald said.
> "Yes, and when you go away you'll feel 'Well, I haven't got the letter but at least I cheered up the poor girl for an hour.' And what d'you suppose *I'll* feel? It's much better for men not to come at all if they're always going to go away and leave me alone. I'm not lonely before they come. I'm only lonely when they go away."

Ronald then asks for the letter simply because she took it. She again declines, this time on the grounds that "it's the first time I've taken anything worth having off a man. And I want to keep it." She then intimates that she'll give him the letter if he will promise to visit her again. This he thinks unlikely and accordingly declines to promise. What wins her over, although not at once, is evident in this exchange:

> "Give it to me for love."
> "What love do I get out of it?"
> "That's not the point."
> "Well, you've got a nerve, I'll say that. But you all come for what you can get."
> "Give it to me for love," Ronald said. "The best type of love to give is sacrificial. It's an embarrassing type of love to receive, if that's any consolation to you. The best type of love you can receive is to be taken for granted as a dependable person and otherwise ignored—that's more comfortable."

Eventually she hands over the letter and they part as friendly strangers. He still thinks it unlikely that he will revisit her. When she then accuses him of snobbery, he replies, "I'm an epileptic. . . . It rather puts one out of the reach of class."

This scene strikes me as altogether remarkable in itself and as even more remarkable in contrast to Patrick's episode (it is hardly a scene) that precedes it. To begin with, each passage focuses on a choice to be justified on the basis of love—but here the similarity ends and the contrast takes over. Patrick's argument to himself depends crucially upon his leaving Alice—whom he must insist upon loving and who must be understood to love him—out of the deliberations. Further, Patrick's one-sided self-persuasion not only cannot afford disinterestedness but must moreover by definition advocate, answer, and judge itself in psychological circumstances allowing of no appeal. He also comes around to making himself believe that really he will be doing Alice a favor in killing her and enabling her spirit to survive without having to drag around her body. Interesting as well is his twisting of spiritual and material considerations in such a way as to suit his purposes. That is, by reading the morality of give and take as he wishes, he is able to justify his plans on the grounds that his love is proven by his having supported Alice rather than having taken money from her, and by his rationalization that taking her life will in fact be giving her spirit freedom from the flesh. This reasoning he regards as spiritual, while taking women's money and respecting their wish to stay alive and bear the children they have conceived he takes as materialistic. Thus he rationalizes, inverts, and—most important—dichotomizes, with the result that his adolescence and thorough self-centeredness emerge plainly. Instinctively, Patrick feels a need to separate matter from spirit, to find spirit good, and to put himself on the side of spirit. In Spark's view of reality, of course, this kind of split cannot be achieved and to attempt it is unnatural. The unnatural is sometimes called evil.

In the succeeding section, Ronald comes out front in saying what he wants (although Elsie already knows what he wants), makes no effort to threaten, blackmail, lie, or otherwise coerce Elsie, declines her own self-interested, blackmailing propositions, and makes no promises. In doing all of these things he tells her matter-of-factly that he made the mistake (i.e., not protecting the letter) which accounts for his being in professional trouble, that she can help or hurt him by her decision, that they two are strangers and that strangers are inappropriate bedfellows, and that materially disinterested love (about which he knows much and to which his vocation as "first-rate epileptic" commits him) is, incidentally, difficult to take and the finest and perhaps hardest kind to give. In this way he adjusts, rights, the Patrick-mess that precedes this section. For Ronald communicates his ideas and his sincerity to another who is indeed a stranger to him and thereby manifests unobtrusively that very kind of love of which he speaks—so that Elsie, whether she knows it or not, is swayed by his love for her (for another person, stranger or not), as well as amusingly thrown off balance by his declining the sexual proposition that she has always found useful and indeed necessary heretofore. Ronald differs from Patrick, then, in bringing out his thoughts as truthfully as he can, in nonhypocritically recommending a love not based on sex—which preachment we know him to practice—and in thereby endorsing a spiritual motive without in the least denying the value of the materially realistic (e.g., his job, her sexual needs). The section is funny in that it finds Elsie starting out as Patrick might, materially, moving from the sexual bribe to that of friendship, and then being confused by Ronald's using the word "love" not as a synonym for "sex" (as she understands it) but as a term to signify human relations in the realm of the larger reality—not necessarily instead of, but only responsibly inclusive of, the physical. In this way Ronald places the sexual (material) within greater reality and thereby endorses Spark's reality principle without patronizing Elsie or making her feel unclean in her physicality. To see this Patrick-Ronald moral distinction clearly, moreover, one has only to observe the mindlessly blind confusion and refusal to face facts that Alice displays even after Patrick's conviction, and to pit these against Elsie's respect for Ronald and herself after he levels with her openly and then leaves her. The two sections are a beautifully economical presentation of moral sensibilities: Patrick's versus Ronald's and Spark's. Giving and taking must be separately discussed but must finally be seen to function so that giving is one with getting.

Tied to this distinction between moral sensibilities, and thus to Spark's reality principle and to the aura of investigation and trial in *The Bachelors*, are various relations with what may conveniently be called *the other*. Ronald remarks that "there are only two religions, the spiritualist and the Catholic" (p. 175). Understandably, he gives rise hereby to a funny response: "I say, that's going a bit far. There's the Greek Orthodox and the Quakers and of course the C. of E. and some people are Buddhists, and—." Ronald doesn't explain but remarks only that his friend "must take it in a figurative sense . . . or leave it." For good reason these assertions puzzle characters to whom they are addressed; the remarks may, however, appear meaningful and by no means puzzling to those readers attentive to the narrator's third-person view.

Ronald is not discussing denominations—at least not primarily. Rather, given the events of the novel, he seems to be intimating a division of psychological types into those who see things his way and those who do not—so that he is concerned with psychology in religious perspective. If I am correct about this inference, then assuredly there *are* two kinds of "religion," and it is not surprising to find either kind at least occasionally thinking the other fraudulent. The two types may perhaps be thought of as the romantically integrated (Blake or Ronald or Spark) and the realistically dual (Crusoe or Patrick). The point is hardly that all Catholics think as Ronald does or that dualism and realism are always conjoinable: the point is rather that Ronald is finding applicable labels from within his own frame of reference, which is the frame of reference regularly found in Spark's novels. Thus, when he remarks that Patrick is very likely "a genuine medium" and that Alice's love for Patrick makes her "obviously a soul-lover" (p. 86), Ronald is commenting implicitly on Patrick's appeal and also noting implicitly a dualistic split that is not Ronald's own doubleness. For Ronald does "affirm the oneness of reality in some form or another" (p. 87). What Ronald's remark may be taken to mean is that Alice ignores evidence—indeed, she *must* ignore evidence—in order to keep her belief in Patrick. She shuts off common sense and the entire realistic investigatory process and insists that her hunches and intuition about Patrick's good soul are right, just as we saw Patrick shutting off communication with Alice in the process of convincing himself that he loves her and will therefore kill her. Each of them is a "spiritualist" as distinct from a "Catholic" (again, in Ronald's sense of the terms) in that each instinctively hangs onto an illusion by means of deliberately avoiding the opportunity to examine or try that illusion. Such behavior, it seems to me, is of a piece with turning out the lights at a séance—that is, closing off avenues testable by the senses, and relying instead upon each individual's collective experience of the purely spiritual as conveyed through a medium. The point here is that we necessarily dwell in the body but that the persons Ronald calls "spiritualists" try to escape the body and even to deny it and transcend it while in fact they hold hands or touch tables or attune their bodily ears to listen to what comes from the supposedly bodiless realm. Paradoxically, they would transcend the flesh even as they sustain their belief in proportion to what their ears convince them they hear coming to them from beyond earshot. Spark's contrasting investigation of the two types labeled by Ronald appears to indicate quite plainly that we are all creatures of the reality seen by Ronald, but that sadly, sickly, tragically, hilariously, we who are "spiritualists" unnaturally attempt self-contradictingly to have things both ways—to use the real body to escape (and somehow to *discover*) reality.

On the contrary, Ronald's view tries to have things both ways by insisting that only a two-footed stance or dual vision can be said to be harmonious with the real—which harmony he calls "Catholic." In this view, it follows that of course one should love the soul (in which Ronald assuredly believes), but that to fasten one's veneration upon any such attribute or essence as the only human quality or *the* good human quality is as ill-conceived and perverted as to attend exclusively to the body. Exclusiveness of either sort is what Ronald resists (he has gently told Elsie—p. 167—that entertainment without sex is a reasonable expectation for men and women alike), for to come down on the side of either flesh or spirit is to deny the reality principle. Indeed, on one occasion when he has painfully encountered himself, figuratively, in the person of another epileptic in seizure, he resists taking his medicine—and thus risks a seizure in his present nervousness—for reasons explained in the narrative: "On occasions of extra stress he rather cherished the feeling of being more alive and conscious than usual, he cherished his tension and liked to see how far he could stand it. . . . [H]e did not take [his drugs], and managed to get a living troubled sleep instead of a dead and peaceful one" (p. 89).

This is the standard mark of Ronald Bridges. Patrick induces a tranced condition in the dark, however genuine the trance may be, and he becomes, fraudulently or genuinely, *the* means of connecting our state with that of spirit(s) and of course allows others to believe that being a medium means that he alone among the group attains to the spiritual realm. But Ronald operates in the daylight, the open, and carefully distinguishes among scientific fact, conjecture, untenable statement, plausible belief, and implausible belief. Ronald believes in the absolute inseparability of real elements from one another, and thus in the necessity of remembering body-soul when speaking of body and soul as distinct. He also pretends to know nothing, where knowledge is understood to be acquired ratiocinatively, about the realm of pure spirit. His is not *that* kind of "religion" but is instead the kind that distinguishes between knowing and believing. He *believes*, of course, in the larger reality but has no pipeline to it and for some unknown reason (which his belief calls grace) has no need to base his belief on a direct contact with sensibly perceivable spirits that light up and talk only in the dark.

What the Patrick-Ronald distinction comes to here is the difference between those ("spiritualists") who talk about spirit, but who are unable to believe in communion with spirit unless that communion is materially, sensible verified, and those ("Catholics") who acknowledge spirit, but who see spirit as that reality in which deceased and predeceased alike dwell, and as that which, because it obviously *is*, assures communion without the necessity (I do not say the possibility) of material verification. In a sense, Patrick's version of spiritualism would be taken by Ronald to be basically self-contradictory in being materialistically based, whereas Ronald's own Catholicism he obviously regards as true—that is, as positing the permanent reality of spirit while keeping a grip on realism's sane conjoining of matter-spirit among the predeceased. Patrick's type talks spirit but wants to *know*, to place its hand in the wounds; Ronald's type talks spirit *and* spirit-matter and prays for grace to go on *believing*, for it understands that knowledge in these matters is inherently unattainable, and that in fact the body's materiality may be considered, not as evil, but as properly and inevitably preclusive of that very awareness which Patrick tries to achieve by means of the body. In short, knowledge may be had of the sensibly and intellectually available, while belief is in the enormous remainder of reality that is not so much left over as it is permeating and informing of the realistic. This distinction is, as Ronald says, "figurative" but it is one more effort—like efforts to place "catholic" within "Catholic" and "realistic" within "reality-conscious" and "human" within "universal"—to unify rather than to set up mutually exclusive dualities. One has either to agree with Patrick that mystery exists but not really, or to agree with Ronald that mystery really exists and would not be called mystery were it accessible to our quite appropriate human endeavors to know more and more. Knowledge and belief have different objects, and any person is classifiable as this or that type of "religionist" according to the need to fight that separateness or the ability to accept it and its consequences as well.

The courtroom battle to which *The Bachelors* builds is concerned, then, with the whole complex of issues and attitudes at war in the Patrick-Ronald contrast, a contrast of which we readers are aware but of which the participants have only their limited separate-charactered sense. Spark manages to arrange the dramatic proceedings so that our greater knowledge of what this criminal investigation stems from and of the true characters of those involved, as well as our outsiders' consequent awareness of there being more at stake than the jury can possibly decide, converge in a way that lets us take the whole thing more seriously than do the characters, even while we see the struggle as a Marx Brothers scene.

Another way to get at this contrast between "real" and "realistic" values is to note the emphasis of the judge when he tells the jury pointedly that everything hinges upon *evidence* (as Robinson insisted), and that one's personal opinions and prejudices are beside the point of justice (p. 216). With this admonition in mind, we look back upon the courtroom drama now being completed, as well as back upon the whole novel that precedes this occasion, and we absolutely must, like Chaucer's Troilus, laugh helplessly at the thorough entanglement of the "facts" presented by the two sides in the trial, and at the human impossibility of relating *whatever* verdicts are reached in all our courts to the doing or ignoring of justice in the larger context. Obviously, Spark's and Ronald's sense of the force of Original Sin bears heavily upon this trial—(Ronald on p. 88: "The Christian economy seems to me to be so ordered that original sin is necessary to salvation.")—so that to the extent that the reader shares imaginatively in that conviction the reader will see that tragedy and comedy—to simplify the possibilities—emerge arbitrarily from the limited human perspective. That is, as we look back upon the lying testimony, the honest conjectures, the concealed or admitted self-interest behind some avowals, and the inevitable limits of human knowledge, we can see no reason other than arbitrariness or irrelevance for the jury to have come down one way rather than another. Spark indeed sees to it that we know justice to have been done, and the novel has a comic ending in that the villain is punished and some other desired events occur. But precisely because the reader—like Troilus—knows what he knows, the reader must decide either that blind chance overcomes pomposity of assurance and leads to unjust or just, happy or unhappy, endings—or that something besides chance or our human projects and policies and choices is operating to outcomes and according to plans of which we can know nothing.

In a sense, then, we get the feeling that we might just as well sit back and let things happen, let events roll over us. But of course, because we are privy to what's at stake in the novel even though we cannot explain what we know, we simultaneously realize, like Oedipus, that to be human means making choices and taking responsibility for them even though we are acutely sensitive to the uncontrollable something else that affirms or alters or contradicts our choices. Such a fully integrated view is frightening, of course, because it reminds us of our frailty, but it is also a source of the fullest laughter, I think, because it frees us from a certain ponderousness characteristic of those who suppose that they must be responsible for knowing and understanding and choosing whatever they do— or whatever happens. One can laugh, not necessarily in despair, if one sees that one cannot be *expected* to know perfectly, although one may acknowledge the responsibility to act upon whatever knowledge one can achieve. The attitude expressed in the words of Ronald and of Elsie—"Take it or leave it"—is what Spark often impresses upon her readers. These words do not mean that the speaker will not bother to explain further, but that he or she has said all that can be known and thus truthfully said with assurance, and that more would be conjecture, presumption, or lying. The novel's inconclusiveness, humor, seemingly accidental comic outcome, and conviction of human limitedness arise alike, then, from Spark's vastness of imagination, rather than from a realist's malnutrition or quirkiness.[7] She uses her omniscient point of view to show us that the more we know, the closer we come to empathy with her reality principle; the closer we come to having things all ways—with Ronald Bridges and William Blake. And the more we grow in this awareness that more knowledge pushes out the walls of the real, the more human we become. The fullest human beings, in Spark's books, are those whose attunement with reality taxes, proportionately, characters and readers whose assumptions are confined to realism.

While not all Spark novels, despite the author's consistent view, are comic structures, the investigation-trial pattern does lead in some other instances— notably in *The Ballad of Peckham Rye* and *The Mandelbaum Gate*—to comic resolutions. In the first of these two books Spark offers us a title that triggers various associations with the odd, the supernatural, the fantastic—for ballads are quite readily compatible with ghosts, devils, extraordinary powers. Yet, as we have seen, in Spark's view of reality there is no incompatibility between realistic characteristics and occurrences usually adjudged odd, crazy, unrealistic: so that associations with balladic events are a shortcut to Spark's usual proceedings, rather than a signal that proceedings here are different from what we expect in her work.

In *Ballad* (1960)[8] Dougal Douglas professes to be engaged in "human research." Whatever this may mean, he is being paid, eventually, by two rival companies, unbeknownst to either of them, to indulge in it. Indeed, everywhere in the novel we encounter doubles, reflections, and the difficulty if not the impossibility of separating analogues from opposites. Dougal Douglas is, for instance, called Douglas Dougal in one of his two personnel jobs. (He also calls himself "Dougal-Douglas" and another character calls him "Mr. Doubtless.") On the one hand he seems an obvious crook, earning high pay, twice, for not much of anything but acting knowledgeable, making people feel important or making them laugh while he plays them as he likes, and in general behaving like a public relations man for himself. In this capacity he enjoys emphasizing his high shoulder, small stature, two apparent protuberances of forehead, and certain oddities of acquired or intuitive knowledge that contribute to his claim that he is "fey," in fact a devil. But on the other hand, shortness and a high shoulder hardly require supernatural explanation, and forehead bumps are neither unusual nor more factual than imagined by those invited to touch them. What we don't know is how he knows some of what he divulges of persons' lives—but a Spark character (like Ronald Bridges) need hardly be a devil or be evil to be capable of such insight. Perhaps most catching about Dougal's doubleness is that when he is asked for help in the form of advice, he offers advice which must be considered sometimes indifferent and inconclusive and sometimes good and right. For example, when Merle Coverdale wants to know how she can end her stultifyingly dependent affair with Druce, her employer, Dougal tells her to walk out, to leave him, even though it will not be easy to leave the job and take a smaller salary elsewhere. This is moral, if common, sense. Similarly, when he tells Humphrey Place that Dixie Morse, Humphrey's fiancée, is eaten up with avarice and will make a miserable wife for him, even Humphrey has to see the truth and the good sense of the observation. Perplexingly, on one occasion when Dougal tells Merle that he has "powers of exorcism," or the "ability to drive devils out of people," and when Merle then retorts that "I thought you said you were a devil yourself," Dougal seals the exchange by saying, "The two states are not incompatible" (pp. 114–15). Of course he doesn't bother to explain (he is a Spark character, after all), but what he may well be implying is that devils induce our resistance to the devil, to evil; that temptation prompts a turning to good instead and thereby a driving out of devils. We don't know that he means this, and if he does mean it we still cannot understand how this creature of balladic rootlessness comes to be situated temporarily in Peckham Rye. But however much he may induce us to make his words and behavior signify, he is double, complex, mysterious. We are into another recognizable Spark novel.

Indeed, although *Ballad* is filled with traits associated with ballads—the old crone Nelly, who roams the streets singing psalms interspersed with snippets of contemporary English, warning Dougal of this or that danger; Dougal's skipping and dancing about in his walks with Merle; Dougal's allowing or causing persons to fear him as someone in league with the supernatural—this novel's pawky occurrences and outcome are quite similar to those of *The Bachelors.* Both books were published in 1960, and in fact Ronald Bridges of the transitional name resembles Dougal Douglas of the reversible appellations in that both characters are dual-visioned. On the other hand a measure of the characters' differences shows up in the way that Ronald not only lives with his epilepsy but in fact uses it for his growth, while Dougal, like Patrick Seton, averts his eyes from illness or death. Ronald's book is more emphatically realistic in manner, but, as we have seen, he too is capable of an angel-devil's vision, of seeing that we interact with something else in reality's manifestations. Again, the difference between these books seems primarily Spark's decision to associate Dougal with ballad conventions, so that his being less recognizably realistic in behavior would have its reasons and its clues without severing him from relations with the familiar world. Because of differing conventions, Ronald's bridging of two realms is more interior and psychological, Dougal's more overt. Both characters' novels, however, come to comically inconclusive ends. Ronald's book, as we know, leaves apparently resolved but genuinely mysterious the workings of variously intentioned humans toward or away from justice; Dougal's leaves couples reconciled and order apparently restored but leaves unanswered for readers and characters alike the question of Dougal's function in the book. He undoubtedly affected the lives of several characters; but nobody knows anything solid about who he was, where he came from, what he meant to do, whether his devil status made him more good demon or more bad demon. The characters and the readers (like characters in and readers of many ballads containing Dougal-like figures) know that some things have happened since or after his functioning among them, but this is far from evidence that he caused things to happen—and is perhaps even farther from evidence that he influenced the characters to cause them. Thus, Ronald may perform in a more realistic novel and he may do his own reflecting about demonic attitudes in conflict with grace, but Dougal's more romantic behavior (like that of Hawthorne's Donatello in *The Marble Faun*) and his cryptic statements about devils lead his novel, also, to comic inconclusiveness. And, again as in *The Bachelors*, we cannot avoid seeing that the arbitrariness by means of which the outcome is socially happy reinforces Spark's point about the arbitrariness, the touch-and-go quality, of any results that humans may be pleased to take credit for. Because in both novels we are acutely aware of both realms, we are left with a sense that matters could readily have come out otherwise, and that if they had done so, we would have been equally as unaware of reasons.[9]

As one final instance of how comedy is somehow made of the inscrutable interworking of human planning and reality's mystery, *The Mandelbaum Gate* (1965)[10] is instructive. This is Spark's longest novel, her most detailed tribute to the realistic tradition.[11] But while the book introduces a sizable assembly of characters and goes into considerable detail about their religious, social, national, psychological backgrounds and expectations, it is involved as are all of this writer's novels with the role of the inexplicable in realism's sweaty doings. In *Gate*, the point of view is again third-person omniscient, and the central character is predictably double and doubly involved. She is Barbara Vaughan, a thirtyish English schoolteacher, her father Gentile, her mother Jewish. Barbara is virtually orphaned but is acutely sensitive to her dual heritage and feels close to both sides of her family, especially to her Jewish cousin Michael Aaronson. To make matters yet more complicated, Barbara is a convert to Catholicism. The book is set in 1961 in both Israeli Jerusalem and Jordanian Jerusalem, the two separated by the Mandelbaum Gate. Obviously, the gate projects various splits: Arab-Israeli, Gentile-Jew, vestigial imperialism-emerging independence, Jewish-Christian-Islamic. For Barbara personally, there is the additional conflict arising from the fact that she is trying to give a certain solidity to her mixed ethnic and religious identity. For her, this period of pilgrimage to the Holy Land is moreover an opportunity to wait out the time to be taken by Vatican courts in deciding whether her fiancé's divorce is to be ecclesiastically acknowledged so that she may marry him within the Church. He, Harry Clegg, is in Rome while she awaits word from him and while she privately decides what she will do in the likely event that Rome will not let her as Catholic marry an undivorced man: her conflict is thus sexual as well as otherwise emotional.

Anyone accustomed to Spark will expect these supposedly larger and smaller issues to become involved with one another, and indeed in the ordeals endured and amusingly suffered by Barbara Vaughan the gate becomes a connector even as it remains a divider. For of course Spark's perennially varied thesis is that doubles can remain double and be seen as in some ways one. To effect such a paradoxical merger is plainly difficult and, as Spark shows here in particular, it involves real risks and considerable danger. But just as we saw Ronald foregoing his medicine in favor of taking a risk alertly in the teeth of hard reality, so Barbara in this book sees that all of life—if one posits values and hierarchies of any kind—necessitates confrontation with danger (no less real for its sometimes being very funny, as when Barbara discovers a sly and dangerous Arab merchant, Joe Ramdez, in bed with Miss Rickward, the Calvinistically forbidding head-mistress of Barbara's school), and she welcomes this danger despite its cost. In fact, danger makes her more conscious than ever of the elements of her identity and of those elements as the only integrated self she can be. The narrator sums up Barbara's awareness:

> For the first time since her arrival in the Middle East she felt all of a piece; Gentile and Jewess, Vaughan and Aaronson; she had caught some of [her friend and English escort] Freddy's madness, having recognized . . . that he had regained some lost or forgotten element in his nature and was now, at last, for some reason, flowering in the full irrational norm of the stock she also derived from: unself-questioning hierarchists, anarchistic imperialists, blood-sporting zoophiles, sceptical believers—the whole paradoxical lark that had secured, among their bones, the sane life for the dead generations of British Islanders.
> She . . . felt all of a piece, a Gentile Jewess, a private-judging Catholic, a shy adventuress. (P. 155)

The expression "for some reason" carries the usual puzzlement at being unable to resolve the *why* and *how* of experience, and the words "irrational norm" convey much of what I have been describing as the unknowableness of reasons other than our own. But beyond these notes, the passage is reminding us that this moment of exhilaration should not blind us—and it does not blind Barbara—to the painful fact that metaphorically and psychologically pulling together the components of a paradox is a union ardently to be pursued and striven for, but that terror emerges because commonly one cannot help coming down on one side or the other of a given hyphen. We can probably see such imbalance as a corollary of Spark's regular demonstration that where balance is achieved, the achievement is not traceable to anything we can label as our own doing: e.g., comic vs. tragic outcome, as previously discussed. Awareness of theoretical unions and of their desirability can thus make even more bitter the likely failure of one's attempts to bring about such unions. More specifically, while it is doubtless well and good to feel, as Barbara does in this passage, spiritually right about her paradoxical self, the future will still pose problems of anti-Semitism, national loyalty, religious tension. Most specific of all, perhaps, is her virtual assurance that she will marry Harry Clegg outside the Church if his suit is rejected by Rome. She knows that this manifestation of her love for Harry will tear her apart because she, a serious Catholic, will be cut off from the sacraments. Thus, just as Patrick Seton's momentary transport beyond the mundane cannot be a permanent escape, so Barbara's intensely authentic moment of integration renders her more than ever aware of the difficulty of making it last.

What remains to be said about this forest-vs.-trees contrast is that, as Ronald Bridges saw, one can do very little about merging one vision with the other, epiphany with mundane temporality, except, in Ronald's view, to pray for grace to believe in both visions separately and in the propriety and desirability of their conjunction apart from human capacity to bring about that union. *The Mandelbaum Gate* supports and indeed expands upon Ronald's view in that this novel shows that the result of trying to go it alone, trying to use human means to unify dualities, effectively neutralizes one. One thus becomes not more fully human but less than human, where to be human means to take risks by making choices and making one's self day by day. In fact, Spark shows, in Freddy's case, that thinking to make a better life by avoiding confrontations and hard decisions makes one a target of God's words in the Apocalypse (cited by Barbara): "Being what thou art, lukewarm, neither hot nor cold, thou wilt make me vomit thee out of my mouth" (p. 20). The Vaughan-Spark point here, of course, is that— given the human inability to match the realistic to its encompassing context— one has either to give up and settle for the realistic less, or to hope and believe that the reconciliation requiring one's participation cannot be accomplished by oneself alone—and may even contradict one's understanding of what is happening at any moment. Be reasonable and expect what happens, Spark's books imply.

What happens here is comic. Barbara's pilgrimage could have led, so far as humans can predict outcomes, to disillusionment and despair rather than to any sort of self-discovery or integration. Similarly, Harry Clegg's "trial" could readily have ended negatively and contributed to Barbara's disillusionment. Perhaps worse, Barbara's revelatory experiences on pilgrimage could have been undercut and violated destructively had she decided to marry Clegg in spite of Rome. What in fact occurs for reasons that cannot be traced beneath the surface (as with *Memento Mori's* phone calls and the trial proceedings in *The Bachelors*) is that Miss Rickward, thinking to hurt Barbara and wrongly supposing that Rome will find against Clegg if he is shown to have been baptized Catholic, viciously searches out and sends to Rome a copy of his baptismal certificate. The result is that, since Harry as Christian had married a non-Christian, the Church sees his marriage as invalid, a fact precluding any need for a divorce. Running contrary to Miss Rickward's intention, then, and indeed accidentally wonderful in Barbara's and Harry's opinion, this piece of evidence—unknown by even Harry until Miss Rickward's detective work—brings about a result that nobody meant or could have foreseen—a comic ending which one kind of psychology has to call an accident and the other kind of psychology sees as accidental only when viewed from a realistic stance.[12]

As the gate connects various values kept separate, and as Barbara's experiences on pilgrimage assist in concretizing some of those values, so a sermon delivered to a group of pilgrims visiting the Holy Sepulchre helps us gain anagogic perspective on the two realms. The priest making the brief remarks addresses believers, those participating in a mass, and is thus not officiously forcing his views upon those I call realists; but interestingly, he does take a second to caution his audience against fake relics and other fraudulence aimed at tourists. His theme, however, goes beyond the range of Patrick Seton, for he employs the biblical and Augustinian distinction betweem cities to make the point we have been developing from Spark's novels:

> "It is the New Jerusalem which we seek with our faith, and which is the goal of our pilgrimage to this old Jerusalem of history. 'What is faith?' said St. Paul. 'It is that which gives substance to our hopes, which convinces us of things we cannot see.'"
>
> . . . .
>
> "We know" [he continues] "the creed of our faith and what we believe. Outside of that it is better to know what is doubtful than to place faith in uncertainties. Doubt is the prerogative of the believer; the unbeliever cannot know doubt. And in what is doubtful we should doubt well. But in whatever touches the human spirit, it is better to believe everything than nothing. Have faith." (P. 189)

The priest reassures his fellow pilgrims that "we know . . . what we believe," although knowledge is not belief. He also tells them not to be surprised or disheartened to find themselves doubting—since only believers, extraknowers, adherents to Muriel Spark's reality principle, *can* doubt (nonbelievers—those who believe in nothing—have nothing to doubt and thus *cannot* doubt). Doubt is to belief as ignorance is to knowledge, he suggests. What he is recommending, amidst the secular clamor and commercial impatience surrounding him, is staunchness in striving for Barbara's experience of epiphany or Ronald's exhausted relief in successfully driving away the temptation to think uncharitably.

Obviously the priest cannot explain his thesis but must, like Spark, strive to manifest it figuratively. To the extent that Spark's novel succeeds, the priest will have succeeded in imaginative communication with the reader. We ought, he says, to "know what is doubtful," and/but try to "believe everything." *Everything,* of course, is that encompassing reality with which we have been dealing.

If we take this sermon's thesis as a tentative guide to Spark's psychology and to her fiction, her novels may be seen as situated along a spectrum of belief, from faith-sustaining comedies at one end (such books as we have discussed to this point) through books of grayer inconclusiveness and confrontation with doubt. As I read Spark, the hypothetical other end of the spectrum—the end of nonbelief (the spectrum is essentially one of belief, after all), of what for her psychology would be tragedy—has been approached intimately only once: in *The Driver's Seat.* Having looked in some detail at the comedies at one extreme, I should like to move along the spectrum through four more of her novels, for varied indeed are the fictional challenges to—and embodiments of—Spark's reality principle.

DARKER SIMULTANEITY

Dante provides us with one model for comic structure—a model less and less recoverable in the living of lives and more and more confined to scholarly reaches. Indeed, literary comedy both before and after Dante tends to mean the kind of conflict that may occur within a particular society, that may become intensified by virtue of real or apparent opposition to that society's code, and that is eventually resolved satisfactorily both on that society's terms and to that society's betterment: comedy has become more and more *realistic* in our sense of that word. Muriel Spark's comedies, as we have seen, show perfectly well what the modern world knows and does not believe, even as her comedies remain true to their author. While she cannot write supernaturally centered epics she can write novels implicitly grounded in Dantean assumptions but rooted in the explicitly social. However, novels such as *The Bachelors, The Ballad of Peckham Rye,* and *The Mandelbaum Gate*—books resulting in welcome social solutions— are atypical of Spark's achievement. In fact, except for *The Mandelbaum Gate* and *Loitering with Intent,* none of Spark's novels written after 1960 is comic as we have been using that term. More precisely, where the books discussed in the previous section of this chapter manifest comic status in their inexplicable coalitions between realism and reality, the later novels are more unsettling in that they both insist upon the two realms and project doubts of various degrees and kinds concerning the likelihood of comic merger—of integrated resolution.[13] Ronald Bridges' faith is that things can go right on both levels simultaneously, and in his book they do so; in the later books not many characters share Ronald's vision, and even though the controlling narrator operates doubly, belief is peripheral, if present at all, and regularly tested. Moreover, although all of Spark's books are well shaped and finished, inconclusiveness concerning actions and characters becomes increasingly the mark of her craft. While reality inevitably remains constant, events are increasingly less likely to result in realism's happily coinciding with reality. Doubts, then, are not about reality, but about the diminishing human penchant for glimpsing that reality. Spark's later books are, like her earlier ones, funny, but they are also grimmer and sadder and credibly more sober in rendering the consequences of operating rather dominantly on realism's premises. Perhaps it would be more nearly accurate to say that, whereas in most Spark novels the point of view is consistently omniscient and psychologically mindful of the reality-realism inclusiveness of which we have been speaking, it is especially true of her books since *The Prime of Miss Jean Brodie* (1961) that the events narrated and the characters' own psychologies reflect dimly if at all the narrator's awareness. In this section I wish to look in some detail at various instances and shades of the more usual sort of Spark novel, lest we suppose her seriousness to be consistently comic.

If we look, for instance, at *The Girls of Slender Means* (1963),[14] we find the familiar doubly aware overview, together with one female character who never doubts it and a more nearly central male character who importantly comes to share it. The other principal women sharing the book's title with Joanna, as well as the few other men in the novel, both harmonize with and contrast to Joanna and Nicholas. What complicates this predictable split between, say, the likes of a Crusoe and a Ronald Bridges, is that the narrative is distanced from us rather in the style of *The Ballad of Peckham Rye*. That is, where "ballad" manner sets up certain expectations for our reading of *Ballad*, expectations that are then both met and averted, so in the case of *Girls* the dated and ageless associations between reader and fairy tale condition us for pleasures, disappointments, shocks, complicated evaluation. More precisely, Spark's narrator begins with "Long ago in 1945 all the nice people in England were poor, allowing for exceptions. . . . All the nice people were poor; at least, that was a general axiom, the best of the rich being poor in spirit" (p. 7). The book's last words, too, are "long ago in 1945" (p. 128). This casually artful blending of childhood tale, scriptural tag, calendar specificity with its World War II reminders, and colloquial humor cutting into both tale and Scripture is neatly suggestive of several attitudes, concerns, and confusions eventually shared by the readers in such a way as to impress upon us the irony in those final words. For of course the long ago, in the novels of Spark or of anyone else successfully aiming for universality, conveys all thens and theres, heres and nows, as well as the timeless, the placeless.

I have said that Joanna Childe, strong Christian and daughter of a clergyman, and Nicholas Farringdon, confused secularist-become-Catholic Brother, fit in with the others in the book and are at odds with them. Spark manages to effect this paradoxical arrangement by virtue, in part, of her fairy-tale frame. By this I mean not only that the narrator introduces the novel and ends it in traditional

Grimm and Andersen language, but that the narrator plays up the spirit of cohesiveness arising from the men's and especially the women's all being young, variously interesting and attractive, relatively poor in worldly goods, and united with so many against such an obviously evil enemy as Germany in World War II. Although the book is narrated externally, much attention is given to Nicholas's admiration for the individuals who are "the girls," and for these women collectively considered. Cold or warm, fat or thin, plain or beautiful, calculatingly sane or balmy, religious or not, blank or bright, all the residents and male guests of Kensington's May of Teck Club (founded by and named after George V's eventual queen, for "Ladies of Slender Means"—pp. 9,13) delight Nicholas and give rise to his (and our) reflections on this community as microcosm *and* anomaly. Nicholas sees, and the fairy-tale frame enables us to see, these characters as set apart, happily at one despite their quarrels and differences; and Nicholas feels at one with that unity despite his own uniqueness. The frame urges us, with much narrative assistance, to see these characters, their situation, and the events in which the girls are engaged as somehow wonderfully happy no matter how the girls get on one another's nerves, bicker, compete for men and rationing coupons, or earn their various wartime livings away from the club. This blissful illusion is traceable, as I say, to Nicholas as well as to the narrator. In particular, the illusion comes from the facts that Nicholas sleeps with Selina Redwood, easily the most beautiful resident of the club, negotiates pleasantly with Jane Wright, an assistant publisher, for the possible publication of his *Sabbath Notebooks*, enjoys religious discussion with the more elderly women in residence, and is fascinated by Joanna's poetic recitations as she gives diction lessons in the club. In fact Nicholas's pleasure in the club and his implicit feeling that it is somehow set apart evoke the specialness—also like that of a fairy tale— of Frank Capra's film version of *You Can't Take It with You.* One almost gets the feeling that youth, high spirits, determination to win through, may be traced to the characters' being forced into this happy individual-collective society and that it will not end.

But of course that it will not end is the principal illusion that Spark's novel is out to break—and indeed we recall that, for good or ill, fairy tales too end. Even when tales end comically, in fact, with "happily ever after" appended, a good deal may qualify their bliss; and we remember that violence and pain are decidedly appropriate to fairy tales. In short, that fairy tales are harmless pap fit for the innocent and those we would keep from the hard world is itself a remarkable illusion. Spark knows this and uses her knowledge to coax us in so that she can show us the foolishness of being thus coaxed and the opportunity to be delighted and instructed once we've been seduced.

After Spark's narrator gets us and Nicholas feeling at home in the world that is the May of Teck Club, allied opposition to Nazism, and youthful and vigorous will to make the world and oneself free again—and well fed and well paid and sexually satisfied—the narrator quite suddenly shows us the value of a specific and emphasized early setting, the better to make us absorb the point of the book. Right after the fairy-tale opening, the narrator had described bombed-out England:

> The streets of the cities were lined with buildings in bad repair or in no repair at all, bomb-sites piled with stony rubble, houses like giant teeth in which decay had been drilled out, leaving only the cavity. Some bomb-ripped buildings looked like the ruins of ancient castles until, at a closer view, the wallpapers of various quite normal rooms would be visible, room above room, exposed, as on a stage, with one wall missing; sometimes a lavatory chain would dangle over nothing from a fourth or fifth-floor ceiling; most of all the staircases survived, like a new art-form, leading up and up to an unspecified destination that made unusual demands on the mind's eye. (P. 7)

These are vivid words, almost analogous to a sharply sketched painting even as they evoke photographs of London during the blitz. As the narrator builds the book, however, the words take on some of that larger significance of physical setting to which Spark has accustomed us. Indeed, the club that has escaped this common fate of buildings surrounding it eventually succumbs to a fire caused by the explosion of an undetected bomb dropped into its garden in 1942. When this time bomb explodes after three years the resulting fire closes the staircase to all the girls living at the top of the club and forces them to escape by way of a skylight in the roof of a lavatory, through which all escape save Joanna, who, in fixed habit and terrible fear, recites the Book of Common Prayer's readings for this twenty-seventh day of the month. When Joanna and the building go down together, after a whole bookful of her recitations of poems (like Hopkins's *Wreck of the Deutschland*) concerned with death and resurrection, the reader harks back to those opening words contrasting decay and collapse to ascending staircases, open sky, and regions of the imagination. The reader then associates the descent-ascent figure attached to 1945 with the castles mentioned in the opening paragraph, so that once again the dated is seen to apply to all times. Then the reader recalls the firemen's reiterated assurances during the rescue operation: "It's just a question of time" (p. 109)—as indeed had been the bomb's exploding and the breaking of the carefully established narrative illusion that Eden might be regained in Kensington.

But the touch-soft popular lyrics—"There were angels dining at the Ritz / And a nightingale sang in Berk'ley Square" (pp. 44, 100)—words that regularly come over the radio—prove no competition for the sacred and secular poetry recited by Joanna: things decay and people die, and no amount of effort to hold fast to realism's yesterday can succeed.[15] Sentimentality is deadly and serves only to remind us of mortality rather than to take our minds from it or to transcend it. Sentimentality is depressing in its self-contradictory addiction to impermanence. In short, Eden is not to be found in London whatever the reader, together with Nicholas, may have been led pleasantly to suppose. Given the terms of the novel as these are presented to Nicholas, one must choose meta-phorically between the emptiness of sentimental assurances that concrete real-ism is imperishable and Joanna's poetic reminders that, however one looks at reality, life, realistically, is inevitably death's prelude and neither more nor less real than death. Joanna's periodic dollops of Shelley's "Ode to the West Wind" or of Hopkins's *Wreck*, taken together with Joanna's fiery demise and Christian belief, help to push readers of any and all persuasions to see the dehumanizing—if poignant—unreality of the "Nightingale"'s lyrics and to reflect instead upon what the narrator may have allowed us to infer from those words, "up and up to an unspecified destination that made unusual demands on the mind's eye."

Primarily the eye in question is that of Nicholas, although obviously the reader's eye will take in and work with what the reader understands to be Nicholas's reactions and motivation. For this reason I think it important to observe in detail the forces at work upon Nicholas—forces influencing his actions, the shape of the book, and our readings. Indeed, this is a conversion novel that has the task of making conversion at least plausible, imaginable. Moreover, this is a conversion story that does not fit the comic pattern discussed in the previous section of this chapter. By following Nicholas's changes, we should be able to chart the narrator's course, Spark's art, and the generic mixedness of the novel.

According to the presumably reliable Rudi Bittesch, Nicholas's longtime acquaintance, Nicholas had for years wavered between extremes. He had had affairs with men and with women, had leaned toward exclusive privacy at one moment and toward collective action at another, had talked monarchy or incipient fascism alternately with anarchism, had talked pacifism and joined the army, had got out of armed service on psychological grounds only to be moved to Intelligence, and "could never make up his mind between suicide and an equally drastic course of action known as Father D'Arcy. . . . [T]he latter was a Jesuit philosopher who had the monopoly for converting the English intellectuals" (p. 48). Plainly, even this thumbnail sketch shows Nicholas's promise as a Spark figure (like Barbara Vaughan) prominently torn between apparent opposites. We should expect the narrative to involve him in the possibility of having things both ways, in Ronald Bridges's fashion. Nicholas does in fact live and die up to our expectations.

Once we know how Nicholas has been tugged at, we can more easily appreci-ate his being taken with the harmonious disarray of the May of Teck Club and can understand his relishing what looks like the incarnation of having-it-both-ways. Moreover, he is gratified to be made apparently a part of the club's life—to gain a most attractive lover, charming friends, amusing opportunities, and a chance to be published—all, crucially, at no cost to himself. That is, he manifests the usual idea that paradise will/would be all get, little or no give, even as his personal split is apparently appeased by the attractive combination of social interaction and youthful individualism. In a moment of high spirits, presumably to see himself in print, Nicholas induces Jane Wright, the publisher's assistant, to forge a letter of compliment from Charles Morgan to Nicholas, praising the manuscript of *The Sabbath Notebooks*.[16] Since Jane is, like Patrick Seton, a skillful forger, Nicholas's worldly career would seem to be in good hands.

With his world looking better and his flesh well tended, Nicholas begins to observe other matters—thereby supporting Rudi's testimony that Nicholas is an inveterate double-seer. He observes, for example, that the poetry recited by Joanna is always of the same sort. Although he does not specify that sort, we realize that the poetry is always concerned with springtime and autumn, with the *carpe diem* theme, with immortality variously conceived. Joanna, as the narrator informs us, has decided to remain constant to her first unmarriable love, to have no other man, and to live for the spirit as exclusively as she can. Nicholas regards her decision as unfortunate and refers to "poor Joanna." On the other hand he observes that while he loves Selina, she does not love him. The assurance of this imbalance comes from the narrator:

> [H]e was quite content with his austere bed-sitting room. With the reckless abandon of a visionary, he pushed his passion for Selina into a desire that she, too, should accept and exploit the outlines of poverty in her life. He loved her as he loved his native country. He wanted Selina to be an ideal society personified amongst her bones, he wanted her beautiful limbs to obey her mind and heart like intelligent men and women, and for these to possess the same grace and beauty as her body. Whereas Selina's desires were comparatively humble, she only wanted . . . a packet of hairgrips which had just disappeared from the shops. . . .
>   It was not the first instance of a man taking a girl to bed with the aim of converting her soul, but he . . . felt it was, and . . . willed and willed the awakening of her social conscience. . . . It was incredible to him that she should not share with him an understanding of the lovely attributes of dispossession and poverty, her body was so austere and economically furnished. (P. 83)

Noting these observations made of Nicholas, the reader is aware that on the one hand Nicholas wants Joanna to be fulfilled, to have some sexual life, and that on the other hand Nicholas cannot make Selina comprehend any sort of life other than the bodily. Countering Joanna's poems of death and renewal is Selina's charm-school formula, which she recites regularly: "Poise is perfect balance, an equanimity of body and mind, complete composure whatever the social scene. Elegant dress, immaculate grooming, and perfect deportment all contribute to the attainment of self-confidence" (p. 45). We note as well, and hardly incidentally, that, like Ronald Bridges, Nicholas convinces us of the genuineness of his concern—his love—for *both* Joanna and Selina neither by going to bed nor by staying out of bed with them, but by thinking, according to his lights, of what it is good for them to be and to have. Nicholas's love for Joanna is evident in his wishing her physically and spiritually well, although he does not desire her; and his love for Selina is evident in his wishing her spiritual life to match the sexual life that he shares with her. As Ronald suggested to Elsie, sex itself neither establishes nor disproves anything else about the reality of a human relationship. Two corollary points are worthy of mention here. First, Joanna's renunciation not of the body but of sex affirms her first love's constancy rather than denies the value of the body. Second, Selina's wish to sleep with only those who do not threaten to possess her individuality may seem to affirm spirit but in fact denies spirit and affirms her intention to remain free to use her sexuality not so much for its own gratifications as for those things of this world which prove difficult to procure otherwise. If each woman is selfish, we are reminded that everyone is naturally selfish and that selfishness requires various, perhaps innumerable, definitions. But the immediate value of our point about the Joanna-Selina contrast as that contrast imperceptibly grows upon Nicholas is that it prepares us for what he eventually experiences and consequently what he chooses to do with his life.

Of two climactic occasions that account for Nicholas's behavior and motives, the first is the fire. In a decidedly minor way, there is something slightly amusing about a group of women huddled in a lavatory and separated into either down-flushable or up-risable according to the accident of their hip measurements: there they are gathered, dressed or undressed, greased in some instances for slithering upward, while the ample Joanna, clearly too large for the only exit immediately available, recites the splendidly appropriate Common Prayer psalms pleading for delivery. Nicholas, seeing all of this from the rooftop where he has gone to pull out anyone slim enough to make it, sees also the lovely Selina as she first pulls herself through the skylight as she had done on many an evening to make love with Nicholas on the roof, then sees her reenter the building in order to help others escape, he supposes, then sees her reascend with a valuable Schiaparelli taffeta dress that the slimmer girls have shared. Her only words are "Is it safe out here?" His reply, the first indication that his Edenic illusion is cracking and that he is a Spark reality-seer, is merely, "Nowhere's safe" (p. 112). This he says in spite of Selina's securing or stealing Anne Baberton's dress and ascending skyward.

On the other hand, Nicholas's background may well have readied him to see Joanna's death as evocative of Hardy's "Convergence of the Twain" or of Hopkins's *Wreck*, as well as of Pentecostal fire in the upper room and Joan of Arc's redemptive burning. He does not share his thoughts with the reader, but the narrator records Nicholas's wonder at Joanna's being pale with terror and mechanically capable of recalling both incantations and responses of the right day of the month, and of supplying, perhaps hypnotically, perhaps consciously, strength of a sort to herself and the others in the midst of fear. No more than

Selina does Joanna have occasion to talk about motive or attitude, but that she has a profound effect (as does Selina) upon Nicholas is undeniable (pp. 112–17).

Both Selina's ascent and Joanna's sinking obviously reinforce Nicholas's instinctive remark that "nowhere's safe," although he cannot account for his improbably making the sign of the cross when Selina scurries out with the dress. Like Lord Marchmain's signing of the cross that contributes to Charles Ryder's conversion in *Brideshead Revisited*, Nicholas's gesture cannot be explained but can be understood as psychologically appropriate because it has been set up in the fiction and can thus be regarded as fitting for the behavior of a character for whom we have been prepared as we have been prepared for Nicholas.

The other incident touching on Nicholas's change occurs during the wild public celebration in London on V-J Day. Amidst the thousands of people thronging the area of Buckingham Palace and Saint James's Park, Nicholas suddenly sees a sailor "[slide] a knife silently between the ribs of a woman who was with him" (p. 127). Nobody else seems to observe this or to hear Nicholas's shouting that the deed has been done and that the perpetrator ought to be apprehended. In such a crowd, the woman cannot even fall and be noticed. Later, Nicholas sees the same sailor in another part of the area and silently slips into his pocket the forged Charles Morgan letter that he had amusedly called the sign of his being "a crook" (p. 88). As we hear from beginning to end of the novel, Nicholas hereafter gives his unpublished *Sabbath Notebooks* to Rudi Bittesch, joins a Catholic missionary order, and is martyred in Haiti—news that Jane's assorted telephone calls to the "girls" perhaps fifteen years after V-J Day sprinkle throughout the novel together with snippets of Joanna's recitations and the other girls' dialogue recollected in bits and pieces.[17] As always, nothing can possibly explain religious conversion—conversion to believing rather than knowing, to awareness of reality as distinct from isolated realism—but such conversion can be experienced by others as imaginatively and emotionally right if care is taken by the narrator in selecting and presenting the sort of event—in the realistic realm—that can be observed and recorded. Enough of such events in the right order can make emotional sense of an otherwise irrecoverable occurrence. It may help us to know, for example, that Nicholas had written in his *Notebooks* a sentence which makes some sense to those of us who, unlike the characters in the novel, know of the knifing and of the letter transfer: "A vision of evil may be as effective to conversion as a vision of good" (p. 126). The words may apply to the knifing and may also clarify Dougal Douglas's reference to devils driving out devils. But we realize that the words apply as well to Selina's sexuality and selfish commitment to matter, starting with her body, and also to Nicholas's new sense of his own previous commitment to matter in having the letter forged and in supposing Joanna to be necessarily stunted without a man (the same mistake that Ryder makes about Cordelia in *Brideshead Revisited*). The good that balances evil is of course Joanna's martyrdom (she had waited for the others to flee before failing to make it herself), a fact that he cannot doubt as proof that he was mistaken about her having lost out in life, and which he cannot explain. Nor can he explain how Selina could miss so much or why he presumably feels that attaching his own guilty letter to a scapegoat will enable Nicholas to atone and maybe alert the murderer to good as Nicholas the evildoer has become aware of good. What Nicholas's string of experiences leads to is a conversion rooted inexplicably in the realization that since "nowhere's safe" (that is, since Original Sin has precluded Eden) one must choose between living for a realism that, however intentioned, is limited to what Nicholas's secular best wishes had wanted for Joanna, Selina, himself, and everyone else, and living so as somehow to recognize a different, ultimately mysterious, reading of the possible. Nicholas opts for the second choice, although one need not infer that what he comes to realize—what converts him—accounts altogether for his formal religious vocation. All we know for sure is that the fiction presents us and Nicholas with a stark contrast between Selina and the sailor on the one hand and Joanna on the other, and that Nicholas, who had not previously thought either extreme possible, feels compelled to choose between the dangers of world and flesh alone and the dangers of world-flesh-spirit. The second is more nearly real to him than the first can any longer be, and he accordingly takes the direction of what he newly sees to be reality—another way to describe conversion.

And yet I have excluded this novel from those discussed under the rubric of comic structure. How can this be, since *Girls* would appear to be the story of Nicholas Farringdon's conversion and apparently willing martyrdom to that reality which Spark consistently expounds? The reason is that this book is not Nicholas's or Joanna's, even to the extent that *The Bachelors* is Ronald Bridges's. True, Joanna and Nicholas seem the only ones to grasp Spark's thesis, but the book is also heavily concerned, obviously, with the full group included in the title—concerned more prominently, too, than *The Bachelors* is concerned with Patrick Seton. That is, where Spark takes Patrick seriously, she leaves no doubt about his being wrong and about his opposition's being right, and she sees to it that Patrick loses; whereas in *Girls*, on the contrary, while one has no doubt about Nicholas's making the right choice based on accurate perception, one shares Nicholas's mixed feelings about the other side. Illusions are never more than illusions, of course; still, when one thinks back to the book's acknowledgment of V-E Day—an acknowledgment in the form of one character's asking a question of another (Nicholas) by quoting "[a]n Alexandrian poet" (Cavafy)—one realizes something of the depth and intensity of a certain kind of illusion created by one's participation in a war that one believes just. The words are:

And now what will become of us without Barbarians?
Those people were some sort of a solution.

(P. 18)

This language evokes something of the spirit reputedly felt by the British as they underwent the blitz and fought back, and the words also intimate something of the spirit that Nicholas both experiences and tries to nurture at the May of Teck Club. For a common enemy, clearly bad, against whom people can honorably expend energy, occasions pulling together self-sacrificingly and uniting for good. The end of such a war, as the poem suggests, destroys the illusion that evil is external and collectively opposable. Instead, one realizes that wartime makes its own effective illusion that one need not remember the personal, internal, individual nemesis inherent in human nature. Everyone is his/her own barbarian, a fact more basic than any social fact and one that guarantees a lifelong battle rather than a temporary if dreadful one. It is this Original Sin that Nicholas neglects in his enchantment—or self-enchantment—with the fetching ways of young women united. Thus, the subsequent experiencing of Joanna, Selina, the sailor, and himself in the midst of noise, struggle, excitement, is this awakening to the truth that personal taint is part of human nature rather than of German or Japanese militarism exclusively.

The book's structure is ironic, then, rather than comic, not for lack of a clear moral awareness socially relevant, but because of so much emphasis on the sadness of loss, of the Fall, of most characters' inability to comprehend what Nicholas comes to find out about realistic shortcomings. His death is gossip to be forgotten tomorrow; moreover, Nancy Riddle's calling him a "poor fellow" recalls Nicholas's own secular misreading of "poor Joanna," so that one is inclined to wonder what good on the realistic level vocation or martyrdom may accomplish. His conversion makes the question as unnecessary as it is unanswerable in the terms on which it is asked; but still there is an abiding sadness both because the girls cannot recreate Eden and because they cannot share his conviction of what therefore will and will not do. Never does a Spark book condescend or scold or puritanically fail to see what's funny in the most terrible moral misreadings, but at the same time, a comic structure works out—at least socially—the way we want it to work out, whereas *Girls* plays up not only the way to think and believe but the sadness of not knowing or glimpsing what's been missed. Looking back over the narrative, we note that novel-time (that is, narrative-time irrespective of exposition and retrospective narration and the future occasion of Nicholas's martyrdom) extends through the summer of 1945: from V-E Day to V-J Day. This period marks for Nicholas the weary end of battle and the gathering of forces to finish up; but one of the other characters remarks on the occasion of the public celebration of V-E Day that "it was something between a wedding and a funeral on a world scale" (p. 16). This language begins to hit home as we become accustomed to Nicholas's doubleness and it lands hard when on V-J Day, the other end of narrative present, we share with Nicholas alone the sailor's murdering of the woman amidst happiness that the barbarians of Europe and Asia have been conquered. What impresses us here is that we, like Nicholas, had been lulled into forgetting the human condition, precisely because an obvious external evil had indirectly complimented us on our own collective virtue and had drawn our attention from taint coeval with the race. Of a piece with the sailor's deed are Nicholas's lying forgery and what the narrator calls Selina's act of "savagery" on the occasion of the fire (p. 54). If, then, the novel presents a "wedding" side in giving us, through Nicholas's eyes, the beautiful youth and Edenic illusion of the girls and in bringing Nicholas to share Spark's awareness, it also gives us a "funeral" side. For it shows the falseness of that lovely illusion, the fleetingness of any occasion to transfer individual taint and responsibility to a common external foe (analogous to Nicholas's futile effort to attach his fraudulence to the murdering sailor), and the unlikelihood of working successfully on the realistic level to cause anyone else to share Nicholas's view. Such things—such conversions—are shown to be effected apart from and against anyone's intention, as Nicholas's experiences demonstrate. It is the reminder of this funeral side of existence that determines my generic qualifying of this novel: because it concludes not socially resolved as a comic structure is resolved, I call it an irony.

As we have seen, romantic and realistic tendencies had alternately swayed Nicholas until he became a reality-seer. In the long run not only is his simple Edenic illusion broken, but his conversion manifests his conviction of how poverty-stricken in spirit humanity is. We recall that in interviewing prospective authors Jane Wright was in the habit of asking, "What is your raison d'être?" (p. 37). This question is delightfully inane, of course, and is meant to put the aspiring author in a hole; but the question is one that Nicholas and the reader are eventually required to ask seriously, as always in Spark's books. In Nicholas's case, as for example in Ronald's, the implicit answer comes in the life chosen, which in turn indicates the "être" and the reality in question. Similarly, the book's title works at various levels. Only the slenderest girls can wear the Schiaparelli dress and slide readily through the skylight to safety (as if, given this novel, that could be the right word), and their incomes are slight and their material opportunities limited accordingly. But the narrative clearly reverses (converts) these readings for Nicholas, so that the sylphlike Selina and the hefty Joanna are viewed in reversed opposition, and the slender means of survival is read otherwise because Nicholas arrives at his "raison d'être" and another idea of what "survival" is and is for. The title is not meant to convey a sense of moral superiority (Nicholas over all except Joanna) but, I think, is meant to suggest the slight means of coping, whatever one's view. That is, precisely because Nicholas sees doubly, he sees that anyone's personal resources are "slender," in short, and Nicholas's conversion is to a way of seeing the different senses in which that assertion is true.

"Nowhere's safe," as he blurts out instinctively, even as he instinctively crosses himself: but the conviction of this fact is exactly what precludes his feeling some sort of moral superiority. Nicholas is not, then, "saved" (to use a word frequently applied, many times by themselves, to converts) but is converted to a sense of the ongoing struggle different from his earlier sense of that struggle: to read the struggle doubly is clearly not to rest in complacent awareness of arrival, but to battle doubly hard to keep one's unified duality in view. Nicholas was, as Nancy Riddle happily speculates on the phone to Jane, "in love with us all" (p. 126), rather than with Selina alone; but the love is eventually Ronald's kind rather than a sentimental attachment to stalwart young women impervious to the blows of the world. His is a love inexplicable in origin and nature as, for instance, is the temporal-timeless harmony of Joanna's probably unconscious recitation of the Anglican liturgy for Day 27, which fits all times and 27 July 1945, and which is right for now and universally right (pp. 113–17). Nicholas's eventual belief follows hard upon his taking in of such moments as this, but no one is in a position to say what exactly *caused* that belief. Nobody can explain belief, but Nicholas knows that it depends in paradoxically large part upon what he surely does not and cannot know. Since this is the case, we may note that, in Nicholas's double view, the slenderness of one's personal means is directly proportionate to one's need to seek other help—grace.

This doubleness, or what I have called an ambivalent irony undercutting comedy, is beautifully evident when Joanna's father, Rector Childe, comes to London at Nicholas's invitation, to hear Nicholas's tape recording of Joanna's reading of Hopkins's *Wreck of the Deutschland* and to view the site of her death. Nicholas discovers that the tape has been erased and that all he can do is insist to Joanna's father that "Joanna had religious strength"—to which the rector replies, "I know that, my boy" (p. 120). Similarly, at the bombsite, this exchange occurs:

> 'There's really nothing to see.'
> "Like my tape-recording,' said Nicholas.
> 'Yes, it's all gone, all elsewhere.' (P. 123)

Clearly we are back with Saint Paul and Barbara Vaughan and the narrator on the last page of *Ballad,* in their insistence upon belief as fitted to what the senses cannot detect, and Rector Childe calmly takes as much for granted whereas Nicholas feels at this point that he has somehow let the old gentleman down in failing to produce realistic sights and sounds. True, Nicholas obviously comes to share the rector's faith; but the darkness or grayness of the novel is in its stark acknowledgment that nothing is sadder about the human condition—the Fall's effects—than its leaving the realist and the reality-seer no way to talk with each other and nothing to talk about. As the converted king notes in Eliot's "Journey of the Magi," birth is a great revelation and joy, but it bears a remarkably grim resemblance to death. This resemblance resides in the believer's altered view of the realistic realm and of "elsewhere," and in his consequent inability to communicate, to share, in the former human way. Thus Joanna and Nicholas cannot communicate, the rector and Nicholas similarly miss each other, and, to come full circle, Nicholas appears not to connect with any of the "girls" who learn of his martyrdom. That this gap is obvious to the reality-seers and in no way impinges adversely on their belief is plainly the case; but the emphatic coldness of the separation precludes, for me, the overall affirmativeness of Nicholas's conversion separately considered.[18]

The progress and outcome of *The Prime of Miss Jean Brodie* (1961)[19] are also mixed, but even more severely grim, less nearly comic, than those of *Girls*. In some ways, the superficial conditions of the two books are similar. *Girls* places Nicholas Farringdon among a group of young women whom he regards as in many ways idyllic, and toward whom his judgments become changed but not quite altogether so, as he himself changes profoundly all unawares. In this way we get Spark's sense of them vs. him-plus-them, a contrast with an effect I call ironic. *Prime*, written two years earlier, deals with a group of young girls as they mature under the tutelage of Jean Brodie. Miss Brodie and the girls join the narrator in regarding this particular teacher-student relationship as often idyllic and seemingly headed for a fortunate outcome desired and foreseen by Miss Brodie. What occurs, however, is a reversal resembling that in *Girls*: one of the young women comes to see things, as does Nicholas, with different eyes, changes in Nicholas's fashion, and brings about an ending that, in honoring doubleness, breaks up comic possibilities. Because the breakup is even more sobering than that in *Girls*, I discuss it later on the scale of increasing starkness.

Like *Girls*, this earlier novel sets up a group that creates for itself and others the illusion (considered by the narrator as a partial reality) of a small world capable of living within the larger world but on the smaller world's own terms to a considerable degree. Indeed, like the young women of the May of Teck Club, the six little girls who at age ten become "the Brodie set" at Edinburgh's Marcia Blaine School in 1930, and who leave that establishment at eighteen in 1938, display distinct differences from one another while remaining to some extent unified—in this case around the central figure of Miss Jean Brodie, although Miss Brodie teaches only the Junior School classes, covering the first two of the girls' eight years at Marcia Blaine. The six girls are in effect, even beyond their two years in Miss Brodie's classroom, a sort of school within a school and thus an instance, designed by their mentor, of an elitist manner of dealing with extramural realism. Jean Brodie sets out to make these girls "the crème de la crème," by which she means a small coterie who will value "art and religion first; then philosophy; lastly science. That is the order of the great subjects of life, that's their order of importance" (p. 39). In fact, Jean herself only thinks she values these subjects, at least as academic or intellectual pursuits; for in practice she encourages the girls in so many words to cram what they know to be necessary for examinations, without regard to retaining any of it thereafter, and—here is the essence of her pedagogy—to model themselves on her. Miss Brodie's regime, her model, her basis for distinguishing among and evaluating and compartmentalizing her six girls, is herself. Thus Giotto is the greatest painter: "He is my favourite" (p. 18). Religion (she appears to mean Christian religion) is important but supposedly ought not to qualify one's individualistic style of life: Roman Catholicism, for instance, is for those who cannot think for themselves. Education means a "leading out" of what is seemingly inherent in each girl; it is an *"e-duco"* rather than in *"in-trudo"*—a breaking into that individuality. One is to pray for, but not to stare at, the poor. The world needs to be saved, and Hitler and Mussolini and Franco are restoring economic order to that end. "Team spirit" is nonetheless out; individualism counts. Posture and pronunciation matter; loyalty is crucial. "Safety first" will not do: "Goodness, Truth and Beauty come first" (p. 17). These are some of Miss Brodie's principles. Given the economic comfort and loyal cohesiveness of the six girls and their mentor in this decade before World War II, and despite quarrels and the general sadistic treatment of the "stupid" Mary Macgregor (one of the six), they do seem in a fair way to making Miss Brodie's plans for them a reality.

But of course the trouble with Miss Brodie's principles is not so much that the outside world will inevitably encroach upon the possibility of their realization as it is the principles themselves. The weakness resides in their randomness and whimsicality, in their being the anti-intellectual, emotionally strong impressions of Miss Brodie. The so-called principles have not been thought out and are in fact self-contradictory, or potentially so in many ways. Miss Brodie's preferences are sometimes addressed to abstract ideas and circumstances, sometimes to the concrete order; they sometimes concern the self considered alone, sometimes imply or overtly account for the rest of the world—people and things; they sometimes limit themselves to realistic matters, sometimes conjure up relations with extrarealistic reality. In other words, as we look back from the end of the novel through its course, we see that the narrator has arranged the history of the thirties and of these characters so that, as in *Girls,* "it is a question of time" before the dream dissipates and this microworld shows itself to have been an impossibility.

In the meanwhile, of course, the pleasures and endearments of this little corner of Edinburgh between wars are many. Indeed, the special pleasures of this novel stem in large part from the narrator's coaxing us into the illusion that Jean Brodie's efforts to have things both ways (to live on her terms, and to train others to embrace and get away with those same terms, even while earning the world's money and eating its bread and playing its game superficially) will pay off. She is singularly strong and tranquil in her battle to keep her teaching position, although Miss Mackay, the headmistress, works ceaselessly to find grounds for removing her. Everything, in fact, given the omniscient narrator's focus on the teacher and her coterie, inclines the reader to sympathize with the Brodie view of reality and thereby to see how the little girls are powerfully affected by that view. We are reliably informed by the narrator, for example, that Miss Brodie's first love, Hugh Carruthers, died (as she tells the girls) in the First World War, that she resists an affair with Teddy Lloyd, the art instructor, because (despite their love for each other) he is a married man, that at least one of her reasons for not marrying Gordon Lowther, the music instructor, is that she doesn't love him, that although she speaks regularly of Miss Mackay as her enemy she will not permit the little girls to speak disloyally of her, that what she gives the girls *does* cause them—even poor Mary—to remember her as the best part of the most impressionable time of their lives, and that they do in fact love her. More importantly, none of these generalizations is merely pronounced and laid down for us; rather, we see in the conduct of the little and growing girls that Jean Brodie provides an example of what to be and do—and of what to resist.

One useful way to imagine the crossroads where comedy splits off from irony is to attend to the question of how far the little girls can go along with Miss Brodie before taking decisions in favor of the ironic road—the road along which circumstances and choice induce Nicholas Farringdon. In the present novel this crisis arises for Sandy Stranger, the girl closest in every way to Jean Brodie's character, the one most imaginatively aware (*because* she is most like Jean Brodie) of what is morally at stake in the lives of Jean and others, and thus the one most sensitive to the inevitability of betraying one set of values or another, no matter whether she chooses to act or to refrain from acting. Where five of the girls—Monica Douglas, Rose Stanley, Eunice Gardiner, Jenny Gray, and Mary Macgregor—all take what Miss Brodie is and what she has to give and then depart to their assorted careers influenced by her but seemingly otherwise tied to Miss Brodie only in memory, Sandy Stranger shares their common girlhood with her mentor *and* undergoes experiences (like Nicholas's) that both tie her future life to her Brodie-set youth and separate her from that part of her life. Another way to say this is to point out that as in Spark's other books, a central character learns the necessity of balancing, living with, realism and reality. Sandy Stranger becomes this novel's Nicholas; she is converted to his way of seeing, which is Spark's way.

More specifically, this novel shows Jean's principles and pronouncements to be self-contradictory. Where Jean thinks herself to be educating each of her girls to be a civilized (European rather than Scots or British) individual in contrast to and defiance of the system (social, religious, political, locally cultural), she in fact would have them become a small separate society of persons like herself, and more crucially she would have them be not their own individual selves at all, but vicarious livers of the life she has wanted for herself. That is, she endorses "*e-duco*" but practices, very likely inadvertently, "*in-trudo.*" As I say, for five of the six girls, this internal contradiction makes no difference, for they appear not to notice it or be affected by it: each goes her own way and fits somehow into the going system without jettisoning fond, deserved memories of her teacher. Sandy Stranger, however, is, like Nicholas, the one character whose difference from the rest makes her centrally important to theme and structure.

Spark's development of Sandy is brilliant. For most of the book Sandy is convincingly shown as a little girl among other girls, coming to love Jean Brodie and to stand in awe of her courageous idiosyncrasies. And indeed Jean Brodie seems to be very successful in "educing" Sandy's imaginative potential: among the funniest passages in the book, for instance, are Sandy's imagined encounters with Alan Breck of *Kidnapped* and Rochester of *Jane Eyre*, and the epistolary and narrative fictions in which she and Jenny fantasize the romantic involvement of Jean Brodie with Hugh Carruthers and Gordon Lowther. But at fifteen Sandy undergoes a psychological-cultural experience that begins with her discovering a connection between the religion of John Knox and the temperament and habits of the Scots people. This discovery is seemingly of no particular religious import, at least initially, but serves rather to help her make other connections among her experiences. For example, it is only after seeing Knox's influence in her sur-roundings and in the institutions and people of Edinburgh that she gives any serious thought to Jean Brodie's eager desire to have Rose Stanley become Teddy Lloyd's mistress and to have Sandy report the affair in detail. Previously, Sandy had seen only that since Jean Brodie and Teddy loved each other fruitlessly, Miss Brodie would like the highly valued girls to be his friends, to be painted by him, to be her platonic links with him. Now, however, Sandy sees that whichever of the girls happens to be his model of the moment, all of their portraits turn out looking like Jean Brodie despite their bearing some resemblance to the models. Sandy also is astounded to realize, following her putting together of Scots religion and Scots behavior to account for the peculiarly guilty glee with which Scots break religious rules, that Jean Brodie is not living vicariously and harmlessly in the girls' relations with Teddy Lloyd but is verily playing God in trying to assign Rose (as one with "instinct") to become a lover and Sandy (with "insight") to become an uninvolved reporter. When, at about the same time (age eighteen) that Sandy, not Rose, has become Teddy's lover, Sandy learns that Miss Brodie has been responsible for sending a student named Joyce Emily Hammond to fight for Franco, events have contributed enough to Sandy's awareness of Jean Brodie to dictate that she must "[put] a stop to Miss Brodie" (p. 182). The point is perhaps not so much that Jean converted Joyce Emily from the Republican side to Franco's as that Joyce Emily, who was in fact killed in an accident before ever reaching the war, is but another victim of Miss Brodie's manipulation—violation—of that very individuality of person about which she generalizes as her reason for teaching.

The fact that all these realizations are Sandy's rather than Miss Brodie's will indicate, quite rightly, that, just as *Girls* shifts from an apparent focus upon its title figures to an emphasis upon one who is converted because, in part, of his experiencing them, so the present novel is less concerned with the character and values of its title figure than with their effects upon Sandy Stranger's conversion. And indeed, just as Spark's method of time-breaking narration made it useful to specify chronologically certain crucial events in Nicholas's course of change, so it will be helpful to trace Sandy's development into Sister Helena of the Transfiguration. For it is Sandy's changing values rather than Jean Brodie's idiosyncratic constancy (sometimes delightful, harmless, invulnerable; sometimes not) with which the narrator is more and more clearly concerned (as was true in Nicholas's case also), and that accordingly become the book's shape and (yes) raison d'être. Thus, to understand Sandy is to understand this novel.

Looking back from the novel's end, we discover that throughout the book we have been given more insight into Sandy than into any of the other girls, a fact which the artfully disrupted chronology has carefully obscured. We learn, for example, that Sandy is perhaps more intelligent and imaginative than most of the other girls and that her kinship with Miss Brodie emerges in the sort of independent, flippant remark which provokes Miss Brodie to retort, foreshadowingly, that "someday you will go too far." We are told that Sandy loves Miss Brodie, and we see this love in Sandy's loyalty in the teeth of Miss Mackay's inquisition. We also see Sandy's fantasy life growing as she tries to put together her notions of romance, the psychological implausibility of intercourse, and indeed the sheer logistics or acrobatics of sex. Then, as we have noted, at fifteen (in 1935) she suddenly becomes interested in her Scots heritage (she is half English) and is drawn to make connections betwen Knox's theology and observable cultural behavior. Like all the other Brodie girls, Sandy spends a good portion of her last years at Marcia Blaine in the company of Teddy Lloyd and his family, often posing for portraits. Then for a few weeks in the summer of 1938 she and Teddy have their affair. We do not know why Sandy begins the affair— whether deliberately to thwart the much-discussed Brodie plan for Rose to play this role, or because she wishes to learn about sex or about what Miss Brodie finds in Teddy, or because, as she tells Miss Brodie, "he interests me" for unspecifiable reasons. Almost certainly, Sandy cannot know, either. As Sandy tells Jean Brodie and the narrator tells us, Sandy soon loses interest in Lloyd but embraces his Catholicism (in 1939), for reasons as mysterious as Nicholas's, but equally prominent in their following a series of selectively emphasized experiences. Also in 1939, Sandy provides miss Mackay with the political means of getting at Miss Brodie, who is thus forced to retire prematurely. In 1946, perhaps a year before Jean's death and Sandy's entering the convent, Sandy and Miss Brodie have lunch together, on which occasion Miss Brodie still wonders which girl betrayed her. Thereafter we learn that Sandy has written a surprisingly famous psychological treatise entitled *The Transfiguration of the Commonplace* and that she replies variously to her former coterie and to the many other outsiders who are permitted, as exceptions to the rule of the cloister, to visit this famous nun. Visitors notice, the narrator often remarks, that Sister Helena clutches the bars of the grille from behind which she speaks with her guests.

The title of Sandy's book and her new name—Sister Helena of the Transfiguration—combine with the rest of her career to make *Prime* her book and, like Nicholas's, a story of conversion and its consequences. Indeed, as the five other girls fade away and Miss Brodie slips, destroyed and hurt more by betrayal than by involuntary early retirement, into her grave, we are forced to consider Sandy's

act of betrayal in its causes and effects. How could Sandy, loving Miss Brodie and knowing what her career meant to her, have betrayed her and ended that career? Although nobody asks this directly of Sandy, several ask it indirectly (whether or not they actually suspect her) and she assuredly asks and answers it for herself.

We may or may not settle for calling Sandy's act one of betrayal, but we can begin our examination of her decision to tell Miss Mackay of Jean's fascist preachments by pointing out that Sandy does what she does because she has been more deeply and permanently influenced by Jean's teaching than have the rest. Indeed, her situation and her decision illuminate Lovelace's words, "I could not love thee, dear, so much, / Loved I not honor more." More specifically, Sandy herself makes three comments on the subject of betrayal. First, without talking about herself in particular, she responds as follows to Miss Brodie's concern to know which of her girls betrayed her: "If you did not betray us it is impossible that you could have been betrayed by us. The word betrayed does not apply" (p. 185). Then, when Monica tells her that the dying Jean Brodie suspected Sandy of betraying her, Sister Helena replies, "It's only possible to betray where loyalty is due" (p. 186). Finally, when Monica asks whether loyalty was not due Miss Brodie, Sister Helena responds, "Only up to a point" (p. 186).

As I see this novel, these comments are far from gratuitous mystification. Indeed, all three comments come to much the same thing, since they stem from the same moral economy. Sandy means that one must distinguish between principle and practice, between generalization and perpetration, between universal value and concrete doer and deed, between the values that Sandy had learned from Miss Brodie and Miss Brodie's own conduct in relation to those values. Thus, Sandy's retort to Jean Brodie means that Jean Brodie's behavior contradicted her own principles and thus canceled out any loyalty owed to herself as the consistent practitioner of those principles. If the spiritual ought to govern the material; if the concretely scientific is really less important than art, religion, and philosophy; if "Goodness, Truth and Beauty come first"—if these principles are to be accepted as Jean has induced Sandy, her most ardent disciple, to accept them, they obviously impose limits upon the extent to which one can possibly owe loyalty to any person, and limits on anyone's individualism. At some point, anyone attempting to attend seriously to all of Jean Brodie's idiosyncrasies put forward as general principles will have to observe that Miss Brodie necessarily contradicts herself and that her followers will have to do the same—not out of meanness or ill will, but simply because of the inherent self-contradictoriness between principles universal and "principles" idiosyncratic. Thus, in answering Jean Brodie on a very general level, Sandy means that "betrayal" is the wrong word for what the two of them are trying to get at; or, as she tells Monica, one can talk about betrayal only where loyalty is due and not paid. Miss Brodie's violation of her own tenet that everyone's individualism is sacred has shown Sandy that Jean Brodie cannot possibly understand what is involved in adhering to her own abstract ideals. In sending Joyce Emily to serve

vicariously for her in Spain, and in sending the others to take her place in Teddy's bed and studio, Jean Brodie, Sandy sees, "intruded" upon their individual selves and thereby pointed up her own inadequacy as God, church, and the embodiment of moral law. "Only up to a point" is loyalty due to any person, and that point is reached, in Sandy's reading, when she, as disciple, experiences the collapse of her "church" in its self-contradictions. When she reaches this point, Sandy (like Nicholas) has to make a choice.

Typically in Spark's work, that choice must be considered in two ways. In the realm of realism the choice—as the narrator and all characters except Sandy/Helena frequently refer to it—is between betraying and not betraying Miss Brodie. In the larger reality, however, as Sandy/Helena herself and as the direction of the novel posit that choice, it is between loyalty on the one hand to universally and concretely applicable and realizable values and loyalty on the other hand to one who contradicts those values and who trains others to do so. Sandy is like Nicholas in her conversion to the former loyalty as the larger one, and away from the latter loyalty as self-contradictory and humanly, morally, destructive. As Sandy sees her choice, it is between *both* and *neither*: for to stop Miss Brodie is to practice independently the Brodie principles, whereas to allow Miss Brodie to continue with children the manipulating that Sandy has become conscious of would be to let Miss Brodie continue violating her own supposed code *and* for Sandy to give up her own adherence to belief in that violated code.

Thus we return to my earlier observation that Sandy may be said in a larger sense to have manifested loyalty to what Miss Brodie taught her even though neither her teacher nor her fellow students appear to understand any moral basis except the first, the realistic. Sandy's act shows her rejection of loyalty to the person at all costs (the loyalty of E. M. Forster and Anthony Blunt) and her acceptance of loyalty to general principles without which loyalty to an individual would become meaningless and arbitrary. If her decision seems not only disloyal but crazy, the reason is that the other characters and most readers are realists rather than reality-seers. Given her lights, however, Sandy acts swiftly and economically: "The course to be taken was the most expedient and most suitable at the time for all the objects in hand" (p. 149). And again, when Sandy leaves Teddy and the city, the two of them congratulate each other on their "economy"—upon which the narrator comments as follows: "Sandy thought, if he knew about my stopping of Miss Brodie, he would think me more economical still. She was more fuming, now, with Christian morals, than John Knox" (p. 183).

This passage not only provides a key to Sandy's motivation. It offers as well an opportunity to compare Sandy's situation to Nicholas's, to observe a variation on the realism-reality theme, and to support my contention that this novel is darker than *Girls*.

For one thing, everything about this novel indicates that one ought not to be smitten with Knoxian morality, and indeed that Jean Brodie's capacity for unpredictable enthusiasms is theoretically counter to Knoxian repression and guilt-fostering. In this connection, and remembering Sandy's central position in the book, we ought to observe that Sandy's sharp swing over perhaps three years from Miss Brodie's brand of flexibility to Knox's brand of inflexibility marks, in its arc from one extreme to another, both Sandy's obvious differences from Jean Brodie and, paradoxically, Sandy's role as disciple and double. This rather odd statement means only that Jean Brodie's character is unstable, that her first principle is, at bottom, a thoroughly unprincipled, pragmatic insistence on rationalizing whatever she wants to be and do. Thus, when Sandy, whose flirtation with Knox is perfectly in keeping with her mentor's notions of trying out everything and keeping oneself open to change, shifts to a repressive frame of reference, she shows the unprincipled principle of her teacher. Moreover, the paradox takes another twist when we realize that Jean's own instability and avowed tolerance contradict her efforts to force her pupils to conform to fixed parts. Thus, remarkably, Sandy is Jean's mirror image as much in relying upon her fancy as in following that fancy into rigid confrontation with its model. Obviously, however, the novel is a great deal more complex than a single eventual battle between teacher and student, each motivated by the same instincts. For the narrator makes it very plain, by stressing Sister Helena's uneasy grasping of her grille, that, while Catholicism answers Sandy's needs better than does Knox, this very fact points to what was wrong with Sandy's action against Jean and therefore indirectly to why she chose Catholicism instead of either Knox or Jean Brodie. If we follow Sandy beyond her conversion to Knox we should be better able to compare her to Nicholas and to place this novel on the scale of irony.

We have had occasion to note that while conversion has its causes, these cannot be discovered and specified on the realistic level. We have also noted that Jean Brodie and Sandy are doubles. These two observations come jointly to mind, rewardingly, when we examine the following passage—and particularly when we recall that it is not the characters but the narrator who herein presumes to judge, to match, beliefs and characters:

> [Miss Brodie] always went to Church on Sunday mornings, she had a rota of different denominations and sects . . . outside the Roman Catholic pale which she might discover. Her disapproval of the Church of Rome was based on her assertions that it was a church of superstition, and that only people who did not want to think for themselves were Roman Catholics. In some ways, her attitude was a strange one, because she was by temperament suited only to the Roman Catholic Church; possibly it could have embraced, even while it disciplined, her soaring and diving spirit, it might even have normalised her. But perhaps this was the reason that she shunned it, lover of Italy though she was, bringing to her support a rigid Edinburgh-born side of herself when the Catholic Church was in question, although this side was not otherwise greatly in evidence. . . . [S]he let everyone know she was in no

doubt, that God was on her side whatever her course, and so she experienced
no difficulty or sense of hypocrisy in worship while at the same time she went
to bed with the singing master [Gordon Lowther]. Just as an excessive sense of
guilt can drive people to excessive action, so was Miss Brodie driven to it by an
excessive lack of guilt.

The side-effects of this condition were exhilarating to her special girls in
that they in some way partook of the general absolution she had assumed to
herself, and it was only in retrospect that they could see Miss Brodie's affair
with Mr. Lowther . . . in a factual light. All the time they were under her
influence she and her actions were outside the context of right and wrong. It
was twenty-five years before Sandy had so far recovered from a creeping vision
of disorder that she could look back and recognise that Miss Brodie's defective
sense of self-criticism had not been without its beneficent and enlarging
effects; by which time Sandy had already betrayed Miss Brodie and Miss
Brodie was laid in her grave. (Pp. 125–26)

Whatever the complex of discernible reasons for Sandy's conversion first to
Knox and then to Rome, those reasons are implicitly suggested by this passage.
The narrator tells us of Jean Brodie's "soaring and diving spirit" and of the self-
contradictory behavior manifesting that spirit. It seems clear that Sandy demonstrates precisely that erratic behavior in veering sharply in her attitude toward
Miss Brodie, her mirror image. Indeed, the narrator's language strongly implies
that this "soaring and diving" is as characteristic of Sandy as of Jean. It is ironic,
of course, that in veering from Jean's view that one is a moral law unto oneself all
the way to Knoxian theocratic repression, Sandy should wipe out her teacher.
But this fact is tricky in that the novel uses it to suggest that in moving past this
occasion and frame of mind, and in becoming Catholic, Sandy is not rejecting
her teacher but following the path which the narrator had seen as desirable if
implausible for Jean. Thus when Sandy is converted ("transfigured") from her
Knoxian furor and absolutism to Catholicism, she is extending Jean Brodie's
career and influence and showing the effectiveness of Jean's example (as Nicholas extends and expands upon Joanna's)—so that Sister Helena is anything but
sentimental in remarking that "a Miss Jean Brodie in her prime" (p. 187) was
the greatest influence upon her, whether one thinks of an influence as an
example to follow or to resist.

Sandy/Helena in fact follows *and* resists. This paradox looks clearer perhaps
when we see that Helena's position in the present is something of a middle
ground between the "excessive lack of guilt" evident in Jean's unprincipled
individualistic preachments and conduct and the "excessive sense of guilt"
evident in Knoxian orthodoxy. Sandy recovers from an early "vision of disorder"
and irresponsibility, swings opposite to narrow theocratic absolutism, and now
occupies a ground that, in the opinion of the narrator, allows individualism
within law and system. It is in first assuming the possibility of getting away with
Jean's version of reality, then in being disillusioned, and finally in converting to
Catholicism that Sandy parallels Nicholas: each is transfigured for the reader,

and for each of them reality becomes transfigured. Almost incidental to this parallel are the facts that Nicholas's conversion causes him to give up his book in favor of other action while Sandy's change accounts for her being enabled to write *The Transfiguration of the Commonplace*, and that Nicholas's change is almost immediate and final while Sandy's is gradual and ongoing. In fact, after we note that neither conversion can be explained, Nicholas's impresses us in its comparative simplicity—for we know nothing of him for fifteen years until he is martyred. Sandy, on the other hand, behaves in a way that pushes us to examine the relations among her denominational switching, her psychological book, her abiding view of Miss Brodie, and her clutching the bars of her grille. The middle ground that the narrator thinks possibly right for Jean is taken by her double but is uneasily occupied.

The reason for Helena's uneasiness is that she is acutely conscious of having behaved with violent severity toward Jean Brodie; of having followed her emotion (in Jean's fashion) with unnecessary haste and cruelty, however justifiable her reason might have been in the abstract. While Jean might eventually have had to be separated from an opportunity to nurture young girls in irresponsibility, Sandy did act on principle alone, without looking for any way to combine the principle with concern for Jean herself. Sandy might well have adhered to the moral aim of removing the evil, while alerting Miss Brodie herself to her intent rather than going directly to Miss Mackay. That is, the most economical means of acting may leave out certain complexities such as duties and responsibilities to persons as well as to tenets: news of an atomic threat might have won the war without requiring Sandy to drop the bomb. But of course Knox's view of moral economy, like Jean's, is partial—which is perhaps one reason why Sister Helena, who now (to her sorrow) knows this limitedness, has embraced (with Teddy's inexplicable aid) the faith recommended by the narrator for her double.

We may infer, at least, that Helena's present position is a sort of middle way between Knox's iron rules and Jean's sometimes hard, sometimes mushy, whimsy. But if Nicholas's giving up on Eden is sad, Helena's second conversion signifies an even grayer awareness. That is, coming down from her Knoxian fervor to the Catholicism suggested by the narrator may very well be Sandy's way of honoring both realism and reality, concretely pragmatic and individual on one hand and universally unchanging and general on the other, but this very alteration in her vision assures her seeing what she has done to Jean Brodie. For Sandy herself, acting to stop Miss Brodie's playing God, played God in presuming to dispose of Jean's life on sheer principle, as if this were Sandy's prerogative. Sandy did indeed "go too far," as Jean had ironically predicted, and whether her becoming Catholic is cause or effect of her realizing this moral grotesqueness, realize it she does: and this is why she clings to the bars. As the narrator remarks, Helena is now conscious (as Sandy was not in her Knoxian heat, in 1938) "that Miss Brodie's defective sense of self-criticism had not been without its beneficent and enlarging effects." But the very Nicholas-like dual vision that now lets her appreciate this truth (presumably the basis of her psychological study as well), and lets her value whatever *is* as dually unified in the manner of Christ's Transfiguration, means inevitably that she will never get over the psychological effects—the guilt attached to playing God and Judas—of crushing Jean Brodie. For even if there had been no other way to "stop . . . Miss Brodie," and even if the principle that one owes loyalty is true "[o]nly up to a point," Helena realizes (as Sandy did not) that Miss Brodie was in many ways a good person and good to and for Sandy and the others. For Jean Brodie *did* teach them to value individualism, she did renounce—on principle not honored by Sandy—an affair with the married man she loved, and she was apparently ignorant of any contradiction in molding others to live her wished-for life. It is because Helena knows that Miss Brodie was basically good that her own attitude behind bars is so expressive. Jean Brodie was and remains the great influence on Helena, having both freed her and imprisoned her. That Helena can now see doubly means that she will never cease to regret Sandy's having seen only singly in her principled and youthful haste.

The point of Sandy/Helena's career is not to suggest that her faith in the unseeable is any less genuine than Ronald's, Barbara's, or Nicholas's, of course, but to observe that Helena's experience is incompatible with comic structure. Spark here, even more emphatically than in Nicholas's case, stresses that seeing dually will become a permanent facility if one is blessed but that one can never afford to regard this gift as an answer to all questions or as an eradicator of all one's choices and problems past and future. Indeed, to acknowledge doubleness is to acknowledge a truth and the need to act on it; but, as in Helena's case, a conversion to this truth means knowing and living with what one has done. It is one thing, in short, to see things and to want things both ways, but a very different thing to have things in congruity with one's vision. Nicholas cannot communicate with the surviving "girls" even in his martyrdom; Helena can neither tell others how doubleness transfigures singleness of view nor alleviate in herself the effects of single-visioned Sandy's choices. In Nicholas's case, the greater evil that apparently aided his conversion was more others' than his; in Sandy's case the evil was others', too, but while *Girls* is structured so as to remove Nicholas between insight and death, *Prime* is structured to compel us to see Sandy's going through three stages, two conversions, and the abiding effects of her own actions at all stages. We know nothing of Nicholas's thinking for fifteen years; but we know, as she does, that Helena's transfiguration assures her living acutely with her past as Sandy. For the reality-seer, past is present is future: all times are now. Such a view is far from Knoxian determinism; it points instead to the continuing struggle to keep one's balance in realism-reality and points indirectly to the function of works together with faith. Sandy's faith and vocation imply all of that, but my point is that both Sandy and this novel insist that seeing and wanting to have things both ways preclude Jean's premise that only one way is viable, challenge Knox's premise that what one may want is beside God's point, and convincingly show that occupying the middle ground is no assurance of having things both ways. Being "normalised" (the narrator's word) ends nothing but recapitulates everything and begins a struggle whose outcome must remain doubtful.[20]

The greater the doubt, the darker the mood of a given novel. Thus the darkest of Spark's books is *The Driver's Seat* (1970).[21] The book is indeed frightening, because, in the manner of *Oedipus Rex* or *King Lear*, it raises standard classical questions associated with tragedy: most specifically, it asks, by means of its title, as well as through character and event, who or what is in charge. It raises again the old poser about the balance between choice and necessity.

In this book, in fact, Spark supposes a universe quite different from the one we have seen in her earlier books. We are asked in effect to forget all about the Christian underpinning of those books and to divorce ourselves from implicit assurances that some character in the book will signal the possibility of metaphysical accord, of ultimate resolution in the larger reality. What we are given instead is a desperately lucid, single-minded seeker after her own death. This death seeker is Lise, whose last day of life on this earth is narrated by a third-person omniscient voice in Spark's familiar present tense. If Lise's present-tense story were the entire book, however, we would be looking at a third-person limited narrative—terrible, to be sure, but lacking Spark's usual concern with dual vision. What applies the Spark brand and substitues "omniscient" for "limited" is the fact that alternating with Lise's story, as Lise occupies the realistic realm and lives out her last mortal day, is the regular narrative assurance that tomorrow the papers will report this or that detail of Lise's death, the police will interrogate her murderer, various persons who met her on that last day will have a number of things to say about her, and so forth. All these details the narrator drops into the present-tense account of Lise's realistic last day, and the narrator does so in the future tense. The ingeniously conceived effect of this alternating temporal current is to reverse what we are pleased as a rule to think of the present and the future. Where we take the present to be sure, concrete, here, real, and the future to be dark, uncertain, there, and "unreal," Spark's narrative method turns things around in giving us a questing central figure, with no groundwork of reasons for her demanding to die, and a consequently puzzled group of explanation-seekers—all these on the one hand in the present tense— and a dead-certain, absolutely surefire view of what's to come—this on the other, future, hand. In short, we have here a refashioning of the ancient encounter between foreknowledge and predestination.

The essential difference between this familiar encounter as depicted in *The Driver's Seat* and Spark's customary interrelating of real and realistic is that in the present instance nothing is seen to suggest even an implied relief in the manner of the interrelating. Characters, events, narrative tone all conspire to give us both the bald facts of realism plus the something else *and* not the least indication that things here have worked out not only as they had to work out, but also as they should have worked out or as we would have liked them to work out. For one thing, we don't know enough about Lise to have an attitude about "should," except that as a rule we don't like people to choose death, quite apart from our usual aversion to seeing people determined to be violently killed. For another thing, Lise's fixation and that of her killer, when joined with the nearly opinionless narrative tone, leave us no opportunity to derive *from the book* evidence of theological or cosmological appropriateness.[22] All we can do is observe Lise's committed searching and the narrator's matter-of-fact descriptions of tomorrow's events. All we can do, that is, is to place ourselves in the classic tragic position—this time without God or gods or narrative inkling of matters' being finally all right. All we can do is note that things are as they had to be and try as always to reconcile that inevitability with much counterweight of will and determination on Lise's side—and on her killer's side, too, for that matter, although, very neatly, in his case the determination is to *avoid* killing her.

We might note, about the tragic quality of this novel, that Spark manages such an effect without incorporating one of the standard ingredients of traditionally "highest" tragedy: the protagonist's awareness, evident to a reader, of the very issues we have conveniently abstracted under the labels "foreknowledge" and "predestination." We have no reason to suppose that Lise sees herself as Lear, Oedipus, or Job, or that she sees herself enmeshed in the tussle between freedom and compulsion. Yet the relentless shot-calling narrator never allows us to forget that this is Lise's situation and that we must engage Lise's questions in her stead. The fiction thus implicitly takes on those who might think Spark's Christian belief an obstacle to her imagining the possibility of tragedy. Moreover, it challenges an engrained belief that the protagonist must be acutely aware to qualify as tragic (not merely unfortunate). Finally, as I hope to establish, Spark successfully implies this proportion: the dual vision in *Driver's Seat* is to that of other Spark fictions as realistic is to real. If this proportion can be shown to obtain, Spark will be seen once more not to have beaten realism at its own game but to have accommodated realism's terms on her own terms; not to have entered into the "either-or" contest, but to have intimated "both-and" while playing once again the only art that matters to her.

From the very beginning of *Driver's Seat* the double view is imposed. For example, we see Lise to be a classic schizophrenic unable on one hand to control her conviction that she must be on guard against those who would laugh at her or otherwise take advantage of her; on the other hand, she appears to be strong-willed and determined to take charge of her own plans—not at all about to be victimized by others. Similarly, she both looks forward to her vacation and reluctantly leaves her desk covered with work left undone. Again, she is dominated by her need to dominate her co-workers and others. She is exactly situated at the office between seven persons below her (five women) and seven above her (five men). Her determination to exercise control over herself and others is

balanced by her exhaustion. Moreover, the narrator assures us that this ambivalence prevails both in the world around Lise and as an extension of her own
state of mind, sometimes independently of Lise. How, for example, are we to be
sure of the facts in such a passage as the following (wherein I have emphasized
the balancing terms): "The [porter] laughs . . . forcing the *evident* point that Lise
is habitually mean with her tips, or *perhaps* never tips the porter at all"? Or what
are we to think finally about Lise's action subsequent to this laughter, as she
neglects to leave some keys with this insulting porter: "Whether she has failed to
leave [these] . . . by intention, or whether through the distraction of the
woman's laughter, one could not tell" (pp. 14–15)? In this manner the narrator
is able to have things both ways: she is both saner and clearer than the
protagonist, and a more reliable reporter of ambivalence and murk precisely
because of that greater lucidity. Her manner cooperates with and extends Lise's
present-tense behavior rather than explains or resolves it.

Other evidence comes easily to mind in support of this premise that assurance
is regularly matched by doubt, the character's or the narrator's indiscriminately.
As we have seen, for instance, the reliable narrative flash-forward guarantees the
future, while Lise's alternating brusqueness and confusion shroud the present in
fog. Similarly, a number of expressions recur with regularity, to keep the reader
wondering. These expressions include: *about* (meaning approximately), *as if,
probably, presumably, might be, possibly, seems, perhaps, it depends, evidently.* We
note too that even when Lise is proven right in saying "I know" or "I'm sure," she
is invariably right by instinct rather than by reasoning. "Who knows her
thoughts? Who can tell?" asks the narrator (p. 53), who obviously could answer
these questions were she not narrating a Spark fiction. Pointed, too, in this
regard, is the repeated contrasting coexistence of—on the one hand—Lise's
willing her quest for what will satisfy her and—on the other—constant references to what she wants, and seems to be in the process of choosing very
painstakingly, as "my type." In this attracting-selecting interplay we get frequent
reminders of the long-standing debate between fate and free will. If, as Bill, the
macrobiotics fanatic, says, "You become what you eat," does one's becoming a
"type" preclude choice or not?

Just as the mood is often subjunctive and as the alternating between temporal
and eternal offers us certainty and perplexity exactly where we do not look for
them, so the book's treatment of place contributes to our interested vertigo.
Lise's apartment, for instance, is fashionable, functional, comfortable; but it is
also one of many like itself, coldly antiseptic in design, and virtually "unin-
habited" (p. 12)—thus a perfect extension of the tormented woman who is at
home both there and nowhere. In the same way, geography itself emphasizes the
acute particularity and universal ramifications of Lise's condition. Specifically,
Lise speaks four languages—none of which she will specify, when asked, as her
native tongue—and comes from "the North" to "the South" on vacation. That
is, the North may be some vague European city and no place in particular, but it

also contains department stores, offices, apartments, merchandise, and much other realistic paraphernalia. Similarly, the South is some other city (Italian, one supposes) but its locale also matters less for concrete urban reasons than for universal spiritual or psychological reasons. At the same time, this city also has its people, its traffic, its hotels, its stores, its parks, and indeed Lise even has a map of the city on which she has marked the pavilion where she will be found dead (the narrator assures us) on the morrow. In this moving between spatial universal and particular, Spark would appear to fall in this book somewhere between Bunyan's allegorical generality and Thackeray's emphasis on particular manifestations of Vanity Fair. Spark is more specific than Bunyan, more consciously universal than Thackeray.

An important effect achieved by all of this unsettling doubleness is precisely the tragic darkness that we have not hitherto encountered in Spark. Where, for example, in *Girls* or in *Prime*—as well as in the obviously comic novels—we had always been offered at least implicitly a bridge in the form of religious belief, here we are given none. That bridge had regularly assured us of the interworkings of real and realistic; the bridge surely guaranteed nothing like mindless jollity or relief from agony, but it did assure us, as faith does, that the components of what is make sense. In *Driver's Seat*, on the other hand, we get something unmistakably Sparkian but starkly different from what we have seen so far. Here we are given Lise and her killer, two present-tense seekers, desirers, wanters, willers, and we find them balanced by a narrative anonymity assuring us of what the future will bring. The crucial difference between this handling of time, place, and occurrence and what we have so far been reading is of course that here we are supplied with no connecting bridge. On one side we have Lise's and Richard's wanting; on the other side we have tomorrow vouched for: what we cannot *know*, and what we are provided with no grounds to *believe in*, is that the characters' wanting and willing had (have) anything to do with *causing* tomorrow's effects. And this inability to know or to believe is of course what makes this fiction Spark's darkest and most classically tragic.

For me the classically tragic—as distinct from what is sometimes called the postmodern—situation arises either because God or gods will not explain why things occur as they do, and will not explain causal connections between themselves and us, or because humans cannot believe in anyone from whom they might at least ask for explanations or hints. The point in this second instance is that humans instinctively retain at least a minimal conviction that there *ought* to be someone of whom such inquiry might be made. The so-called postmodern, on the other hand, is the attitude that takes for granted no God or gods, no plans in the universe which would underpin the real-realistic interworkings of Spark's world, and—most crucially—no reason to hope that answers ought to be forthcoming. That is, where classical tragedy is still possible up through such prominent modernists as Woolf, Eliot, and Joyce, it ceases to be possible for such postmodernists as Sartre, Ionesco, and Pinter because of the difference in kind between persons who hold that all does or should make sense and persons whose reasons for resisting suicide begin after despair has been accepted.

On the basis of this distinction, I would like to place Spark's *Driver's Seat*. The book is certainly not overtly theistic, but neither is it postmodern; it posits neither God nor Apollo on the one hand, nor the assurance of mere accident on the other. The question of the Divinity simply never arises seriously; the question of accidental occurrence frequently arises and is rejected either pointedly or inadvertently. That is, Lise may not know who her "type" is, but she believes she has a type and that she will recognize him when she meets him, "around the corner somewhere, now, any time" (p. 76). She is sure her "friend's going to turn up soon. . . . Apart from that I have no plans" (p. 74). This limited but fixed confidence ironically illuminates such a throwaway line as Mrs. Fiedke's, concerning traffic problems: "You mustn't think of accidents" (p. 59). Such a casual comment is Spark's means here of reinforcing the book's support of Mrs. Fiedke's advice: Lise may operate very largely on hunch, but the hunch, regardless of what it leads to, is right. And this of course signals the really decisive element that keeps this fiction out of the postmodern maelstrom: the narrator's detached assurance that the future will be precisely so.[23]

The narrator's statements—not predictions—of the future keep a reader feeling that since there is to be a future, and since the future can be *imagined* at least to have resulted from a combination of Lise's choosing and Lise's being oxymoronically compelled to "choose," reality is still conceivable on the old familiar, no less painful, terms that enraged and broke Lear. That is, to the extent that the narrator drums into us that the future is a sure thing, we are at least troubled in our temptation to conclude that, oh well, things just happen and after all what can we expect? Spark's narrator will not tell us that our choices plainly establish the future or that we in fact really choose; but neither will the narrator tell us that our wills are only illusorily availing and effective. In this way the narrator keeps before us the possibilities that something larger than our experiences is operative, that freedom may be more than an illusion, and that the indiscernibility of a bridge does not necessarily establish the nonexistence of a bridge. A reader cannot prove "accident" here. Indeed, another exchange between Mrs. Fiedke and Lise suggests the place of this fiction, by means of our rather negative route, in the traditionally tragic camp. Speaking of Lise's conviction that she will soon meet her "type," Mrs. Fiedke asks, "Will you feel a presence? Is that how you'll know?" Lise's response is tellingly vague: "Not really a presence. . . . The lack of an absence, that's what it is. I know I'll find it" (p. 76). The quickened sense that the absence of an absence not only is worth wanting but amounts as well to "the time of my life" (p. 7) looks no doubt like the coldest possible comfort; but cold or not, it keeps ajar the door to the possibility that reality is eventually one and makes sense.

The point here is assuredly not to diminish the awareness of suffering intense enough to make one want death by violence so single-mindedly as to devote oneself to seeking it out. Any comfort that this narrative may supply must accommodate suffering's reality, just as any discomfort may be traceable to the narrative's preventing a reader from simply and finally dismissing the whole problem of causality. "I've no definite plans. It's foolish to have plans" (pp. 54–55), says Lise, in a pair of sentences typical of Spark's two-way viewing. On the one hand we know that Lise has one plan; on the other hand we hear her sounding more insightful than she means to sound, in that this book shows how foolish it would be for anyone to be sure that outcomes or events are the result of our plans; *that* causal bridge this fiction will not let us build; any other causal bridge this book will encourage us to think about building but will not let us think definitely buildable. Although Lise and Mrs. Fiedke "happen" to meet, and although each is seeking—unbeknownst to the other—the man, Richard, who is Mrs. Fiedke's nephew (by "chance"), and although we may therefore wonder how Richard "happens" to be in this city (a Samarra that he might have tried to avoid), we cannot reach firm conclusions about the language I have here placed in quotations. We end up unable to establish accident or coincidence, but equally unable to nail down cause or causes in their stead. This inability to be sure of who or what is in "the driver's seat" is the familiar tragic problem.

It is to this tragic status that we must now look in examining my earlier contention that the dual vision in this book is to the dual vision of other Spark books as realistic is to real. What I mean is that *Driver's Seat* comes closer than other Spark fictions to effecting an illusion wherein the views of central character and of narrator agree; an illusion that, however much it allows for the mysterious in experience, nonetheless finds the narrator entertaining and perhaps endorsing the classic secular view that puzzles end with the extinction which is death. Neither Lise nor the narrator allows for appeals to higher causes, and neither accuses such causes, as Job and Oedipus are inclined to do. Lise wants to die, to encounter the killer who will embody that presence which will simply and finally render her extinct—and the narrator's terminal note of "fear and pity, pity and fear" (p. 117) would seem to suggest agreement with Lise that such pain and inexplicability make understandable anyone's longing for annihilation.

Everything along the trail that describes Lise's final day contributes to the conclusion that she seeks the permanent absence of self as the sole means of topping all the terrible absences she knows. In predictable anticomedy fashion, she finds love and money—the essentials of comedy, of living socially—to be inadequate and even tormenting. All day she disregards money, and of love she speaks thus revealingly: "It's all right at the time and it's all right before . . . but the problem is afterwards. That is, if you aren't just an animal. Most of the time, afterwards is pretty sad" (p. 113). To be accurate, it is sex, not love, to which she refers here: but that only plays up the absence of love from her bare existence. She is almost totally alone, even to the point of being isolated in the present by the narrator, who never makes any attempt to explain background or to account for Lise's condition. The effect of such narrative noncommitment is of course to suggest that this is the universal human condition and not merely Lise's here-and-now. Once again Spark's present-tense narrative both keeps us grounded and inclines us to generalize. What we see quite convincingly is the basis of despair. We see that such suffering and isolation—whatever may have caused them—make plausible Lise's shedding of her material possessions during the day: not only money, luggage, and the stuff with which we all fill up our lives and that enables us to forget about nonstuff, but also her passport, that mocking pretense that age, sex, shape, and itinerary constitute identification of self.

If I am right about Lise's view of her predicament, and about the narrator's clinical detachment and aloof universalizing, then this is the only decidedly tragic Spark book; the only book that raises speculation about mystery with no effect save that of intensifying our sense of having to endure suffering in ignorance. (*The Only Problem* invites the same speculation, but the tone and effects of that novel place it quite outside direct confrontation with the question of tragedy—as we shall see in chapter 3, below.) Pity and fear are indeed in order as responses to such illusion. Moreover, I assume that such an illusion is close to what most readers take tragedy to be—close to what most readers regard as *realistic*, nonfanciful, antispeculative, unconcerned with notions of afterlife, salvation, and the like. Finally, then, if this reading of *Driver's Seat* alone and then against Spark's other books is correct, it will by now be clear that this book stops short of Spark's usual suggestions of the *real* precisely because it deliberately limits itself to the *realistic*, the hard everyday now that Lise successfully escapes from.

Does all of this mean that Spark in the present instance abandons her usual theistic romantic psychology and operates from a different set of assumptions? I think not. In my opinion this book shows Spark's ability to imagine the situation of anyone—believer or not—who is pushed to the edge. *The Driver's Seat* is simply not a comedy such as *The Ballad of Peckham Rye* nor is it a generic mixture such as *The Girls of Slender Means*; and it does not employ an assortment of characters in order to marvel at reality's plenty and the conversion of one character to a theistic stance. Rather, as we have seen, it focuses exclusively upon a single desperate character whose only company is a fellow compulsive, a silly food-faddist, a lecher or two, a kindly but unthinking *ficelle*, and a coolly detached narrator whose function is apparently to make Lise's plight universal rather than to qualify it in any way. Spark has imagined a tragedy, a situation wherein Lise's condition is the book, and whereon it is important that reality's variousness be unable to impinge. The only truth that Lise knows—and that the book presents—of concrete realism or mysterious reality is that they are terrible, and the nature of this book precludes the introduction of other possibilities. Such unrelieved awareness of the terrible is of the tragic essence.

Lise's suicidal isolation from others and from any other view of reality is, then, the condition of the only tragedy Spark has written. And the generic label also helps to make some sense of my proportion: for if Lise exists in psychological and spiritual solitude, and if she gets no help from her narrator to imply that she needn't live this way, her tragic condition is by definition cut off from what we have seen in Spark's imagining of other genres and hence is similarly cut off from what Spark elsewhere presents or suggests as wider, vaster, nonclaustrophobic views. Far from implying that she works from a basically different set of assumptions, then, this book more plausibly demonstrates to me that Spark's usual realism-reality premises are seen to be irrelevant to Lise—and, implicitly, to much human experience. Such recognition, however, does not constitute a changing of the author's mind. Rather, when seen in the context of her other fictional illusions, it both points up powerful empathy with and compassion for such prevalent torment and implies that tragedy may be rooted in the inability to see anything beyond realism—beyond the hyphen. *The Driver's Seat* is thus Spark's one tragedy because its lone character's narrated situation stops helplessly short of any larger reality.

So ends my proportion-talk: the double vision in this book, because that vision seems to support generally what Lise sees particularly, is to the double vision in other Spark fictions as realistic is to real. Tragedy is darkest when it supposes that what is real is solipsistically confined. Spark very effectively images such confinement and induces pity and fear more poignantly when we consider her tragedy within the context of her other imaginings.

The Driver's Seat addresses either head-on or obliquely a number of paradoxical pairs. These include plans vs. eventualities (in each case, whose?); choices vs. compulsions or needs; law and order vs. Law and Order; solving of crimes vs. standing in helpless awe, in an attitude of pity and fear, in confrontation with unnameable occurrence; macrobiotic self-building vs. hushed sense of universal patterning; questioning vs. the futility of inquiry. Knowledge and belief being absent, Lise, the narrator, and the reader tragically find no way to balance paradoxical pairs or even to weigh them together. Such is tragedy, as I have tried to say, and such is why this book occupies the end of the spectrum opposite comedies like *Ballad* and *Bachelors*. Darkness more profound than this neither Spark nor others could conceivably give us.

Nonetheless, I wish to conclude this section of the discussion with a book much concerned with darkness even though that darkness is intensified largely to give meaning to the light that follows. The fiction in question is *The Hothouse by the East River* (1973),[24] a book that fits here because in a way it starts where *The Driver's Seat* ends (if one can really talk in such linear terms about Spark's work) in that *Hothouse*'s characters are dead, but which, because it goes beyond the fact of death, should offer a means of transition to other matters.

In *Hothouse* we have a third-person narrator who starts off with "If it were only true that all's well that ends well, if only it were true" (p. 3), and who then develops with and for us an attitude emerging from the premises that (1) such a wish could make sense only if based on something other than the assumptions of this novel, and that (2) such a wish, when this novel is adequately understood, is not only unmakeable but meaningless—because to be dead is not to cease being but is to be differently. Thus, according to this second premise, "ends" makes no sense: nobody *can* end. Perhaps it should also be said that, however much we may know of Muriel Spark's Catholicism and however clearly this novel assumes human immortality, the focus of narrator and characters alike is not specifically religious or doctrinal, but psychological. The book's moral seriousness is never ponderous or preachy but comes across as a tantalizingly lucid, plainly opaque, soberly funny, mazed and well-reasoned conundrum. Such paradoxical procedure is perfectly consistent with Spark's orthodoxy, of course; the point is only to indicate here that her fiction is concerned with its first task: the establishing of an illusion most convincing when its fundamental assumptions are understood imaginatively, apart from writer's or reader's extranovelistic commitments.

Those fundamental assumptions are two traditional standpoints—one *sub specie temporis* and the other *sub specie aeternitatis*. The novel may be puzzling to some readers because we are accustomed in many cases to taking the temporal for granted in our unfamiliarity with the eternal, or because we regard the temporal as the proper domain of fiction however we think of the eternal, or because we tend to think the two quite separate and thus manageable. If, for instance, the illusion created by *Pride and Prejudice* and thousands of other books in its tradition has conditioned us to regard societal particulars and plotted development of character as *the* novel's manner of proceeding, we will likely not be ready for Spark. Or, again, if we recall how plays such as *Our Town* or *Carousel* neatly divide the deceased from the living, we know that it is possible for a single vehicle to convey a sense of both realms. The problem is not difficult in these cases, for in fact it is the audience rather than the characters who know about and must register the significance of any interaction between living and dead: the realms are kept separate and far from equal. Aside from differences between drama and prose fiction, however, Spark's *Hothouse* presents very different tasks for a reader.

For one thing, Spark's "dead" characters seem as tangible as her "living" ones and would appear to function as tangibly as the "living" both among themselves and in mixed company. Unsegregated, both sets of characters apparently eat, dress, talk, think, make love, plot, dance, remember, forget, desire, spend money, and perform alike the familiar everyday activities of those we usually call the living. Moreover, chapters and subsections are arranged like two halves of a deck of playing cards that the narrator so to speak shuffles into the form of a single deck which is the book. In this case the halves represent the past (1944) and the present—both halves, however, rendered in Spark's familiar present tense, so that narrative manner in effect makes all times Now. Or one may see the metaphorical relevance in this context of the narrator's reference to British Intelligence's "scrambler" telephone, so called "because the connection is heavily jammed with jangling caterwauls to protect the conversation against eavesdropping . . . but once the knack [of listening] is mastered it is easy to hear the voice at the other end giving . . . information" (p. 55). Third-person anonymity, in any event, not only builds implicit reliability but does so for both past and present, while in addition virtually compelling us to suppose that, in the absence of any denial, the principal characters remember events as the speaker narrates them. We believe the voice, then, and we also almost inadvertently find ourselves making a single deck of past and present halves, with the result that Spark lures us into merging, blurring, was and is.

Further to distinguish the illusion of, say, *Our Town* from that of *Hothouse,* we observe that Spark's characters not only speak and act with one another but are said in two instances to be married parents with children (dead and living generations respectively), although we learn by reading cards from the other half of the deck (the past) that death in 1944 came to Elsa and Paul before they married and became parents of Pierre and Katerina. Thus, where Wilder's *Our Town* gives us characters readily sortable because they function discretely while occupying the same stage, Spark provides us with a narrator whose procedure forces us actively to consider how these characters can be possible since in fact they *cannot* be separated from one another. In short, we ask what this book is positing about death and the dead, and what views it encourages us to imagine. How can the dead past be said to have had a future and perhaps to have yet more or another future, as the book's last pages suggest is the case?

The answer, I think, is that Spark requires us to see both halves of the deck not discretely or alternately, but simultaneously. Spark plays with a full deck unfamiliar to those who know only the realist's game. It is quite likely that if we suppose death to mean annihilation pure and simple, or if we think the spiritual all right in its supposedly nonnovelistic place, or if we insist that a writer must make up her mind to write either a novel or a fairy tale, we will throw this book out the window. I do not presume to tell anyone *how* to see both halves of the deck—both levels of activity and both settings and both times, to say nothing of times and places of whatever may have "happened" *between* past and present—simultaneously; but that is nonetheless the way things must be seen, I think, for book and reader to come together. Hence the value of thinking about temporal and eternal: the value not of a blueprint or map but of a traditionally suggestive way to prod the imagination. Accordingly, I want to discuss both of these levels, necessarily *as if* they were separable, much as we misleadingly but helplessly treat form and content or style and meaning. We anatomize to reconstruct and unify. Such anatomizing will revive, too, some of the general premises discussed in the first chapter of this study.

By the temporal level, then, I mean the commonsensical complex of temporal-spatial thinking, the complex we usually label as reality or the real. We mean, I believe, that reality necessarily entails the sensible-intellectual ability to "place" oneself and others spatially, socially, psychologically, morally, and so forth, and to understand experience sequentially. We want to know where we are outside of the book we're reading and where the characters in that book are; we want to know what time of day, year, life this is when we read or do anything else, and we expect writers to let us know what time it is in their books: not only days, hours, years, centuries, but past, present, future. And we want to be able to assign reasons, motives, causes for characters' behavior and development. Further, we think automatically that this sorting-out can be readily done, and we expect such sorting-out from novelists. We incline to disallow a novelist the right to leave such matters unclear or unsettled, although we may well give leeway to writers otherwise labeled: science-fictioneers, fantasists, escapists, romancers, et al. Our implicitly rigorous expectations lead us as casual readers, as academics, or as reviewers to accept or reject books according to whether they meet our often unconscious demands. So instinctive may be our conviction of what novelists may and may not do that we may entertain no idea of reality at all outside the bounds of what I here call the temporal.[25]

If, then, a writer asks us to imagine the extratemporal, and to keep on imagining it steadily for the duration of a novel, some readers may become outraged—and indeed the request is an odd one for a novelist to make, especially perhaps today. What Muriel Spark in this instance requires is that we suppose placelessness and timelessness to be possible and fictionally viable. This means that reality—what is—when viewed *sub specie aeternitatis,* cannot be confined to the limitations specified and suggested by the temporal view. The commonsensical alone not only won't do but will prevent our getting the point. Where the temporal view takes the "normal," human, sequentially plotted ordering of reality for granted, the extratemporal view recasts the meaning of "normal" and "real" and "human" and does so as if from a preternatural overview. Thus, from such an angle, whoever is must be said merely to participate in being (or Being) and cannot cease to be, any more than his/her generating source can cease to be or can even be diminished. From such a point of view it would follow that time and place—while properly remaining crucial concerns of the temporal view and realm—take on the look of limited realities within limitless reality. If we posit that Being (God) must always have been, is, must always be, cannot not be, what we've said is that, given the nature and viewpoint of Being, all times are in a sense one—are Now (for all beings in time's changing participate in Being's changeless Now)—and all places may be seen as merely the personal limits of this or that created participant-in-being. What exists, then, by definition does so in the permanent Now, the unchangeable present tense; and as it goes on present-tensing forever (immortally), the place where it exists may be spoken of not as a geographical location but as a function of its "is-ing." One "is-es" without particular regard to the temporal notion of defined place (which notion distinguishes between occupied position and the occupier thereof); rather, one's "place" is specificable as the boundaries of one's capacity to share in being. One's place, then, has much to do with one's capacity to grow, to change, by imagining—to exercise and expand the same kind of creative faculty, as creature, that caused one to be created: the extent of one's moral imagination is a measure of one's place in, share of, being.

But of course Muriel Spark is not writing this sort of abstract theological-philosophical treatise. What she asks is that we share with her an idea much more familiar and more novelistic, but ultimately more difficult to cope with than we suppose the novel usually to require of us. She asks that we read and imagine these two levels together. In practice, what this means is that we suppose it possible for six characters killed in 1944 in England to find author and narrator for their circulating temporally and spatially in New York today, in the company of one another and of characters not yet dead; and for two not-dead characters to have been begotten extratemporally by two of the already killed principals. In my opinion, such a fictional illusion is possible only if we keep in mind the temporal-eternal split that Spark's narrator requires us to mend imaginatively. As Being causes, contains, and sustains all actual and potential beings, and thus must be thought a larger reality within which temporal-spatial reality exists, so the six principals of this book are shown to be immortal (i.e., literally not subject to extinction) as they necessarily share in Being, even while their nature as human creatures compels them to speak of their past, of the future they wanted and would seem to be having, of the existence to which they go at the book's close, and of the day-to-day requirements of what we refer to as the present, or daily living. Spark is showing us that a larger circle (Being) contains, without in the least contradicting, the smaller ones (individual beings). Therefore, beings limited only by their moral natures are both to be thought of as having had past lives in other locations and to have present lives across a tangible ocean thirty years later. Since nothing *is* beyond Being and Now, spatial-temporal beings must necessarily be imagined as quite real within that All—for what could possibly be anywhere else at any time? In short, the realms may be thought of discretely, but only when we further see the novel as manifestation of the creative imagination's merging of two realms.

What, however, does all this come to as a novel? Reading the two halves of our deck, or observing our smaller circles within the larger one, and disregarding the niceties of alternating times, places, and characters' behavior, we see ourselves presented with a group of characters in wealthy middle life in New York—characters who are eventually said to have interacted or *maybe* to have interacted with one another in wartime England. Two of them, Paul Hazlett and Elsa, his co-worker in British Intelligence, plan marriage and emigration to New York after the war, when he is assured of a position on the staff of Columbia University and when they are promised an apartment on the East River. These two and three of their colleagues in Intelligence are instantly killed by a rocket bomb in 1944, and/but are peopling New York's novelistic present together with a German prisoner of war whom all five knew and who was supposedly executed six years after the war (1951?)—executed, perhaps, through the efforts of the apparently late Paul Hazlett. Elsa is "now" (this sort of temporal term must be used, whatever the hazard of causing greater confusion) Elsa Hazlett, Pierre and Katerina are at least in their twenties, Princess Poppy Xavier, Colonel Tylden, and Miles Bunting (the three colleagues), as well as a character who is probably Helmut Kiel (the prisoner of war), may all be seen as well preserved in middle age, and the lot operate with a number of other characters who haven't yet died. This sketch of Spark's two-realmed fiction is delicately concretized by assorted details that suggest both classic and Christian versions of life-after-death. For instance, Paul and Elsa's overheated apartment connotes "hothouse" conditions for preserving the occupants extratemporally ("out of season," as it were) and for inducing growth. Heat also suggests purgatorially punitive flames—symbol of suffering in aid of healthy growth.[26] Poppy Xavier's rather grotesque generating of silkworms suggests a corpse's maggot-producing capacity. The hothouse's situation on the East River carries overtones of Styx and Lethe, and the latter river is associated with the wish to forget, to reinforce the novel's opening wish. Again, while all the principals cast shadows, Elsa's shadow falls "the wrong way," as lore would have shadows of the dead fall (although Elsa's mirror image is seemingly usual). As may be seen, one who keeps circles and playing cards straight will have to take Spark seriously and will very likely also be amused by unpredictables.

But, one may ask, why do a thing like this to readers? The answer is dual, I think. For one thing, Muriel Spark wants both to write prose fiction and to write about things as she sees them. She has said that conversion was fairly easy for her, since far from requiring that she give up her way of viewing reality, allegiance to Catholicism meant formally confirming her established way of seeing things.[27] As for writing, she has also said that she writes fiction which she does not intend to be taken for truth, but that she is decidedly interested in "absolute truth."[28] These two statements combine to mean that she is writing fiction (not, for example, autobiography or philosophy or apologetics); that she does not write entirely within the conventions of fictional realism; and that her fiction is to be taken thoughtfully, as any concern for truth is to be taken. Thus, for instance, the fact that she makes it impossible to find out or even to ask about what went on for those years between England and New York, or to find out how the dead can function corporeally (in and outside of their overheated residence), or where the six are going for "peace" when the book closes (I dare not say "ends")—such facts of frustration do not preclude, and indeed they bolster, a reader's awareness that the meaning of death and of the dead is handled delicately, reflectively, brilliantly.

Spark is writing a fiction about death, that most obvious fact of life which, like all facts in her view, escapes the manner of realistic fiction and calls for a method to do justice to mysteriousness. We can clear up some apparent mysteries if we keep our circles in mind, but the possibilities of narrating *as if* extratemporally are limited, so that mystery persists.

Within clarifiable range, however, the circle-distinction at once spotlights

Paul's remarks to a potential knifer, " 'You can't kill us' . . . . 'We're dead already' " (p. 139). Again, our distinction makes some sense of passages wherein Paul's heart beats in its "coffin" and cries, " 'Let me out!' " (pp. 14, 133)—for it is unnatural that the immortal go on having to behave corporeally, as if the body were not yet dead: unnatural for one state of being to pose as another. This awkwardness may in fact lend credence to the notion that the six principals exist purgatorially (I decline to say "in Purgatory," for fear of undoing my efforts to associate place with personal state of being rather than with locus); that is, the six may be seen to be in transition from one condition of existence to another, so long as we understand the transition to mean change from one attitude to another. Or, by means of our circle-distinction, we can make some sense of Paul's telling Elsa, as she gazes from her window across the East River, " 'There's nothing there' " (p. 8). He does not mean, temporally, that everything east of New York has vanished; rather, his words suggest, extratemporally, that beyond what *is*, which includes one's participation therein, anything else, including a world elsewhere, cannot be. Accordingly, Elsa can (temporally) take planes between New York and Zurich, while (extratemporally) joining the other five principals, as the book makes its concluding point, in agreement that " 'we can't go on like this' " (p. 140). This in turn means not that they are too old to go dancing from nightspot to nightspot and must therefore go home to the apartment; instead, it means that, since Paul and Elsa now agree (as they had not done) that they died in 1944, they can stop this in-between living death of pretense and can join the other four in seeking possible "peace" (pp. 139–46).

In this connection, and among more nearly solvable mysteries, we may note the use to which Barrie's *Peter Pan* is put. In a sense it is droll to cast the play with actors aged at least sixty. But in the book's full context, this is a fine way to underline the novel's moral support for the characters' opinion that the play is inherently obscene (pp. 65, 92–97). For, like the Tithonus myth or Gulliver's encounter with the Struldbruggs, *Peter Pan* shows what is wrong with wishful thinking that, in its desire to counter one extreme—fear of death as extinction—goes to the other extreme of wanting immortality to be of the physical body (whether permanently young or endlessly withering). The word "obscene" here means unnatural, so that the *Peter Pan* references in this book are a virtual microcosm of what is unnatural in the six characters' immortality's being distorted by their persisting in the flesh. "Peace" may come when their attitudes alter; when they are "purged" of that attachment to flesh and worldly things which accounts for their purgatorial, transitional wandering unnaturally on the face of the earth—like Peter and the Lost Boys in Never-Never Land. " 'Sick is real,' " says the psychiatrist who is the book's scapegoat-spokesman for the exclusively temporal notion of reality (p. 95); but of course the book shows that while his words carry truth, they do so only up to the point at which the six Pirandellesque characters (in search of their Author) recognize that they are not stuck with this version of reality but can and must accept their death if they are to live their immortality naturally. The breakthrough, purging's end, comes because Paul and Elsa both admit to being dead, agree that they will very likely never know the full truth of their own and each other's emotional attachment to Helmut Kiel in 1944, and that the only way to seek peace is to be reconciled with the inevitability of mystery: whatever they've had, been, done cannot cease to be, cannot be fully known or understood, cannot do other than live in timeless Now, as their lives, their tenseless beings. Thus the only sane thing to do is to surrender to the full meaning of the real, accept their limits as finite beings, and sever connections with bodies that cast shadows in one or another direction (one thinks of Eliot's temporal present as "fear in a handful of dust"—fear that is worse than shadows before and behind, future and past). For the dead, temporal now is unnatural; extratemporal Now is natural, normal. The novel plots its characters' resistance to the natural; the novel stops when they choose to accept the finite conditions of their immortality.

Like others planning to "go," Paul and Elsa regard what they leave. They watch their apartment building being demolished and pay visits to their children and the old woman, Melly, who arranged for the New York job and apartment decades ago. Like everything else in the book, these incidents work on two levels. Temporal urban demolition and renewal signify extratemporal appropriateness in abandoning that which houses bodies (a detail symbolically parallel to Paul's heart's being released from the "coffin" of his body). Similarly, farewell to Melly and to posttemporally conceived children enables Paul to ask Pierre, " 'Do you exist?' " (p. 141), a question he has already answered for Katerina with " 'I caused you' " (p. 31). This pair of remarks is perfect. Temporally, commonsensically, the dead do not beget children. But just as finite creatures, beings of past-present-future, are consistent within a larger, containing realm of infinite, uncreated Being Now, so one may think of begetting as other than physiological: one may think of Pierre and Katerina (and Paul so thinks of them) as real manifestations of an idea—real *conceptions*—begotten of Paul and Elsa's love, just as the six dead characters' being in New York manifests their onetime *idea* of their future. And, given the notion of Now, the question of literally when, by the calendar, love's idea of marriage and children got around to buying the license and sending children back from beyond the grave becomes obviously unaskable. Pierre and Katerina are incarnations of the mystery of how any idea can come to be realized; the oddity, or apparent oddity, here arises because we are asked to imagine two realms simultaneously—to disregard the clock and to see ideas literally embodied. As Pierre says, again in the narrative's double-cutting way, absurdity vs. intelligence is the only conflict left (p. 65). This opposition may also be expressed as eternal vs. temporal, insane vs. sane, mad vs. reasonable, irrational vs. rational. But however the opposition may be specified, Spark's novel requires us in each instance to see the first term—from our limited point of view—as larger reality containing (not resisting) the second term's proliferation of separate realities. Clearly, such matters are necessarily among mysteries felt and fictionally set forth rather than resolved.[29]

If my reading is valid to this point, then the narrator's opening wish—"If it were only true that all's well that ends well"—must be read in relation to smaller and larger realities. Temporally, it means at least two things: (1) death would be welcome as the end of being, and (2) preferably, such an end would occur in the midst of comparative pleasure. (At a party just before the 1944 bomb falls, one character says, "'If it's a direct hit . . . nothing can save you'" [p. 130].) Extratemporally, the wish is meaningless since ceasing to be is intrinsically impossible. However, given the fact of eternity, wherein human life is immortal, can that opening wish make any sense?

If this book were avowedly religious rather than philosophically fictional, the answer would be negative. That is, if Spark were talking specifically about orthodox Christian ideas of hell, purgatory, and heaven as conditions of immortal existence, it would be nonsense for a narrator from such a position to yearn for nonbeing rather than for perfection to the fullness of personal capacity; to prefer dissolution to fullness of being within Being. But this is not an avowedly religious book, however it may coincide philosophically and psychologically with formal religious doctrine. And this is why the narrator's initial desire makes a kind of sense. What the narrator may be taken to convey, even extratemporally speaking, is that, precisely because one cannot non-be, one must suffer uncertainty, ignorance, after death as before—and that one then might well entertain a preference for nonexistence. The attitude is purgatorial; in fact it demonstrates what makes the idea of purgation feasible. If we think of life on earth as plagued with doubts, loose ends, questions, problems, unresolved issues (a series of terms mostly quotable from this novel, by the way), we imply our opinion that to be able to ask is reasonably to expect answers. To die then and find unanswerability eternal might well cause one to wish oneself out of "is-ness." But surely this is why purgation is needed: it is not natural, these characters learn, to expect always to know when and what you want to know. It is in fact grotesque, hyperhubristic, to insist, not that there must be a reason or a cause for effects, but that since reasons and causes exist we ought to know them. Mystery is natural.

Spark's fictional illusion requires, then, that we imagine the reality of two realms, one within the other, and that we suppose what an extratemporal overview would give us. But because we, like narrator and characters assumed by a human author, are contingent beings restricted to an "as if" identification with extratemporality, the turning point for the principals of this novel is shown to come not when they reach eternal peace, but when they are conscious of the Peter Pan-like unnaturalness (obscenity) of trying to find peace—to have all things, always, in all ways—their way. The novel is concerned with what won't do rather than with presenting an illusion of perfection. The book as illusion is directed toward the disillusioning of its principals (and of its readers) with the idea that life ends at death and with the further idea that immortality denotes endlessness on one's own terms. When the principals reach this dual awareness—with some sadness mixed in, to be sure—the book (unlike these characters) can end. To take it further would be to attempt the *Paradiso,* whereas Spark's interest here is in the psychology of the *Purgatorio.* In sum, the fact that beings are neither Being nor capable of nonbeing is chastening—but sadness would seem considerably alleviated by the realization that (contra Sartre's *No Exit*) inability to exist in every way as in our predead days we wanted to exist is no block to awareness, choice, and change for the better, the natural. Elsa "trails her faithful and lithe cloud of unknowing" off the last page of the novel (p. 146), but such is the only way to "go," and she chooses as she must.

3

Comic Texture: Echoes Golden to Leaden

The previous chapter dwelt upon gross anatomy, process, and outcome—in short, upon generic and structural concerns. In the present chapter I want to emphasize varieties of comic texture. This is not to suggest that structure and texture are perfectly separable, or that their fusion is anything but happy when a given book is successful; rather, this pseudoseparation is strictly for purposes of critical discussion, and indeed the better the structure and texture are wedded, the greater, appropriately, will be my difficulty in isolating specific textural qualities for discussion. Process and outcome will hardly be ignored, then, but will be subordinated to matters of tone and style. Specifically, I will look fairly closely at *Memento Mori, The Abbess of Crewe, The Takeover, Territorial Rights,* and *The Only Problem* in order to discern wherein Spark may be considered funny, satiric, wry, and so forth. Moreover, since one of these is an early book and the others are late, we may gain some insight into the ways in which Spark's textural qualities in general complement such broader structural traits as we have already seen.

Memento Mori (1959) is in several ways a typical Spark book. Most—not all—of its moral direction is supplied by women characters. Waugh-like breaks in its pages indicate abrupt, clipped, economically developed plot- and character-lines. Tone is heavily a function of the third-person narration working on and with a group—not bachelors or young women or schoolgirls in this instance, but old people between the ages of seventy and ninety. Mystery or puzzle is at the book's center, and readings of reality underlie events.

This novel exists because several elderly British men and women receive anonymous telephone calls: "Remember you must die," says a voice to each of these persons, which words echo the title of the book in English translation. What makes the book go is the reactions of the listeners to this message, for these reactions are of course character development and they thereby delight us in their diversity as they are serving to make the book's point: in the delight is the instruction. Something of the diversity to which we will be treated is suggested by Spark's three epigraphs:

What shall I do with this absurdity—
O heart, O troubled heart—this caricature,
Decrepit age that has been tied to me
As to a dog's tail?

—W. B. Yeats, *The Tower*

O what venerable and reverent creatures did
the aged seem! Immortal Cherubims!

—Thomas Traherne, *Centuries of Meditation*

Q. What are the four last things to be ever remembered?
A. The four last things to be ever remembered are Death,
Judgment, Hell, and Heaven.

—*The Penny Catechism*

Obviously, each of these epigraphs is truth-telling, and our experience of Spark's
ideas of reality has perhaps sufficiently conditioned us to suppose, rightly, that
the implications of each epigraph will be pursued and demonstrated.

Structurally and psychologically and morally the book ranges from the completely materialistic to that spiritual-material combination which regularly signifies Spark's ideas of human health and well-being. At one end of the continuum, for example, are Dame Lettie Colston and her brother, Godfrey, who
regard the words of the title as a criminal threat to take their lives, and who
demand that Scotland Yard find and apprehend the caller. At the other end are
Godfrey's wife, Charmian, and Jean Taylor, Charmian's former secretary and
companion. Both women are Catholics and what they attend to is the need to
remember rather than the reminder itself as a scandal or a threat. Charmian tells
the caller that she regularly reminds herself of her death as she ends each day,
and the caller replies that he is glad to hear this. Jean receives no calls but
remarks that her voluntary presence among the other old women in the Maud
Long Ward is the equivalent of a telephone call, and she reminds her old friend
and one-time lover, Alec Warner, a gerontologist, that "a good death . . .
doesn't reside in the dignity of bearing but in the disposition of soul" (p. 171).
Jean, like Charmian, is in much pain—so that her spiritual comments are
anything but unmindful of the hard facts of bodily reality. She is not a disembodied spirit but is fully aware of the difficulty of arranging the suffering body's
accommodation within her reading of the "disposition of soul" (stiff upper lip
and "dignity of bearing" are beside her point: when the nurses are slow with the
chamber pot she wets the bed; when she hurts she cries out).

Between the fearful and pathetic Lettie on one end and the accepting
Charmian and Jean on the other are several other characters, each credible,
entertaining, and instructive on his or her own terms. Alec Warner, for instance, asks the caller to repeat the message so that he can get it straight for his
file cards and then privately speculates on whether mass hysteria is afflicting his
whole crowd of oldsters: his attitude is consistent with his implicit scientific

demand that rationality—his—be served. Guy Leet, a lifelong reprobate, tells the caller to go to hell: Guy is too busy living to think about ceasing to do so, or to suppose that giving a thought to death will serve any purpose. Henry Mortimer, who is a retired police officer accustomed to dealing with crank calls and criminals, advises the old people to think about complying with the words instead of attending to their origin: Henry is apparently not motivated by religion as are Jean and Charmian, but he nevertheless comes through as happily adjusted and ready to die. Mabel Pettigrew, practiced in deceit, actually succeeds in making herself forget that she has received several calls: her fear is akin to Lettie's.

The main point being established about this cast of characters—most of whom have known one another for much of their long adult lives—is that they answer indirectly one of Cardinal Newman's questions, pondered professionally by Alec Warner and reasked by the narrator through Alec, in Victorian-novel fashion, at book's end: "What were they sick, what did they die, of?" (pp. 63, 224). The book's answer to this query is that everyone dies of his or her own life; that everyone is necessarily indicating an attitude toward death in the process of living; that living *is* dying. And a corollary of this weighty generalization is that the telephone calls show the reader who the characters really are: that is, what lives they've lived and how they regard death—as annihilation, or as inevitable if not desirable, or as part of a life process that is unendable (as in *Hothouse by the East River*). In other words, we, like Hamlet, find out about various views of death by discovering answers that Alec's Horatian code does not consider, and thereby we appreciate life's and this book's variety of attitudes.[1]

We know how the characters think and what motivates them, and we are enabled to arrange the characters' qualities on a continuum, as I have suggested, because a third-person omniscient narrator assures us reliably that the old people are not simply imagining things but are fully lucid and are behaving in this or that way for specific reasons; and because the narrator describes the circumstances of a given character's last years or last minutes—and so places these narratively—to compel us to find Charmian, Jean, and Mortimer better off than Lettie or Mabel Pettigrew. In other words, we have a reliable narrator here, rather than the freedom to suppose that the oldsters are feebleminded and thus dismissible. The telephones ring, the voice—different for each hearer—does say those words, and the characters die as the narrator tells us they die.

At the same time, wonderfully, this is a book of obvious comic texture, an extremely funny book. Where we might well expect a heavy sermon or a grim tract, we are given instead a very serious book that is simultaneously warm, compassionate, and sometimes hilarious. How, we may well ask, has Spark managed to combine such amusement with stark reminders of human decline and death? And to what end has she done so?

Consideration of these questions begins and ends with the kind of omniscient narrator encountered in *Memento Mori*. This narrator skips adroitly from character to character, from episode to episode, in such a way as to assure our deriving a particular touch of nastiness, a bit of fellow feeling, a glimmer of malice, lust, greed, envy, some shadow of former or current friendship. In other words, this book belongs to no main character but makes its points primarily and heavily because it ranges over a sizable group to give us more than mere caricatures, but also something other than satellite characters assembled around one or two shimmering principals. Spark assuredly achieves universality, of the sort experienced in parables or fairy tales, by keeping us interested in a number of characters in their assembled activities, rather than by focusing her narrative upon one or two characters. Hierarchy is evident, as my continuum indicates, but that ordering is derived from the collective actions of many. Much of the book's effect is thus traceable to its panoramic use of the omniscient narrator, a narrator who goes unobtrusively *in* by seeming to go only *wide*.

If, for instance, the narrator describes first the elderly Mabel Pettigrew and then the young Olive Mannering displaying their garter-tips to Godfrey Colston and shows us as well that each woman acquires money for catering to what remains of Godfrey's lustful indulgence, the same narrator makes clear a number of differences between the two women's motives and attitudes. For Mabel, this practice is a way to pick up the odd pound or two while she waits and works for bigger financial gains. Plainly she has perfect contempt for Godfrey in his need and seeks to get him within her power so that she can blackmail him and have his will altered in her favor. She is presented, with narrative reliability, as a grasping, furtive, bad-tempered, self-centered person with nothing redeeming about her except possibly an ingrained malice that renders her sad in her helplessness against it or indeed in her very ignorance of it. Olive Mannering, on the other hand, while she also gains money for this curious brand of prostitution, turns most of it over to Eric Colston, the son whom Godfrey no longer supports and who is comparatively needy. Moreover, although Olive needs money apparently more than Mabel does, and in fact eventually marries some of it belonging to the widowered Ronald Sidebottome, she genuinely likes Godfrey and the other old fellows who call upon her for news, companionship, research purposes, and other reasons besides lingering libido, and the uses to which she puts her visitors have nothing to do with gaining power over them and for herself: even when she marries Ronald it is hardly at others' expense, including Ronald's. Mabel, then, is awful—and pathetic for that very reason, while Olive is matey and generous, if hardly disinterested. The narrator will not settle for single motives and accordingly will not settle for simple monotone. We can be sympathetic, at least a little, to the greedy as to the lustful, and we can appreciate the self-serving quality immersed in real concern for others.

This same ambivalent reading must be given to the other relationships and character contrasts and orderings of events in the book. If Godfrey, for instance, is irascible, vindictive, jealous, and promiscuous—and he is and has been all of these—he is also understood to have acted as he has for reasons rendering him more understandable than merely monstrous. He has paid a certain price for his life—a price that causes us to be pleased when he learns of his wife's infidelity years ago, and when he can therefore cease to feel so unrelievedly guilty for his own transgressions and so fearful that Charmian (who has known of them all along) will find him out. By corollary, Charmian is admirable in her serene acceptance of death and is heroic in her resistance against Mabel Pettigrew and Godfrey as well as in her fight to remain lucid and capable when she might well collapse in debility. She has also been tricky and deceptive and manipulative, however, with respect to Godfrey all these years (allowing him to suppose that *he* was the one getting away with something, and thereby keeping him on a guilt hook). We are accordingly satisfied, then, when the truth of Charmian's affair with Guy Leet is revealed to Godfrey, for this truth cannot damage Charmian or Guy, and its emergence relieves Godfrey's last days considerably. Finally, on this point, we note that Jean Taylor's decision to tell Godfrey about Charmian is also double-edged. That decision may be, and likely is, motivated by compassion for Godfrey in his needless guilt, but at the same time it may be partially motivated by a trace of envy—that is, by Jean's lifelong subservience to Charmian. Who can finally sort out the complications of Jean's or anyone's reasons?[2]

This same ambivalence carries over to our readings of other characters and of their behavior over the decades. Guy Leet, for example, is a grotesque reminder of himself as rake, and he is not the least bit repentant, whatever the mismatch between his age and his rambunctious, uncensored inclinations. But Guy is a great pleasure as character and is altogether admirable when taken on his own terms. He has sympathy for this world alone, apparently regards any other view as incomprehensible, and—most important—manifests the courage of his life-long convictions. Guy believes in loyalty, bears his obvious infirmity with persistent if needling humor, adheres to the doctrine that art makes truth, and can take the trouble to soothe the sensibility of poor Percy Mannering. Or, to look at one other member of this cast, we observe the quality of Alec Warner's life. He has remained for the most part emotionally detached and scientifically cool: he takes his notes in three forms, registers his reactions to them, and continues to anticipate the day when these notes shall have become the definitive study of the aged. One admires his efforts at objectivity, but one also realizes that objectivity cannot be and that, furthermore, his book is not likely to be written since the research can never be complete. Thus, while we may appreciate Alec's scientific commitment, we also appreciate that the fire which destroys his notes likewise destroys his life. Like the other characters, Alec serves to impress us with Spark's point that you are what you eat—that is, anyone's life is his or her death. To the extent that characters know this and accept this explicitly or implicitly as sane, they are seen to be likeable—whatever their qualities and regardless of what enables them to accept this sane view. On the other hand, those who cannot handle the fact of death are shown to be finally more pitiable than dreadful or detestable. In short, Jean, Charmian, Mortimer, and Guy Leet, whatever the particular terms of their own lives, can handle death on its own terms as part of a process—while Mabel Pettigrew and Lettie and Godfrey Colston are sad rather than merely malicious or disgusting in their inability to respond appropriately to their phone calls.

Such pronounced ambivalence, while it is of course structural, soaks right down into the texture of the novel and affects intimately the entire tonal quality of the narrative. More specifically, Spark's comic texture is at one with her narrator's omniscience and panoramic viewing, as well as with her spirit of charity. The texture of this fiction differs from that of *The Driver's Seat* (also an omnisciently narrated book), for instance, because in *The Driver's Seat* the omniscience is so heavily concentrated upon Lise as substantially the book's sole character, and because in that book concentration upon Lise is concomitant with the narrative premise that Lise is to be presented and studied in Greek tragic terms. In *Memento Mori*, on the contrary, not only is the narrative interest spread among many characters, but the underlying premise is Spark's more customary view that reality is mysterious but ultimately patterned and credible (if not understandable) in Christian terms. As a result of this very different narrative assumption underlying the point of view, the tone of *The Driver's Seat* is frightening in its presentation of the inexplicable, while *Memento Mori*, every bit as serious in coping with mystery, is comic.

That the fiction is comic and Christian is perfectly compatible with the ambivalence I have been stressing. As we have seen in discussing structure, Spark's duality is by definition emphatically inclusive rather than exclusive. In *Memento Mori* the inclusiveness shows up as a quality of tolerance toward anyone who (like Guy Leet) lives according to his or her best lights, or who (like Dame Lettie) is too frightened to turn on the lights. The texture is complexly comic because, while it certainly allows for what is funny and ridiculous and foolish, it also delicately avoids the note of condescension or of strained insincere camaraderie. Like any true charity, presumably, the tone here is never censuring or adulatory or patronizing or superior or unctuously self-congratulatory. The narrative trick, successfully turned, in my opinion, is to convince us that, while the Christian view of a Jean Taylor may be, absolutely speaking, the view closest to reconciling realism and the larger reality, the very ability to imagine as Jean does necessitates an attitude of charity to every other view. What basis better than a conviction of the reality of human limitation—Original Sin—to compel one to see others with compassion in one's role as omniscient narrator? For that matter, what reason better than a recollection of one's own presumption in narrating all-knowingly to keep one's narrative pride in check?[3]

The omniscient panorama of this point of view thus makes it possible for the narrator to spot stupidity, venality, silliness, kindness, courage, and any number of other vices and virtues—but without succumbing to hubris or despair or mockery of various characters. Every opportunity is available to the reader to note human strengths and weaknesses, but always implicit is the narrator's refraining from judgment, precisely because a sense of the larger reality's mystery induces humility and awe. Of course Godfrey Colston is delightfully Dickensian in his taking pride in the retention of his "faculties," whereas everyone else seems to him to be slipping in this respect. And of course the reader sees the dopiness in Dame Lettie's taking such great pains in barring everyone from her house that inevitably she literally opens the door to the very disaster she would bar. Similarly, the old women in the Maud Long Ward are amusing in their varied eccentricities—their bickering, their little vengeances, their cagey-if-senile suspicions. Again, Guy Leet is ugly in his leering recollection of his days of sexual prowess, and Percy Mannering appears moronically disgusting as he rants and raves through green teeth about the beauties of Dowson's verse. But inevitably the narrator, like Ronald Bridges, offers some balancing evidence, some sympathetic explanation (not necessarily apology or exoneration) to complicate all simple readings. Thus, for example, Godfrey's behavior is at least partly qualified by what Charmian has done to him and to their marriage. And if Lettie is self-defeating, we are at least as inclined to remember her battered corpse as to dwell on accusations of dim-wittedness. Similarly, the old women in the ward may be odd, but surely their surviving spirit and their considerable bonhomie against the world of younger persons are attractive in a way. And as we have seen, Guy is consistently loyal and capable of love and fellow feeling, despite his apparent atrociousness and his real adultery—just as Mannering is admirable in his defense of a lifelong ideal of beauty.

The value of all this panoramic viewing and double-seeing is, among other things, that we are made conscious of universal relevance: calendar age is beside the point that one's life is a dying. The telephone tolls for us, too; if death comes for Lettie as a thief in the night, for whom does it not so come? Who but a fool, whether believer or unbeliever, would deny or ignore the phone call? And is not such foolishness, likely rooted in fear, more lamentable than contemptible? Spark's narrative distance seems thus to me to force us to identify with the splendid individuality of her wide-ranging selection of characters and attitudes, and to empathize with the universal applicability of that very diversity. Delight and instruction are so well combined in this book as to provide yet another reading for Mortimer's thematic statement that "if you look for one thing . . . you frequently find another" (p. 210).

The eccentricities and quirks of old people, then, are responsible for much of the book's delight. But when we have said this, and when we have realized that these traits are remarkably like the quirks of age forty or age twenty—like yours and mine at any time—and that such qualities are herein adroitly modified by other considerations, then we confront the limits of Spark's satiric inclinations in this book. Comic and satiric textures commonly overlap, of course, and in this case the extent of that overlap is instructive.

Satirical import is there, all right. We have no doubt that this book could not have been written without a quite clear sense that much human behavior is deplorable and in need of reform or obliteration if we are to be a better human community. And the portrayal of much conduct of this ugly or idiotic or destructive or malicious sort is of that amusing variety with which we commonly associate satire: that is, we laugh at characters who are obviously at fault, to the extent that we do not recognize ourselves in them. But Spark's book simply will not work out as a satire, despite certain satirical elements. For one thing, we cannot read the book rightly without qualifying the laughter and seeing ourselves in the characters' quirkiness; for another thing, Swift-like Tom-Dick-Harry concreteness is so merged with universal humanity as to prevent our escaping exclusively to an abstract level of reading and emotional involvement. But perhaps the major obstacle to outright satire is that the narrative is imbued with an attitude which, while it inevitably and rightly concerns society, predictably transcends the social. In other words, satirical elements are perfectly at home as components of this comic texture or ambience, even as concrete and abstract are at one here; but the satirical is immersed and transformed because the book is ultimately, inclusively, dealing with a fallen world in many ways satirically funny, but potentially lost in its particulars as well, and in any event not salvageable by means of such social reforms as satire customarily and appropriately strives for.

Possibly a clearer way to get at this slippery point is to indicate that narrative point of view alone makes the essential difference between the balance, tolerance, charity, and "divine" comedy of *Memento Mori* and the alienation, imbalance, terror and pity, helpless compassion, and tragedy of *The Driver's Seat*. Seeing these two omnisciently contrasting books together helps one to see that they imply each other and indeed are each other except for the separate authorial choices of narrative technique, which make all the textural difference. Lise insists upon dying alone, terribly and gratefully; all the characters of *Memento Mori* die alone, too, but this book is shaped to make a comic texture of what is fetching or endearing in each character's style, rather than to play up individual deathbed torments. Lise's narrative terrifies us with the mystery of cosmic design and individual agony, while the old people's narrative stresses snippets of process rather than questioning the outcome of an ordeal, and in this manner makes for comic texture *and* a sense of mystery and design as support for that comic texture. In any case, the world of each book is the same fallen world, however varied may be the treatment of the consequences thereof. And the point in *Memento Mori* is that social reform cannot change the ultimate nature or character of such a world. Satire, as a method well suited to the reform of particular social habits and institutions, is understandably beside the ultimate significance of *Memento Mori*. The only means to change, as seen and offered in this book, is grace: those who don't know or, to be accurate, believe this are to be appreciated for themselves (sometimes deplored in their actions but never patronized); those who do believe it are to be seen as no less entangled in the world's concreteness, are hardly to be complimented for the faith which they must attribute to grace unearned and undeserved, but are to be seen as the characters whose moral *values* are the book's norm. For these reasons the book is not generically satiric and justifies the label "divine" comedy, however much the quotation marks may undercut comparisons to Dantean grandeur and scope.

Having attempted to specify the limits of the satirical, however, we must now say something more precise about the quality of comic texture to be experienced in this book. In a sense, we have here the usual elements to be discovered in a work called a comedy. That is, we are presented with a limited group all belonging to the same comparatively comfortable class; all of them are old; all of them are pronouncedly British. Moreover, like characters in many comedies, these characters are much taken up with the problems of sex and money (much ado about wills and the making and changing of wills). Socially, then, the details of the fiction conform to those of traditional comedy—and in addition rewards and punishments, temporally speaking, are arranged as we expect them to be meted out in comedy. And the fact that the principals are aged is, as we have seen, primarily useful as a ploy to make us suppose, wrongly, that not we, but only the elderly, are the book's central concern. As in most comedy, then, we are eventually able to see what the book has to do with ourselves, and we also find that resolutions (not weddings in this case) are made to appear inevitable if not especially or necessarily deserved.

But just as we have seen that satire extends only so far into the narrative endeavor here, so we observe that what must be said of the comic texture in *Memento Mori* has hardly been approached when we have made such observations as we rightly make of Fielding's or Shaw's works. And the reason for this inadequacy is not, of course, that comedy is unserious or unimportant, but that comedy is traditionally concerned with social matters which can in fact be treated and indeed contained and compromised and resolved on society's own terms. Thinking of *Memento Mori* along such lines, as we have seen, gets us only so far and surely does less than justice to the book. And this is why I have lifted Dante's modifier, however qualifiedly, and applied it to the texture in question. Spark is everywhere a reveler in concrete details of social tone, dress, furnishings, language, appearance, and foible. But what makes the label *comic* applicable to this book, I think, is the abiding security, consolation, assurance arising from the narrative overview given of Mortimer, Charmian, Jean Taylor in their attitudes. Comedy in this sense has nothing to do with amusement inherently, although amusement is not precluded. Moreover, such comic texture, arising as it does from faith and a deep appreciation of the unknown (which can as readily crush as soothe), cannot be said to stem from complacency or a feeling that since so much of the real controls and escapes us, our efforts are fruitless and uncalled-for. On the contrary, the word comic in the present case assumes all the iffiness associated with the mysterious. It may or may not imply laughter or laughableness. It precludes social resolution and denies access to those who would limit it to the social, temporal, societal, political order of things. The word *comic* here means that narrator and reader can more fully appreciate (not depreciate or deny reality to) social and temporal matters, can relish such matters more deeply, precisely because such matters occur in a context of reality larger than the socially comic. That these temporal events are not socially resolved is, then, of no great moment because they are not seen to be limited to the moment or to this or that place. Social comedy is to "divine" comedy, then, as realism is to the larger reality. One does not preclude the other, but the assumptions of works *centered* upon one or the other are remarkably different. As we have seen, centering narrative attention upon mystery that must be believed in rather than known can make for tragic texture, as in *The Driver's Seat*. On the other hand, such centering can also make for comic texture, as in *Memento Mori*. Both books are eminently serious, both come out of the same sensibility, but *Memento Mori* tends more to emphasize suitable demise, the pleasure derived from characters' individuality, and the fact of the need to die as that fact impinges on a group—rather than focusing upon a broken Lise, whose *demand to die* makes for a very different psychological interest and reaction. In sum, sin, pain, death, and hell are parts of Dante's reality, which in turn is a comedy because it makes sense to his faith, has a pattern, is redeemed, and offers redemption. Spark imagines, in *The Driver's Seat*, mystery proffering no redemption; in *Memento Mori*, on the other hand, her narrator shares Dante's assumptions and makes sense of Troilus's laughter.

Memento Mori is, then, a comic texture not because it ignores the material or focuses entirely on spirituality and the next world, and not because it laughs at those whose life is geared to that world or because it is unconcerned about what must seem the limitations of life so geared. Nor is this book texturally comic because it supposes risk impossible and salvation assured because of faith in the larger reality. *Memento Mori* is complexly comic because in fact it does none of these things and adopts none of these attitudes. Rather, the book delights in the unexpected and in concrete everyday experience and relishes what Hopkins specified as "dappled things" and Chaucer called "God's plenty" (indeed, Chaucer's *Pardoner's Tale* comes to mind when we consider Mortimer's thematic observation about looking for one thing and finding another). Such pleasure is perfectly compatible with awareness that some views are fuller than others and that the vaster one's view of the real, the greater one's sense of what is at stake in life. To know what's risked, what may be lost or gained, is the measure, not of something comfortably secured by virtue of one's largely fortuitous faith, but of paradoxical belief to be regularly tested in the life-death process. The comic texture derives not from a turning away from assortment and difference, then, but from the conviction that something explains or makes final sense of such particularity: effects are caused. Jean Taylor, like Samuel Johnson defying Berkeley, points to gravestones to prove to her scientifically rational friend and antagonist Alec Warner that absolute idealism won't do; that "other people are real" (p. 71). The pattern exists; paradoxes are usual; the unexpected is impossible in the larger view; the frame of meaning is real.

And that is what I mean by evoking Troilus's cosmic laughter: like Paul and Elsa in *Hothouse,* Troilus now sees and knows what he would before death have had to believe or miss out on altogether. Similarly, Spark, like Chaucer and Dante, gives us not "the real thing," of course (surely we've labored sufficiently at the impossibility of any art's doing *that*). She gives us instead a narrative overview of a fictional world wherein varieties of faith and nonfaith coexist on a continuum less aware or more aware of the full-frame ramifications of paradoxical tensions between, for instance, concrete and universal, relative and absolute, rational and commonsensical, funny and comic, tangible and spiritual. *Memento Mori* appropriately ends with the narrator's telling us two things that give us the book in little: on the one hand, Alec Warner re-asks Newman's question, "What were they sick, what did they die, of?" To this question he ticks off his friends' names and recites words like pneumonia, arteriosclerosis, carcinoma, coronary thrombosis. Then in the last paragraph, on the other hand, the narrator says, "Jean Taylor lingered for a time, employing her pain to magnify the Lord, and meditating sometimes confidingly upon Death, the first of the Four Last Things to be ever remembered." The point is that both attitudes address reality and return us to the variety of the real suggested in the three epigraphs. Of course we die of physical ailments, the narrative sanely reminds us; but equally sane is the narrative reminder that the particulars of this or that physical demise are only the means to "the first of the Four Last Things." Whatever is, is real; but while Jean Taylor's reality and Alec Warner's coexist and qualify each other, hers includes his.[4]

If the comic texture of *Memento Mori* is rooted in cosmic inclusiveness, in a sense that however messy the particulars may be, things fit, the comic texture of *The Abbess of Crewe* (1974)[5] is quite a different matter. In the *Abbess,* written nearly two decades after *Memento Mori,* Spark gives us a book that, much as it implies the familiar orthodox Christian psychological view of reality, establishes emphases with which the earlier book had little to do. Once again, the epigraph is a useful clue to what we find. Spark here cites Yeats's "Nineteen Hundred and Nineteen":

Come let us mock at the great
That had such burdens on the mind
And toiled so hard and late
To leave some monument behind,
Nor thought of the levelling wind. . . .

Mock mockers after that
That would not lift a hand maybe
To help good, wise or great

To bar that foul storm out, for we
Traffic in mockery.

(Part 5)

These lines are a sort of microcosm of the long Yeats poem, and, when they are seen in context, tempt one to read *The Abbess of Crewe* as nearly an ecclesiastical-political analogue of that poem. The temptation is to be avoided as misleadingly tidy, but the moods, implications, flirtations with despair, and even particulars of imagery are close in these two works. To elaborate on this generalization will be to distinguish between the comic texture of *Memento Mori* and that of the *Abbess*.

Yeats's poem is likely motivated by the Irish troubles and is of course concerned more generally than particularly with the demise of the West, and with the First World War as sign and symptom thereof. As in much of his work, he here anticipates the inevitability of total collapse when the current two-thousand-year cycle shall have run its course. His mood is anything but comic, where *comic* means amused; nor does he suggest the possibility of redeeming the time or restoring past hopes. In the course of prophesying doomsday and giving us the apparently totally cynical advice to mock everything and everyone including ourselves and all other mockers, he can offer only the following masochistically consoling alleviation—hardly permanent or descriptive of what we might consider redemptive of the human condition:

Some moralist or mythological poet
Compares the solitary soul to a swan;
I am satisfied with that,
Satisfied if a troubled mirror show it,
Before that brief gleam of its life be gone,
An image of its state;
The wings half spread for flight,
The breast thrust out in pride
Whether to play, or to ride
Those winds that clamour of approaching night.

(Part 3)

Pessimism is thus unavoidable. No hope appears for the many, for society. The only dim exception to the otherwise universal gloom lies in the unique individual's ability to take some self-tormenting pleasure in an accurate picture of himself and his world. The dying swan relishes its solitariness, its dying, and the precisely imaged lineaments of its hopeless condition. Seeing it clearly necessitates "solitude" and this seeing in turn suggests that only self-reflective (self-addressed?) art makes life bearable. It is impossible to see such an attitude as comic in the larger sense of that word: offering resolution, holding out hope despite actual and potential tragic reality.

Yet Spark uses this poem up front, in spite of her notions of the real, and she uses it to good purpose. And in many ways her book echoes and compares to Yeats's poem. *The Abbess of Crewe* is unlike *Memento Mori* in that its third-person point of view concentrates heavily upon the title figure much as *The Driver's Seat* is concerned with Lise. At the same time, the *Abbess* is omnisciently narrated, so that we get not only the main figure but narrative clues to the real—as is Spark's customary procedure. Proximity to the Yeats poem available by this method is manifold. Spark's fiction gives us plenty of reason to despair of the modern world and of all of us within it.

In its simplest plot-terms, this is a fiction about conditions prevailing at the Abbey of Crewe in England, in our time, shortly before and shortly after a new abbess is elected by the forty or fifty nuns in residence. Sister Alexandra is the nun of the title, and her close colleagues are Sisters Walburga and Mildred. Their legwoman is Sister Winifrede, and Alexandra's rival for the position of abbess is Sister Felicity. The campaign—which, as such, is forbidden by the unique Benedictine-Jesuit Rule under which these nuns live—is between the tall and graceful Alexandra's traditional values and the short and perky Felicity's innovative wishes (in particular for "love" in its physical manifestations). The sides appear fairly balanced, according to Alexandra's reports (which are based on electronic bugging of the abbey and much of the grounds), until Alexandra is enabled to take unconscionably unfair advantage of her already heavy electronic edge and thereby win by a landslide. Thereafter, Alexandra's defeated, departed, and excommunicated enemy draws sufficient attention to the abbey's affairs to give considerable scandal and to cause Alexandra to be summoned to Rome for some explanation of her abbey's management. The book ends as Alexandra prepares to sail for the Continent. She looks, on this occasion, much like Yeats's swan.

So much for bare bones. Perhaps the most attention-getting quality of these occurrences and characters, at least initially, is that they evoke the recent political history of the United States—in particular, they are tied to the person-ages and experiences collectively labeled "Watergate." In many respects and up to a clearly discernible point, Alexandra acts out the Nixon role, Walburga and Mildred play Ehrlichman and Haldeman, Winifrede does Dean, Sister Gertrude, the missionary sister, is Kissinger, and Felicity remotely apes McGovern. Ca-reerism is everything, to the extent that the book cannot afford to dwell on why these women are in the ostensibly religious life at all. As a parable of Watergate, including bugging, break-ins, blackmail payoffs, editing of tapes, newspaper and television scenario-planning, looking for scapegoats, and even some of the same language ("scenario" is an example; Alexandra also describes her two principal aides as "two of the finest nuns I have ever had the privilege to know" [p. 99]; other instances abound)—in these ways, Spark is able not only to arouse the inevitable guffaw, but also to rely upon drawing from us the feelings associated with Watergate (assuming that we're not too weary of the subject to pay attention). We may experience resentment, fascination, anger, collective nau-

sea, zeal for reform, pained curiosity about where we went wrong, some amusement, fear for political structures, perhaps doubts and fears about our
willingness, energy, and ability to make substantial changes rooted in convictions, and so forth. The Watergate trappings are useful and functional, then,
because an author can get much mileage immediately from these as from any
means likely to evoke stock responses and thereby to make the authorial task
more economical.

At the same time, however, it is absolutely essential to indicate the ephemeral
status of these trappings. Anyone, in fact, who has seen the film *Nasty Habits*
(adapted from the *Abbess*) will see clearly what I mean by this importance. *Nasty
Habits* is *nothing but* an effort to put nuns' habits on the principals of Watergate.
The abbey has been transplanted in Philadelphia, the nuns swear and smoke
cigars, Mafia-links with the Vatican are introduced, United States vulgarisms are
prominent even while Glenda Jackson plays the lead and must therefore im-
plausibly be accounted for as someone whose British presence has other than
box-office explanation. The film is a vulgar bore. But the point is that this is an
indication of what can happen if we take the fiction to be no more than an effort
to draw laughs and profits from making us see how funny the Watergaters are
when we imagine them as nuns. Comic texture of a certain level does result, but
it is of the sort that might conceivably come of casting Groucho, Chico, and
Harpo in a film of *The Brothers Karamazov*. Such an enterprise as *Nasty Habits* is
obvious as satire (who needs it?) and stands forth as what it is—frosting gouged
from a substantial cake, and embellished with obviousness after the gouging.
The value of the Watergate parallel is only remotely related to such pratfalling
zestlessness.

In my opinion, the seriousness and farther-reaching interaction of this book
can be traced to that which the Watergate trimming plays up. Indeed, I am going
to project what I suspect will become clearer as the particulars of current politics
fade: if Watergate obscures what matters here, I suspect that someday footnotes
will be needed to spell out the details of this very scandal which to us is so plain
as almost to get in the way of the point. That point is Yeats's, where general
cultural and social and political values of the West are concerned, but it is
additionally Spark's own where religious and ecclesiastical buttressing of those
Yeatsian concerns is at stake. *The Abbess of Crewe* assuredly comments on
Watergate, but the effect of the commentary on Watergate in the context of
religious life is to demonstrate a profound fear and loathing of the narrative view
offered for our contemplation. Watergate is but a minor symptom of what is
deeply wrong, and I do not think that the narrator of this fiction is at all
interchangeable with the narrator of *Memento Mori*.

" 'What are we here for?' says Alexandra. 'What are we doing here?' " (p. 29).
These questions are not given much attention by Alexandra's colleagues, but
they are as important to this fiction as are Newman's queries to *Memento Mori*.
Everything about Spark's book is shaped and toned to remind us that the

questions have proper answers quite contrary to those implicit in the lives being lived in this abbey. The right answers in some way would touch on the dedication to a comparatively selfless calling: a vocation of prayer, self-denial, fasting, praise, and love of things spiritual—all for the welfare of not only the individual nun involved, but also the whole fallen world. That at any rate is a beginning answer, and it contrasts sharply to the life at Crewe, or at least in Crewe's upper rooms: a life not only grossly close to Watergate, but wretchedly worse in that it espouses so much more and such differences. Somewhere along the line the answers to these basic questions have been forgotten, with the result that life inside the walls is not only the same secular opportunism that prevails outside but is moreover depraved because of the effort of hypocrisy required to keep up the front.

But the book is not a diatribe or a jeremiad. Rather, the narrator maintains Spark's customary detached and cool wit and presents us with a very good if depressing reason for the disinclination to shout in the wilderness. That reason is an underlying confusion implicit in the principal characters and in the very texture of the narrative itself. These nuns in high places are indeed amusing in spite of their Watergate affinities, as the unexpected tends often to be amusing if we are not its victims. Indeed, Spark is ingenious in arranging for Alexandra to compel the nuns' allegiances and win their votes, while all the time reminding them that campaigning is against their Rule, as true ladies know. And the various other uses to which Machiavellian maneuvering is put, usually on the advice of the deep-voiced Germanic Gertrude, are comic. But this drollery is not dominant. What pervades is our awareness that these quick-witted leaders no longer know what they are doing here rather than outside; and what intensifies this awareness is the arrangement of the narrative to signify a similar, quite conscious, confusion in the bones of the book.

To be more specific, the narrative is patched together as most Spark books are stitched. But where the stitching is readable as constituting a decided pattern, at least in the earlier books, here such comic effects as we gain are beside the point of the overall narrative direction. We know how to make parts fit the whole in *Memento Mori* (or in other Spark books before *The Public Image*), but that Dantean assurance, in the teeth of tragedy, is not to be found here. In fact deception and confusion are not always separable in the *Abbess*. It is clear that Alexandra is simply hypocritical in justifying the development of electronics laboratories in conjunction with traditional spiritual concerns of the abbey, on the grounds that "we are told in the Scriptures 'to watch and to pray'" (p. 24). And it is also clear that Alexandra abuses traditional concepts of religious authority out of some quite self-interested notion of law and order, not to say oppression. But once we get beyond the realm of the topical, matters are less decipherable. For instance, if we are inclined to suppose automatically that the book adds up to some platitude such as that Nixon is bad and McGovern is good, we are soon caught short. The narrator displays undoubted fondness for much of what Alexandra stands for, even while making Alexandra's offenses plain. Similarly, Felicity, as the rival of these Machiavellian forces, is herself scheming and is moreover personally anything but attractive to the narrator even as Alexandra is quite attractive. The book will not hold up as merely a parable of Watergate. Nor is this only a single abbey gone bad. If all we met here in the way of moral offense were the instance of one place where sexual vigilance had been allowed to drop or where one group of spoiled and wealthy nuns indulged in worldliness, the book would be much slighter and less consequential than it is. What seem instead to underlie the fiction are genuine doubt and fear about the Church as spiritual force and guide in the modern world. That doubt has apparently come about since the earlier books, and much in the *Abbess* would seem to make the Second Vatican Council responsible for weakening religious and moral force in the Church.

When Nixon and Company fade out, what we have is a battle between what often passes for traditional Roman Catholicism and what Vatican II is often found responsible for encouraging. Alexandra espouses tradition and the narrative makes her remarkably appealing in this role—or rather, the narrative makes tradition appealing, although it is abused mightily by Alexandra, who pretends to endorse it. On the other hand, where Felicity might be expected to look good in her opposition to Alexandra's corruption, she is not only presented as shallow, small-minded, and as little genuinely religious as Alexandra, but she is shown to be the mouthpiece of a version of post-Vatican II Catholicism at least as shallow, shortsighted, and—most pronouncedly—vulgar as Felicity. Neither woman is religious or motivated by religious calling, so that we have to view both secularly. When we do so we must try to choose between an intelligent and hypocritical snobbish totalitarian on the one hand and a small-minded and equally hypocritical espouser of a drab-looking new day on the other hand. When this controversy is seen, because of the narrative structure and the comments of the reliable narrator, to extend beyond this fictional situation and indeed to the West and to humanity at large, matters are sufficiently grim. Where are we to turn? Where is that comic conviction encountered in previous books? How indeed can we choose between such unacceptable extremes? If we mock both doers and nondoers, where will our mocking cease?

An answer is to be sought first, I think, in the meager consolation specified by Yeats. This may be only a beginning response, but nonetheless it is impossible not to note Alexandra's own solipsistic relishing of herself as work of art, as self-created identity, as aesthetically beautiful artifact to be contemplated.[6] This tendency fits her Nixon power madness as well as marking her closeness to Yeats's lyric speaker: implicitly at least, the object of one's life is to make an object of one's life. More importantly, this tendency also marks Alexandra's failed vocation—her need to make meaning from within rather than both conforming to a believed-in objective reality and making one's individuality signify because of that recognition and such acts as proceed from it. Alexandra's involuted perspective is never more evident than, for instance, in her attitude toward and treatment of tradition. On the one hand she wants not to change the abbey's medieval practice of stopping everything else in order to offer collective prayer every three hours. But on the other hand it is evident that her reasons for this wish are suspect and peculiar to herself. This routine gives her a chance to locate everyone else once in three hours, to indulge her fondness for medieval and Renaissance English as well as for Latin, and to continue creating her own identity as the central attraction for a ritual intended obviously as prayer to God rather than as moments for her to display her grace and beauty, and to relish her own recitation of fine poetry, before a captive audience. (The contrast between Joanna's and Selina's public recitations in *Girls* is instructive here.) Alexandra needs to be in charge and to be appreciated as such: but in every other sense she plays self-sufficient Creator contemplating herself as handiwork and finding it always and everywhere good and beautiful.

For all of her insistence upon tradition, by the way, Alexandra absents herself from ritual whenever something else presents itself as more important (here we recall "national security," no doubt), and she regularly leans to the side of Benedictine or of Jesuit tradition as she sees need to rationalize her will on various morally defensible grounds. We see such coping with paradox in all Spark books, but in this case what Alexandra presents is a hypocritical violation of two traditions simply for her own advancement rather than shifting to one or the other traditional emphasis (ascetic or worldly) out of a need to struggle in good faith with complexity. Like everything else she does, this manipulation serves to effect and reflect Alexandra's own image and in this respect, again, to exemplify that mirroring which Yeats's speaker thinks enough, or satisfying.

To some extent this mirror-working on Alexandra's part is crafty and adroitly intelligent, even witty. But beyond all that, such endeavor sometimes resembles more than a little the behavior of a doubtfully sane person. After a time, the effort of trying to deal with her immediate charges as well as with pressures from outside the walls raises doubts in us about the mental competence of Alexandra. Her thinking of and treatment of history and mythology are perhaps the surest source of the trouble we may have in distinguishing between the rationally quick-witted and the possibly deranged Alexandra. We can make this distinguishing at least a bit simpler, I think, if we readjust the time sequence in the book so as to see Alexandra's changes more accurately. As the fiction is presented, its six chapters are laid out temporally thus: chapter 1 is penultimately present—after Alexandra's election as abbess, but before what is to come of the mess into which the abbey has fallen; chapters 2 and 3 are prior to the election—during the few weeks between the death of the Abbess Hildegarde and Alexandra's elevation; chapters 4 through 6 are immediately present—after the events of chapter 1. In short, we have a book that begins *in medias res*. Such a structure has many uses, of course, but I think that my present purposes will be best served if we rearrange events the better to see Alexandra's altering conduct.

I will therefore look at the book, here, as if it were set out thus, by chapter: 2, 3, 1, 4–6.

When we view things in this order, we divide them effectively into pre- and postelection events (the election itself is anticlimactically mentioned in a single paragraph beginning chapter 4). Alexandra in black (only the abbess wears white) speaks to her cohort of her destiny to be elected abbess (p. 30), while nonetheless striving to fulfill that destiny. Moreover, it is clear that underlying her intention to see this fate realized is a proud aristocratic spirit about which she is quite open in discussions with Walburga and Mildred and in chanting the canonical hours in chapel. While others chant Latin or English scriptural passages, Alexandra, perhaps unconsciously, is very likely to chant something more suited to her present state of mind. The aristocratic pride of that mind is evident on one occasion, for instance, when the community pleads collectively:

> Hear, O God, my supplication:
>   be attentive to my prayers.
> From the ends of the earth I cry to thee:
>   when my heart fails me.
> Thou wilt set me high upon a rock, thou wilt
>   give me rest:
>   thou art my fortress, a tower of strength
>   against the face of the enemy.

On this note, a familiarly beautiful turning of the "me" to general or community purposes, so that the various selves are joined together and submerged in unity, Alexandra is instead singing what is on her own mind alone:

> For I am homesick after mine own kind
> And ordinary people touch me not.
>   And I am homesick
> After my own kind. . . .

(P. 59)

Such instances, together with the fact that the select dine on paté and French wine while their sisters eat dog and cat food and drink water, anticostively warmed, show plainly what Alexandra thinks of herself and others and set up that foundation of hypocrisy to which we have referred. The point is that Alexandra behaves so much as electable leaders may be expected to behave that we hardly consider her other than shrewd in her pride—although she looks a bit odd, maybe, in an abbey. Her crowning campaign achievement, however, again eminently predictable and politically adroit, is her address to the assembled nuns. Mark Antony did it earlier, but Alexandra learned his art well.

She begins her pitch (for thus it must be called) by reminding her sisters of the distinguished and ever-absent Sister Gertrude, who brings such renown to the abbey, and goes on to say that Gertrude has instructed her to speak with them and to appeal to their higher instincts concerning the recent break-in and theft of Sister Felicity's thimble. In this way she implicitly undercuts any objection that she is making a campaign speech, she pretends to be speaking in behalf of another, and, most importantly, she flatters her audience into thinking that Gertrude thinks of them on her own level and as persons with, indeed, higher instincts. What follows is an elegantly malicious attack on Felicity as *bourgeoise*, and a graceful challenge to the community to identify itself either with the commonness of Felicity or with the *noblesse* of such real ladies as their founder, Gertrude, and Alexandra's cohort. In other words, she defeats Felicity by appealing to snobbery, a very low instinct indeed—and in the entire performance she is never once required to mention the name of her rival. Thus, because to side with Felicity will make them common little things, all the nuns side with Alexandra (perhaps without ever realizing how she has served her own ends) and make the eventual election a formality.

So much for chapters 2 and 3, the preelection sections. Up to this point Alexandra is very much in shrewd control and is behaving in depressingly recognizable campaigner's ways. However despicable and scandalous to the religious life, she knows what she wants and adjusts her hypocritical conduct accordingly. After the election, however, things begin to change.

Beginning two years after the election (chapters 1, 4–6), the line grows fainter between Alexandra's assured control of events and the force exercised by events themselves in controlling Alexandra. Noises made by the departed Felicity have brought television, press, police, and church authorities to the abbey, with the result that Alexandra's continuing vocation to the creation of her own identity has become more harried, even a bit frantic: she begins to appear more and more as victim rather than maker of her own destiny. Early in chapter 1 it is evident that Alexandra's two years as abbess have been spent in seeing to it that the abbey's routine shall become an extension of her self-creation. She implies as much to Walburga and Mildred:

> 'It is absurd in modern times that the nuns have to get up twice in the middle of the night to sing the Matins and the Lauds. But modern times come into a historical context, and as far as I'm concerned history doesn't work. Here, in the Abbey of Crewe, we have discarded history. We have entered the realm, dear Sisters, of mythology. My nuns love it. Who doesn't yearn to be part of a myth at whatever the price in comfort? The monastic system is in revolt throughout the rest of the world, thanks to historical development. Here, within the ambience of mythology, we have consummate satisfaction, we have peace.' (P. 12)

Alexandra's similarity to Dougal Douglas and Jean Brodie is manifest in what is fundamentally wrong with her vision and intent: she wants to control others' lives in order to establish her role as creator. She plays God, violates Spark's much-valued notion of individual privacy, and of course sets herself up for failure. She would throw larger and smaller realities out of balance by denying the here and now, the historical. As she remarks later: "Mythology is nothing more than history garbled; likewise history is mythology garbled and it is nothing more in all the history of man. Who are we to alter the nature of things? So far as we are concerned . . . to look for the truth of the matter will be like looking for the lost limbs, toes and fingernails of a body blown to pieces in an air crash" (pp. 92–93). The paradox that is standardly the more impressive in Spark's books because of efforts to merge larger and lesser, outer and inner, material and spiritual, is here cynically abused by Alexandra (in the manner of Tom Wells) in order to deceive others about what has been going on in the abbey. Like Nixon, to be sure, but, more important, like anyone who strives, like Jean Brodie or Dougal Douglas or Patrick Seton, and overreaches, Alexandra works to make reality into something emanating from herself, even as she attempts to turn a similar trick with her own person. To the extent that she actually comes to believe she can get away with remaking reality so that she is now Prime Mover, she demonstrates the dementia suggested earlier. The point is not that she cannot manage this feat, but that objective reality makes the feat impossible. As Jean Brodie's fiats and Dougal Douglas's or Patrick Seton's inability to live with what is—ugliness and sickness, for instance—signify their being out of touch with the real, so Alexandra's exclusiveness, her compulsion to change her swan-white garments twice daily, her drive to withdraw to the artificially old world that will mirror her self-generative power—so all these traits indicate her drifting sanity.

Even in the first chapter, in medias res, signs of stress accumulate, although these can best be appreciated, as we have suggested, when we reach the middle chapters and find where Alexandra has been. Here at the start of the book and two years into her tenure, however, we hear her speaking on the phone to Gertrude about "the Abbess of Crewe [who] continues to perform her part in the drama of The Abbess of Crewe" (p. 22). Or again:

> The Abbess from her high seat [in chapel] looks with a kind of wonder at her shadowy chapel of nuns, she listens with a fine joy to the keen plainchant [O Lord, our Lord, how wonderful/is thy name in all the earth. . . .], as if upon a certain newly created world. She contemplates and sees it is good. Her lips move with the Latin of the psalm. She stands before her high chair as one exalted by what she sees and thinks, as it might be she is contemplating the full existence of the Abbess of Crewe.
>
> *Et fecisti eum paulo minorem Angelis:*
> *Gloria et honore coronasti eum.*
>
> Soon she is whispering the melodious responses in other words of her great liking:
>
> *Every farthing of the cost,*
> *All the dreaded cards foretell,*

Shall be paid, but from this night
Not a whisper, not a thought,
Not a kiss nor look be lost.

(Pp. 26–27)

Remarkable passages like these point plainly to such contrasts as those between controlling Creator and rambling pseudocreator; between language put to selfless worship and language called forth by educated taste but regardless of other purpose or of occasion; between the recognition of humankind's place, below God and angels, and the disturbing illusion that a unique human person tops this hierarchy; between liturgical uses of canonical hours and the enjoyment of tradition's trappings as framing security for one's creative mania. To the extent that Alexandra (like Miss Brodie) believes (not merely tries to make the world believe) that reality is herself, and that that's what she gets back in the mirror into which Yeats's speaker gazes, she is as crazy as Nixon or Louis XIV, to be sure. And that in turn means that she is different from the calculating practical politician of chapters 2 and 3.

Of course the facts of history are not deniable, however mythological (i.e., garbled) a situation may become. When Alexandra goes on about "truly moving in a mythological context" and asserts that "the facts of the matter are with us no longer, but have returned to God who gave them. We can't be excommunicated without the facts. . . . You cannot bring a charge against Agamemnon or subpoena Clytemnestra," Walburga looks at her "as if at a new person. 'You can,' she says, 'if you are an actor in the drama yourself'" (p. 16). This means that there may be a Watergate-like slipup, true, but it also suggests that there is something at least a little deranged about not so much trying to hide the truth as recreating the truth by scenario and coming actually to believe in your own garble. Eternally speaking, everything is now; but otherwise, past and present are separable. Small wonder that Walburga looks oddly at her superior: the Machiavellian rational mind—such as Alexandra's before the election—knows that muddying that past is far different from believing that the past was (is) not.

Predictably, the facts of history come to impinge upon facts and persons Alexandra had regarded as creatures in her own drama. Since Alexandra is not God, she cannot continue to regard her desires as her destiny and as that of everyone else. The ridiculous break-in and theft of Felicity's silver thimble precipitate publicity, Felicity's blabbing, demands for investigations, and other inevitable signs that only a kind of madness could have supposed Alexandra's providence to have been all-embracingly competent to accommodate every contingency or possibility. History will not die in spite of myth-making ingenuity. Truth is. Alexandra, however, goes on insisting that history cannot touch her: she is her own abiding, ongoing mythological entity. As the book ends, Alexandra has seemingly fooled the bishops and the television audience and is on her way to Rome to defend herself. Gertrude assures her that she "won't get the mythological approach from Rome. In Rome, they deal with realities" (p.

113). Alexandra, however, remains convinced that her tapes are herself, or that they will be when once the recitation of English verse is removed and the blank spaces are marked "Poetry deleted." Her instructions to her nuns are that they "sedulously expurgate all such trivial fond records, and entitle the compilation *The Abbess of Crewe*" (p. 116). As I read this passage, which is Alexandra's implicit defense against Rome's eventual interest in reality, I find Alexandra's shrewdness evident, but I think the course of the fiction coupled with this ending shows that political agility is at last overcome by mental derangement. No matter what Alexandra may wish others to think or, more frighteningly, may force herself to think, she is not God, and the tapes, doctored or not, are not Alexandra. Outer layers of reality exist, as always in Spark's work.

Yet the next layer, that of the narrator, while it certainly prevents our taking Alexandra on her own terms, is not the same as what we have seen in *Memento Mori*. Where in the earlier book the narrator settled things, characters, events into their places in the larger, cosmically comic pattern, here in *The Abbess of Crewe* narrative assurance is more remote and comic design more nearly implicit, more faintly patterned.

As we have seen, the book defeats our reading it as the events of Watergate in nuns' garb. Again, it is plain that the narrator in some ways endorses Alexandra's view of things and presents Felicity as whining, narrow-minded, vindictive, and potentially destructive of beautiful, efficient, dignified, noble tradition. Moreover, the narrator's own language and habits of selecting particular psalms chanted by the sisterly community are a strong endorsement of the values for which Alexandra and her cohort are supposed to be fighting in the battle against Felicity's innovations. An extension of this endorsement is the narrator's own avowal that the nuns are for the most part debased creatures with no minds of their own and no imagination—creatures who deserve to be fed dog and cat food. The book's central problem, and assuredly the central question for anyone trying to specify comic basis, is this: if one side disregards the values and lessons of history and would make freedom into license, while the other side wishes to deny history in the interests of its own mythology surrounded by ancient trappings and would distort freedom in the interests of its own exercise of power, what does the narrator do to break this deadlock between unacceptables? What is to be learned from the narrator's support of some of Alexandra's views but not of Alexandra? of neither Felicity nor her values?

The answer is implicit in the narrative composition: the narrator cherishes tradition as embodying the fullest possible view of the real. Thus the narrator is sympathetic to the orthodox belief that the race is fallen and needs to be vigilant and sober lest it surrender to the devil and damn itself; that prayer, fasting, and ritually regular devotion are necessary for the individual and for the human community; that privacy and quiet are requisite to the foregoing needs and are moreover always needed for the exercise of intelligence and imagination as well as fitting in the light of individual human uniqueness. The narrative's texture further implies that voluntary submission to rightful authority certainly ought to enhance rather than to preclude human growth and development; that form must be one with content if the real is to be evoked and contemplated (the disastrous opposite occurs when the liturgy, say, degenerates into mere form, with the result that content also dies); and in short that belief in the real is abiding, whatever the situation of the believer. This distinction between narrator and characters, between the belief and assorted violations of it, makes sense of Spark's use of Yeats's poem.

We have already seen that while Yeats's narrator may derive satisfaction from seeing himself in the mirror and getting clear what he sees himself and his own dyspeptic view of the world to be, Spark shows Alexandra's efforts at the same thing to be self-delusive and destructive. Spark's book in fact "mocks" both the innovative Felicity and the traditional Alexandra. But mockery of the mockers does not mean that all ends in mockery; rather, Spark carries things beyond the solipsistic near-despair of Yeats's speaker and fits her book into the comic frame—if not so snugly as with *Memento Mori*. What matters is what could be and by implication what was. Spark's narrative quotes the magnificence of the psalms in English—much as in *Girls of Slender Means*—and itself comes at us in gracefully poetic language, not to indicate what is no more, but to show what abides from the past and what language still today can be. Again, if the community are meekly blind and semimoronic, that is because of the state of contemporary vocations and a lack of guidance rather than because the religious life inherently demands dehumanized subservience. Felicity is wrong not in opposing Alexandra but in thinking that true freedom means "doing your own thing." Of Alexandra's wrongs we have said enough. The significance of all these distinctions is that we cannot afford merely to join cynically in the general mocking, when we are presented (as is not the case in "Nineteen Hundred and Nineteen") with indications that this terrible state of affairs need not be and ought not to be. The mirror is inadequate. It is not enough to think, as Alexandra does in speaking to Gertrude, that "I have become an object of art, the end of which is to give pleasure" (p. 113). Instead, the reader is compelled to ask, with Walburga, "Where will it all end?" (p. 89). Walburga refers to the snares they've set for themselves, but the narrative texture implies the familiar struggle to coordinate historical actors and action, the Church as reflector and redeemer of these, and the larger reality as that to which belief dictates that everything else, including the institutional Church, ought to conform. Thus, by offering the past's dedication to an ideal and the present's neglect or mangling of that ideal—that belief—the narrator implies genuine concern for where "it [will] end" when we've discarded the lunacy of self-worship in the looking glass, and for how indeed the abbess, summoned to post-Vatican II Rome, will fare.

This is a very serious book in asking what one is to do when one sees one's beliefs in large part undermined by the very body to which, one further believes, they are entrusted. The comic frame is not much in evidence. It is here, all

right, but only as a trace of what we saw in *Memento Mori*. Emphasis there was
on the firmness of outer realm including inner particulars; in the *Abbess*—the
narrator's book rather than Alexandra's own—particulars are prominent in all
their diversity and confusion and delightfulness and dismaying awfulness, while
the frame is only implicit in the narrator's careful juxtaposing of secular and
sacred texts, traditional language and contemporary jargon, Alexandra's mirror
view and the narrator's opinion of this lady in the context of past, present,
eternal. In *Memento Mori* Jean Taylor and some others embody the narrative
attitude, whereas here no character assists the narrator save by negative example. The narrator's success in using Yeats's poem in order to transcend all the
evidence supporting that poem, and to enforce once more a comic frame that
measures current falling-off, is therefore considerable. Without ever preaching,
the narrator's shaping of texture cautions us that we have once more to get
through the looking glass, so to speak, to an effective awareness of the larger
reality, and that cynicism, mockery, and self-centeredness can neither obliterate
nor adequately respond to such need. The book is minimally about Watergate,
then, but eventually about the historical Church's adequacy to its spiritual
mission, and about whether the historical Church can avoid failing those who
share its beliefs in that comic frame. To become fully conscious of that frame is
no little matter, however obvious the pattern may be to the narrator; for, to
quote the book in a different context, "It is like being told, and all the time
knowing, that the Eyes of God are upon us; it means everything and therefore
nothing" (p. 58). Perhaps we may see the problem of the book as the need to
make every thing signify in the realm of everything.

The genuine if implicit comic structure of *The Abbess of Crewe* is a function of
a comic texture less good-humored and happy than the texture of *Memento Mori*
and other early fictions such as *The Ballad of Peckham Rye*, *The Bachelors*, *The
Prime of Miss Jean Brodie*, and *The Girls of Slender Means*. The comic texture of
Abbess is also more heavily topical in its satirical elements than are those other
books, and the aura of Watergate operates together with narrative fears and
doubts about general cultural breakdown and the fruits of Vatican II to tinge the
comic texture with considerable sobriety. The jokes, wordplay, crafty manipulating of humans by other humans, brilliantly crooked strivings to make for
seeming straightness—all of these Sparkian uses of wit are in evidence as comic
texture; but all of them are inevitably and appropriately dampened by structural
implications.

Another way to set forth this change between early and later Sparkian comic
textures is to remark that the balance between joy taken in awareness of "God's
plenty" and jitters experienced in one's belief that ours is a fallen race is less and
less readily maintained. The omnisciently narrated *The Takeover* (as well as the
subsequent *Territorial Rights* and *The Only Problem*), like *The Abbess of Crewe*,
manifests this increasingly difficult balancing act.

In *The Takeover* (1976)[7] Spark carefully establishes the *milieu* of the Beautiful

People in the stereotyped terms with which we are all familiar if we have been reading the newspapers since President Kennedy's election in 1960 and have seen films directed by Antonioni and Fellini. Indeed, the part of Spark's sensibility that is realistically inclined has been especially interested in extending her reach to the international scene—from *The Mandelbaum Gate* (her eighth novel), obviously set in the two Jerusalems, through *The Public Image* (Italian setting with an international cast), *The Driver's Seat* (mostly Italian, presumably, but plainly universal), *Not to Disturb* (Swiss but again international), *The Hothouse by the East River* (Anglo-American but boundless as well), and *The Abbess of Crewe* (British, worldwide, Catholic), to *The Takeover*, whose immediate settings are Italian and broadly European, but whose significance, like that of its predecessors, is barely suggested by this sort of realistic clue to local setting. Significance likewise transcends the Italian locus of *Territorial Rights* and the southern French setting of *The Only Problem*. Whether or how this international tendency is related to Spark's own expatriation matters less, I think, than that Spark has plain ties to literary realism, and that those social and moral ties of late are more international than British (*Loitering with Intent* is set in London). At the same time, however, Spark is, as always, persuaded of the reality of timelessness and determined to immerse her fiction in the experience derived from her sense of this interwinding of temporal and eternal.

Specifically, the title accurately implies much in common with the efforts of the Abbess Alexandra to extend and confirm her power. Primarily, the title refers to the endeavors of Hubert Mallindaine, an English homosexual, to deprive an American, Maggie Radcliffe (currently the Marchesa di Tullio-Friole, since her third marriage), of as much as possible of her property. A large portion of this property is at Diana's Sacred Grove at Nemi and includes a house and such other valuables as furniture and paintings. Speaking still of this primary sense of the title, we may note that nearly everyone else in the book is similarly occupied in trying to acquire, by theft or fraud, not only Maggie's material wealth but any other material wealth that seems available to effort and ingenuity. We are clearly shown *la dolce vita* looking at least as loathesome and humanly destructive as in Antonioni's version. Words like *desire, appetite, passion, love, sex* are used interchangeably and meaninglessly. The only way of life that happens for these characters is simply bored, acquisitive promiscuity, like the accumulation of real estate and stock and jewelry, or like the tediously regular vacations (from what?) identical with the routines of yesterday and tomorrow in their suntanned, capital-cushioned wavering between torpor and hysteria in the hunt for something novel.

Grim as such a state may be, it is very funny as well. Hubert's schemes to defraud Maggie and to turn her objections legally or at least scandalously against herself are ingenious: Hubert and the reader learn much about the disinterestedly passionate nest-feathering skills of society at all levels and on both sides of the nominal law in Machiavelli's native land. Spark has always taken an interest in the wiles of blackmailers and in this instance delves to a depth that shows the Abbess Alexandra to have been something of a novice. Also, the character of Mary Radcliffe, Maggie's newly married daughter-in-law, is delightful in a cretinous way. Mary is a predictably bronzed, slim, long-legged Californian who vacuously agrees sincerely with anything said by anyone, and whose sharing the favors of the houseboy, Lauro, with both her parents-in-law and her own husband is tranquilly compatible with her repeated declaration that she is "trying to make a success of [her] marriage." She amusingly resembles the character played by Marilyn Monroe in *The Seven-Year Itch.* In short, the acquiring, languishing, pampering, handsome, drifting characters treat people and things indistinguishably and imagine nothing beyond this merger.

On a secondary plane, once again predictably, the title refers simultaneously to something broader than Hubert's thieving and to something farther-reaching than mere capitalistic acquisition, legal or otherwise. Relativism has led to the decay of meaning in life and language; "the Dark Ages II" are foreshadowed. The "takeover" in this other sense is the demonstrable conquering of Christian and humanistic values by their pagan predecessors (Hubert, not incidentally, claims to be descended directly from the union between Diana of Nemi and the Emperor Caligula, and thus to own by direct descent and divine right the ground on which Maggie has built the house he occupies). On this plane it is clearly the third-person narrator, operating directly and indirectly, who orders our perceptions. Such a steering role is certainly not played by two American Jesuits— Fathers Cuthbert Plaice and Gerard Harvey, who are interested in ecology, uninvolved observation including a touch of voyeurism, pagan mythology, and some participation in the jet set's affluence. The demise of Hellenic-Judaeo-Christian values is variously manifest. Law serves its practitioners or apparently any interest other than that of justice. Matter, things, are not questioned save as to quantity, market value, and the constant precaution required to protect them from other people. Only the narrator displays Spark's customary theistic, psychological interest in the interworkings of temporal and timeless, or in juxtaposing cause-effect relationships seen both temporally and eternally, or in raising old-style questions like that of the involvement of spirit with matter. Whence and whither never take interrogative shape among these characters but are of course implicit in the narrator's funny-ominous insistence upon diversion, flow, process, the hoped-for new and different as their own reason for being, among the members of this set.

The book lays heavy stress upon Frazer's reporting in *The Golden Bough* of the priests serving Diana in her Sacred Grove at Nemi, and of their being replaceable only by rival aspirants to the priestly function who succeeded in killing them. Thus, built into this worship was an element of violent sexual rivalry indistinguishable from whatever else characterized the pagan religious impulse— or so Frazer's and Spark's books would lead us to believe. Spark's narrator speaks as follows of the inevitable demise of one of the two rival aspirants to priesthood in Diana's service: "This tragedy was only so in the classical and dramatic sense; its participants were in perfect collusion. In the historic sense it was a pathetic and greedy affair. The recurrent performance of the tragedy began before the dates of knowledge, in mythology, but repeating itself tenaciously well into known history" (pp. 55–56). In this tightly declarative passage the narrator offers us the paradox that fits not only the ancient rivalry but also the abiding malice-affection that ties such apparent opposites and enemies as Hubert and Maggie—counter to each other in nearly every way, including the sexual. We also see in this passage a foreshadowing of the fascinating and ever-dangerous blur that occurs when history and mythology, always coexistent, struggle (as in the *Abbess*) to break their balance and to dominate or eliminate each other. Such a struggle is a version of the illusion-reality tussle, of course, and of late Spark's work has given the names of history and mythology to the combatants. Thus, we are here provided with the familiar Spark pattern. Allowing history to dominate our reading (as concrete realism would direct us to do), we see "a pathetic and greedy affair"—and here the comic texture is most obvious. Conversely, allowing mythology to dominate our reading (thereby ignoring concrete reality and demanding make-believe and lies) can, in the realm of the larger and permeating reality, induce tragedy. In other words this narrator is enabling us to read—compelling us to read—*The Takeover* as we read *The Abbess of Crewe*: as a comic texture that is potentially if not yet structurally tragic. What this abstract encounter comes to in specific terms we may now consider.

Keeping in mind Spark's two realms of reality, and Frazer's version of the service of Diana, we get a fuller appreciation of this splendidly patterned novel and its texture: symbolic, to be sure, although anything but mechanical or overtly didactic in merging structure and texture. We might expect Hubert and Maggie to serve as more than rivals in acquisition and retention of material goods (he of hers, she of everyone's), and we are not disappointed. Indeed, as the book ends, Hubert and Maggie are not merely continuing rivals but are shown to be close friends and to respect each other as prizefighters respect each other's moves and prowess. Hubert and Maggie happen to meet, in the last pages, almost as priest and goddess (I say almost, because, while Hubert is priest, Maggie is both goddess figure and priestess—which dual role is appropriate to her self-worship), in the Grove at Nemi, and the reader is taken with the gen-uineness of their commitment to the same goals. Hubert has bilked Maggie egregiously—and seems thereby to have done the only thing possible to arouse in her what I have called respect. For her part, however, Maggie remains the champion, for she has retained—indeed, she has outburgled and outsmarted all the other thieves and frauds on display in order to *reacquire*—a far greater fortune than Hubert has stolen from her. What we thus see in the end is that these two pagans deserve each other and admire each other for being very good at what they do. Maggie's hilarity in the last scene clarifies what Hubert had earlier described as his "laughter demon": as the narrator says, this "perfect collusion" contributes to "a pathetic and greedy affair." What we may now add is that comic texture is confined to what is viewed and presented thus historically. Historically and comically speaking, then, these two are not rivals only but are seen as enjoyers of mutual laughter at being so much better at the game than are the others around them.

If, on this historical level, danger lurks and the comic is threatened, the reason is not in the least that the larger reality impinges or that the acquisitive instinct experiences a challenge from something spiritual. Rather, as the narrator remarks, the year 1973 was the time when drastic change was introduced because players more powerful than Maggie and Hubert began to influence events. In other words, this was the time of the Arab oil embargo, the beginning of the end for certain European-American plutocratic presumptions. Such a change is of course merely one of degree if we view it extrarealistically, or rather if we once again merge history and mythology and come in this way to realize that a new set of players cannot alter the nature of the dangerous social comedy. The stakes may rise and the big winners become a different group, but the game is still capitalistic acquisition of money-power.

To view the book's events as implying possible tragedy, it is necessary to regard these matters "in the classical and dramatic sense"; that is, to see them in the context of the larger reality. The narrator remarks, of changes wrought by increasing Middle Eastern prominence, that "the new world which was arising out of the ashes of the old, avid for immaterialism, had begun to sprout forth its responsive worshippers" (p. 148). What Spark does with this desire for the immaterial, however, is to show how Hubert cleverly exploits it—"capitalizes" is the apt word, plainly—and cynically uses his kinship with Diana to attract a following among those genuinely seeking either spiritual reality or just a new kind of mind-clouding escape. Once again, we see hereby a parallel with the *Abbess.* The striving for matters spiritual and more largely real is always presented as good in Spark's fictions: what is wrong or askew, as in *Abbess* or *Bachelors,* is that the mythology offered as spiritual guide or key is inevitably at least as bad in its own kind as is the gross materialism which it is ostensibly replacing. The extent to which Hubert may come actually to believe his own mythology is not the point (as it was not the point in Patrick Seton's or in Alexandra's case). What matters here is that any theory or system of belief which attempts to root itself in the longing to escape and forget history, the concrete, the stuff of realism, is bound to go astray and of course is very likely to destroy those who accept such premises. Hubert, like Alexandra, is nearly always a conscious charlatan, but that fact concerns our reading of much of his activity as the matter of comedy in that hypocrisy always aids comic action. The scurrilousness matters little to the overall effects of this kind of belief as distinct from belief that accommodates both matter and spirit, the here-and-now as well as abstract reality.

The direction of the book, on its second level, is away from magic and superstition, with which are associated all efforts to escape matter and fly to the spiritual alone. Magic and superstition are snares because they try to satisfy the longing for "the immaterial" by closing eyes to the rest of the real. Whether the leaders be fools or knaves, then, the end is still wretched for the followers, and Spark's books—from *The Bachelors* to *Memento Mori* to *Peckham Rye* to *Jean Brodie* to the *Abbess* to *Takeover*—regularly make this point. Patrick Seton's spiritualism ignores matter; Dougal Douglas tips his weak hand the minute he shows us that he cannot abide the facts of illness; Alec Warner's Berkeleyan doubts about the reality of matter are of this same enfeebling sort; Jean Brodie assumes that the reality of other people's individual historicism may be overridden with impunity; the abbess cooks scenarios and moreover tries to justify this private mythology on the grounds that "history doesn't work"; and Hubert is a con man in a toga whose appeal is that of drink and drug: he takes people's minds off history. That a market for undeliverable nonmaterial payoffs exists in a fallen, bored, desperate world is "only to be expected." As we have seen in these books, however, the beautiful irony is that such magical endeavors to avoid matter are themselves always necessarily given away by their inevitable fixedness in that every matter which they would disavow.

The potential tragedy suggested in *The Takeover*, then, is not that the West's money is running out so that life-styles will have to change. Nor is it that the Middle East's foreignness may take over. Nor is it that what Maggie and her plutocratic elite would prefer to regard as their domain and their way of life is shown instead to be what everybody in a capitalistic world has invariably had to strive for (as Marx, Shaw, Conrad, Graham Greene, and hordes of others have asked, what is the point of distinguishing between dirty and clean money when we're all in the capitalistic game together?). The book is not puritanical or especially anticapitalist and certainly advocates no other socioeconomic system, because that is not what Spark is about. This book is following the *Abbess* in making clear the danger of allowing any unbalanced concern—whether with matter alone or with nonmatter alone—to take over. As we have seen in book after book, exaggeration or extremes can yield comic results; but violation of human purposes threatens tragic effects if we allow the comic frame to become much more shadowy in our consciousness. The laughter that we mentioned in discussing *Memento Mori*—the laughter of Chaucer's Troilus—is not at all what Maggie and Hubert indulge in at the close of *The Takeover*. Twenty years later in Spark's career, as in the case of the *Abbess*, there is no suggestion that cosmic resolution is quite as readily available as ever, at least where the characters of the action are concerned. Rather, we get laughter signifying pleasure taken in expertise at the only stakes to be played for: mythology is ahistorical and empty, and other people's wits are no match for Hubert's and Maggie's at fleecing—at least (the narrator suggests) until the Arabs get a firmer footing. And as in the *Abbess*, here too we find no character parallel to Jean Taylor or Ronald Bridges who can act out these points or state them to other characters. The narrator does all the work and thereby measures both the pathetic circular futility of money and power's passing endlessly from one burgled party to another, and the distance between Troilus's vision of reality's oneness and the two charlatans' taking time out to guffaw before returning to more of the same pursuit of passing the booty from one unsafe place to another. As at the end of the *Abbess,* so here too we may well ask, "Where will it all end?"—especially since, as we recall, "Nowhere's safe."

Clearly, the implications of the book extend beyond the values and conduct of the Beautiful People, who of course are only those comparatively few who play the game best. Maggie and Hubert are with a vengeance children of darkness wiser than children of light in their own generation. Everyone in the book is an unjust steward of what is only his or hers on loan. The comic texture resides in the adroitly arranged interacting according to the rules of this game. When we grant the players their rules, as of course we must and do, then we distinguish among degrees of expertise. Their varying flurries of witty and of outwitting intrigue make for a grimly fascinating novel.

Frazer, we remember, writing at the turn of the century, optimistically predicted that, as magic had yielded to religion, so religion would give way to science, which he saw as the means of achieving a credible salvation—heaven on earth. Spark, who sees magic and superstition as bases of materialism, is giving us a cool, prolonged, funny, merciless, questioning view of our Western values and daring us to deny that we are all battling one another to become top priests and priestesses in Diana's bloody and tormentedly wakeful retinue. We cannot doubt where the reliable narrator stands or what she sees. In one remarkable passage, for example, when two servants, the fat and dour Clara and the young, pretty and pregnant Agata, meet in the center of town, the narrator thus merges temporal and eternal:

> The two women were greeted occasionally by busy shoppers who passed and swept a glance . . . at Agata's hard-done-by belly of shame, while the whole of eternal life carried on regardless, invisible and implacable, this being what no skinny craving cat with its gleaming eyes by night had ever pounced upon, no tender mole of the earth in the hills above had ever discovered down there under the damp soil, no lucky spider had caught, nor the white flocks of little clouds could reveal when they separated continually, eternal life untraceable and persistent, that not even the excavators, long-dead, who had dug up the fields of Diana's sanctuary had found; they had taken away the statues and the effigies, the votive offerings to the goddess of fertility, terracotta replicas of private parts and public parts, but eternal life had never been shipped off with the loot; and even the lizard on the cliff-rocks in its jerky fits had never been startled by the shadow or motion of that eternal life which remained, past all accounting, while Clara and Agata chattered on. . . . (Pp. 180–81)

The ending of the book is severely noncommittal—Spark's art is always trimly economical—but the book leaves us in no doubt of the doped condition of our "twenty centuries of stony sleep." The novel's somber open-endedness leaves in doubt (assuming that we see what is at issue in the book) only our reaction to this moribund state.

Territorial Rights (1979)[8] is another manifestation—zany and sober— of this moribund condition. Like *Memento Mori,* this novel offers no central figure, but a group, all of whom contribute collectively to the theme, which, in view of the title, seems to me best expressed in the language of 1 Chronicles 29:15: "For we are strangers before thee, and sojourners, as were all our fathers: our days on the earth are as a shadow, and there is none abiding."

In setting forth this theme, *Territorial Rights* appears to be an extension—its texture grayer, its aura more pessimistic—of *The Takeover.* Intimations of stability are few and harder to find than in earlier Spark novels. The title itself ironically keeps before us both the acquisitive drive of most of the characters and the prominent fact that none of these characters belongs anywhere. They are all nomads, so internationally involved in their pursuit of sex and money (the customary motivation of comedy) as to be safe at home nowhere. The principal setting for the book—Venice—admirably establishes this theme. Venice is a vestige of high civilization, sacred and secular, encroached upon by water. Like all else terrestrial, Venice is threatened by flux. As readers we are regularly prodded to wonder what, if anything, abides. The main characters are Italian, American, British, Bulgarian. They have lived not only in their native countries but in Germany, Canada, and France as well. They speak their native languages, sometimes one another's languages, and, in the case of Lina Pancev (a Bulgarian), delightful violations of English. "What does [Robert Leaver] do?" someone asks Lina. Lina replies: "Only loves me. He's a student but not very much. . . . I'm not in rivalry never with no one" (p. 101).

Any number of particulars impose the idea of transitoriness, acquisitive furor, directionless process, absence of norm. Mark Curran, an American billionaire and homosexual, probably worked for the Germans in World War II in Italy and France, while serving in the American forces. He now paints a little, collects art, buys young men, and travels. Robert Leaver is a young English bisexual. He has prostituted himself in Paris, been kept by Curran, discovers his other side with Lina, indulges enthusiastically in high-level blackmail, and moves on to bank robbery, terrorism, and murder. Arnold Leaver, Robert's father, is a retired headmaster who has come to Venice for a rest, leaving his wife in Birmingham and taking with him (to pay the bills) the school's former cook, Mary Tiller, winner of a football pool. Lina Pancev fled Bulgaria, ostensibly for the freedom to paint her own kind of pictures. In fact, she sought such "freedom" as she envisioned in the account given her of economic opportunity and sexual license in Hampstead. She is in Venice to find the grave of her father, Victor Pancev, also a political refugee from Bulgaria—in World War II—and apparently the lover at that time of Mark Curran, of two daughters of a Venetian hotelier (they are Eufemia and Katerina), and of the Countess Violet de Winter, American wife

of an Italian nobleman. Such details as these will suggest well enough the ways
in which the characters are interrelated and will indicate that causes such as
monarchism, fascism, Nazism, democracy, capitalism, communism merely front
for the pleasure principle in driving such characters. As in *Abbess*, "scenarios"
(see especially pp. 147–57) make or threaten to break reputations and underlie
successful blackmail schemes. And as in *The Public Image*, blackmail letters are a
prominent feature of a third-person narrative.

The realistic plot turns on the attempt by Robert Leaver and his Italian
colleagues to extort millions of dollars from Curran. Robert is eventually successful because he knows that Curran, Violet, Eufemia, and Katerina (Victor
Pancev's lovers of thirty years ago) assisted in the killing, dismembering, and
burial of Pancev in the garden of the Pensione Sofia in 1945. The point is made
clear that regardless of the accuracy of the scenario that Robert threatens to
make public, and even though those involved may not remember the details,
what concerns them is their reputations. That is, like Alexandra and like
Frederick's mistaken image of Annabel Christopher *(The Public Image)*, these
harassed characters never give a thought to the acts that they were responsible
for; rather, they consider exclusively what people may think. The peripheral, the
transitory, is thus emphasized as the focus of the characters' attention and
purpose. As Dame Lettie ignores the message and seeks to eliminate the caller,
and as Alexandra whitens her sepulcher and shuns the spiritual verities that she
is ostensibly carrying forward, so the present group attend exclusively to their
public images rather than to the intrinsic significance of their deeds. This sort of
lopsidedness draws attention to what might otherwise have seemed a narrative
throwaway comment upon an observation offered by Anthea, Arnold Leaver's
stay-at-home wife: " 'God and public opinion will judge,' Anthea said, as if the
two were one and the same" (p. 61). Just as in *The Takeover*, the main purpose of
existence would appear to be the accumulation of more and more wealth and
power, both for their own sake and for purposes of acquiring "freedom" from the
wealth and power of others.

Evidence to the contrary is less accessible than in other Spark books, but it is
definitely to be found, sometimes explicitly and more often by implication. For
instance, there is Lina's ingrained anti-Semitism. When she discovers that she
has been sleeping with a Jew, she throws herself into the canal to cleanse herself
of this taint. Humorously, she requires antibiotics to ward off the possible effects
of Venetian canal water. More importantly, she never gives a thought to her
promiscuity as the reason she got into the predicament in the first place. In this
way, familiarly, Spark builds a comic texture even as she comments indirectly on
racial prejudice and sexual license. We gain an insight into an absent good by
virtue of observing evil (to paraphrase Nicholas Farringdon). Amusingly, Lina
also delivers an orthodox punch line on the subject of marital fidelity. She says
to Arnold that "it is all right for you to enjoy your holiday without a wife, but
Mrs. Tiller should not have come with you" and adds that "I can also see the

point of view of the good and faded wife. In my country where I come from, there is two points of view, and we are taught to look upon both of them" (p. 186). Lina's country in this instance is Spark's "nevertheless territory," as we may say. Such making of distinctions may recur when we read another character's query, "What's marriage these days? It's only a bit of paper" (p. 64). Or again, when we read that Robert and Anna ("I Bonnie e Clyde d'Italia") have a "talent" for their criminal activities (pp. 214, 232, 238), we may well ask questions about the purposes of their acts rather than about their personal aptitudes for those acts. Then we realize that, of course, the monstrousness of the world Spark shows us lies in its having no ends in mind as proper or improper: all is process, endless save by death. We are left to discover what "turns us on," and then to "do our own things," as in Takeover—if we settle for Robert's view.

To settle for Robert's attitude would, of course, do an injustice to Spark's theme. Indeed she shows materialism run berserk, but the comic texture is not always and everywhere leaden. We get some of the earlier assurance that meaning persists in spite of ourselves. The examples in the previous paragraph contribute to making this point, and there are other signs as well. For instance, when Lina dances with Robert's father unknowingly upon the grave of Lina's father, Robert and his friend Anna laugh. But we are at the same time reminded of affection and other values that *ought* to connect the generations, and that come to our minds by virtue of their absence here (we may recall Lise's idea that the absence of an absence would be a presence). Or again, we run into fiction as lie vs. fiction as attempted truth—the difference between Tom Wells's version and January Marlow's. In the present instance, however, the contrast is not quite what we saw in Robinson. Instead of simple lie as opposed to inevitably inadequate expression, we get here misuse and elaboration of assorted historical bits (as in Robert's blackmail letters and scenario, akin to Alexandra's mythmaking), *and* snippets from a long novel of "tough-guy" romantic realism that Anthea is reading in her Birmingham solitude, *and* excerpts from Scots poetry that Anthea remembers from her grandmother's recitations. These different fictions are instructive and predictably important to the book.

Robert's blackmail letters deliberately invent material to go along with other matter known to be true. This combination, like any fiction, appears plausible or at least raises fears among the victims that possible readers will believe it. Such letters are truth plus lies intended to be taken as fact. The closemouthed, unsmiling, beer-drinking, indiscriminately entangled soap-opera characters of Anthea's novel, on the other hand, manifest nothing true except on their surfaces. We see them and their kitchens and dishes, but we are left on our own to dredge meaning from their pretentious and cryptic dialogue. This is empty fiction posing as hypertruthful human communication—what we might get if a French phenomenologist were trying to parody Hemingway. Finally, we are given Anthea's selective recollection of her grandmother's rendering of some Scots ballads. These excerpts strike us as genuine in their emotion primarily because of their simplicity. We note that the emotions they commemorate are love, long-ing, sadness at loss, determination to gain riches with which to adorn "my Highland lass" (pp. 51, 172), and regret that a young handsome man of many excellent qualities has left the city and all the young women, especially because he was so well set off by his worldly possessions:

> Weel-featur'd, weel-tocher'd, weel-mounted and braw;
> But chiefly the siller, that gars him gang till her,
> The pennie's the jewel that beautifies a'.
>   . . . the pennie's the jewel . . .
>   . . . the jewel. . . .

(P. 237)

What seems true about these few snippets is not only their simplicity, but the clearly expressed emotions they set out, and the interesting marriage of universal spiritual qualities to universal material fascination. Spark in her usual way is showing us that while older expression was often more nearly genuine and filled with intangible values, its universality is signified by material longings as well as by spiritual. Leaving the blackmail letters aside, then, as patent invention maliciously doctored, we observe the contrast between a realistic fiction that tells lies in pretending to proffer human significance and formally simple ballads that get close to the truth because they embrace both spirit and matter. By laying out *exempla* thus, without narrative comment, Spark invites us into the fiction-making process and challenges us to supply what is missing from the lives of the characters in her plot. As in the case of the Joanna-Selina recitations set forth throughout *Girls of Slender Means*, we infer here what is not specified but what has been seldom so well implied about Spark's perennial dual vision. Spark is undeniably drawn to the accouterments of wealth as to states of soul. What she satirizes and laments is extremes of either, abuses of one or the other.[9]

In the present cast of characters, no one serves as mouthpiece. All are mixed. Anyone is therefore likely to appear foolish on one occasion and to blurt out a home truth thereafter. As we have seen, Lina is hypocritical and prejudiced, but she also voices Spark's orthodox marital morality. In like fashion, Anthea buries her head and refuses to think that her son, Robert, could be anything worse than temporarily confused (e.g., pp. 170–71, 239); she may be afraid to suppose herself to blame for his condition. But on the other hand, Anthea displays some traditional moral common sense. Thus she reports to her blackmailing detective acquaintance, Mr. B., concerning the telephone messages from Venice by her friend, Grace Gregory: "Grace . . . makes out that right is wrong. . . . She went to Venice to fetch my husband home. Now she tells me that Mary Tiller's a nice sort of woman and that Arnold's in good hands and that my son . . . has gone off all on his own, nobody knows where. She makes out all this is normal" (p. 164). Anthea also introduces the question of evil into the goings-on of this novel. She asks Mr. B., "Human nature is evil, isn't it?" He responds, "I wouldn't call it evil. Human nature is human nature as far as I'm concerned" (p. 60). In this way the subject is brought into the book and presented for our consideration. Mr. B.'s answer, noncommital rather than negative, does not relieve us of responsibility for thinking about the question. Anthea and the book would have us ponder what is "normal." Only such hints as I have been enumerating would lead us to suppose that the term means anything at all. In fact purpose is hard to come by, if one tries to look beyond the superficial to long-range reason why. Lina asks, for instance, and without reaching an answer, "What have we defected for?" (pp. 78–79). Under the surface, these characters are unequipped to make moral distinctions that establish significance for them.

It is the narrator—as in most later Spark novels—who finds *ars longa* (p. 240); who burrows and intimates, as a final example will serve to demonstrate. Out of the blue, two characters are made to observe a funeral floating by. Here the narrator takes over:

> A Venetian funeral is intended not to be missed. Even the motor of the barge chugs with a mournful dignity. On the tip of the prow is a gilded ball with flame-like wings, signifying who knows what pagan or civic concept, but certainly symbolising eternity. Next on either side of the wide black boat come two gold lions *couchant*. Then the windscreen, surmounted by vivid masses of flowers under which is posted the sombre, steady-eyed driver. Close behind the driver the men of the family stand, hatted, in dark suits. Then the coffin in the middle of the hearse, the lid covered with bright yellow and red flowers, and the wooden sides glittering with elaborate carvings. More enormous-headed flowers cover the cabin at the stern where the women mourn with black veils and white handkerchiefs. Another ball of eternal flames at the stern gives moral support to the general idea. And all this is reflected in the water beneath it: the stately merchandise and arrogance of Venetian death, as of old, when money was weighty and haste was vile. (Pp. 106–7)

This passage serves much the same function as does the encounter between Agata and Clara in *The Takeover*. The narrator reminds us of the here-and-now, which passes (flowers, coffin, gold trappings, wealth), as well as of vestiges of the historical past (lions, as well as impressions conveyed after the final colon). In addition, the temporal and temporary are parenthetically contained between winged globes, the symbols of eternity, at stem and stern. Finally, the whole emblematic reminder is awash in the flux that reverts to the theme of the book as projected earlier in this discussion, and to the irony of the title. The passage is more elaborate than the image of the father buried in the garden. Like the Agata-Clara encounter or the poetry that dots *Abbess* or the bomb buried in the garden in *Girls*, this funeral boat joins the levels and focuses the narrator's dual view. And in keeping with the tendency in these later books, the characters seem unaware almost always of anything approaching Spark's universality. The reader observes, nonetheless, that this "funeral is intended not to be missed."

The texture is comic, then, but I think of it as leaden rather than as golden (i.e., unlike *Memento Mori*) because, for all the fun and ingenuity and delight in things of this world, readers depend entirely upon the narrator (and on themselves) to establish Spark's meaning. No character follows hints, as becomes clear in the Victorian epilogue (pp. 238–40), where all the characters are off "doing their own things," innocently or otherwise, and unconcerned with their *choices* except as *their* choices.[10]

This "me-generation" mentality likewise permeates Spark's most recent book, *The Only Problem* (1984),[11] a third-person narrative largely attentive to the figure of Harvey Gotham, a Canadian in southern France. The title refers to Job's question asked of God: why does a good God permit the innocent to suffer (and the evil to prosper)? This problem concerns Harvey, who is writing a monograph on the Book of Job. Indeed the Book of Job functions as a sort of subtext for *Problem*, as *Robinson Crusoe* underlies *Robinson*, as *The Golden Bough* shadows *The Takeover*, and as the liturgy and canonical hours anchor the Watergate silliness of *The Abbess of Crewe*. Subtexts serve different purposes, of course, as we have noted in discussing the instances cited. I should like to look now at how Job operates on Spark's narrative.

First, Spark's plot. We find again—as commonly in books since *The Public Image* (1968)—an ingenious assortment of self-exiled connivers, their personal object the accumulation of money, their lack of any traditional moral sense prominent. Floundering or cautious opportunism creates unpredictability for readers, who are likely to entertain expectations based on at least a recollection of moral standards. Whim, however, seems normal here, as we see clearly in marital-familial-social arrangements, to take one example.

Harvey Gotham, a multimillionaire, leaves his wife, Effie, who has stolen two chocolate bars as a sort of socialist egalitarian gesture of protest against capitalism. Effie then moves in with Ernie Howe, an English electronics expert, and they beget a daughter, Clara. Ruth Jensen, Effie's sister, leaves her husband, Edward (who had once had a brief affair with Effie), and moves in with Harvey. She brings Clara with her, for Ernie and Effie have now split up and Effie has reportedly joined a terrorist group (cf. *Territorial Rights*). When the terrorists grow active in Harvey's southern French neighborhood, he agrees with the police that Ruth and the baby should seek safety elsewhere (he insists upon staying to finish his manuscript and to be near the Epinal *Musée*, which houses Georges de La Tour's seventeenth-century inspirational painting of *Job visité par sa femme*). Ruth, now pregnant by Harvey, takes Effie's baby to London rather than to Harvey's relatives in Canada, where Harvey had intended them to go. Ruth moves in with Ernie Howe in London, Effie is killed in a shoot-out with the Paris police (her latest lover, Nathan Fox, one of Ruth's and Edward's protégés, is arrested), Ruth will likely move back to Harvey's château and bring Clara with her (Ernie wants nothing to do with a terrorist's child), Edward appears set to continue his successful acting career in England, and Harvey completes his Job study. Among minor characters are Stewart Cowper (Harvey's British lawyer) and Harvey's Auntie Pet, latest in Spark's string of delightful old persons.

The constant in this giddy round of sexual exchanges and indiscriminate procreation is Harvey's dedication to his monograph on Job. But what are we to make of this dedication? Spark makes our task difficult by seeing to it that we derive only a superficial sense of Harvey, her protagonist. He acts and reacts but he is apparently quite empty of serious motive except for his drive to complete his manuscript. Most of his other actions—supporting Edward, Ruth, Clara, Nathan; living with and buying a château for Ruth; cooperating or at least interacting with police and press, who suppose him to be financing the terrorists; offering to adopt Clara and undertaking responsibility for his and Ruth's unborn child—all these actions are left undiscussed by characters and narrator alike. Sometimes Harvey seems merely to take the line of least resistance (the "why not?" attitude so prevalent in a rootless era), while at other times he *may* feel responsibility. We cannot know. We do know that he misses and desires Effie (although he does not want her back), that he does not love Ruth or even like her much, that he values privacy, and that he is genuinely interested in Job's problem.

Given the persistence with which Harvey discusses Job with Cowper, Edward, and others, we wonder about the particulars of his belief in God and about his occasional inclination to identify with Job. The narrator's assurance that "Harvey believed in God, and this was what tormented him" (p. 22) is the first of few indications that Harvey is more than academically taken with Job's trouble. Harvey's lending of money, providing of food and lodging, willingness (not eagerness or demand) to raise two children—the motives for these choices are not clear: charity? responsibility? economical reluctance to wear himself out with debate and harangue? He remains opaque although paradoxically central in "his" book. On one occasion, however, he does admit to himself that he simply declines involvement with others: "I should have said [to the intrusive Nathan] I wanted Ruth and the baby to myself for Christmas. Why didn't I?—Because I don't want them to myself. I don't want them enough; not basically. . . . I can't hold these women, Harvey thought. Neither Effie nor Ruth. My mind isn't on them enough, and they resent it, just as I resent it when they put something else before me, a person, an idea. Yes, it's understandable" (pp. 62–63).

If Harvey is "tormented," the book offers slight evidence beyond the narrator's assurance. If Harvey identifies with Job, the basis of the identification does not seem to be spiritual, psychological, or physical suffering. Indeed, when Cowper offers Harvey our own commonsense observation that Harvey does not appear to suffer, Harvey counters with the point that the press batters him more severely than it does Effie (p. 119). This would seem rather lame evidence of suffering. It is certainly not on Job's scale. Moreover, it appears that lawyers protect Harvey from nearly all the normal violations of that privacy which he craves, that he requires little human contact, and that his money cushions him well.

And yet the book offers one extraordinary moment of introspection that
qualifies the case for Harvey's blatant separation from Job. When he happens to
see a man in a police station waiting room, Harvey thinks as follows:

> Patience, pallor and deep anxiety: there goes suffering. . . . And I found him
> interesting. Is it only by recognizing how flat would be the world without the
> sufferings of others that we know how desperately becalmed our own lives
> would be without suffering? Do I suffer on Effie's account? Yes, and perhaps I
> can live by that experience. We all need something to suffer about. But *Job*,
> my work on *Job*, all interrupted and neglected, probed into and interfered with
> [by press and police]: that is experience, too; real experience, not vicarious, as
> is often assumed. To study, to think, is to live and suffer painfully. (P. 147)

Temporary upheaval is Harvey's lot: "I'm not even sure that I suffer, I only
endure distress. But why should I analyse myself? I am analysing the God of *Job*"
(p. 171, in a letter to Edward). For this reason Harvey's pain hardly compares to
Job's, his "comforters" resemble Job's only remotely, and Harvey never enters into
discussion with God or accuses himself of vileness or specifies for us the outcome
of his study of Job. He does say to Edward, however, at some moment before the
time of the narrative proper, that "the only logical answer to the problem of
suffering is that the individual soul has made a pact with God before he is born,
that he will suffer during his lifetime. We are born forgetful of this pact. . . .
Sufferers would, in this hypothesis, be pre-conscious volunteers" (p. 30). This
sort of collective individuality is Harvey's version of Adam and Eve's representative Fall.

What nevertheless draws us up short and forces us to pay serious attention to
what otherwise bears all the marks of another pointless chaotic tracking of the
Beautiful People, modern terrorists, and flagrant opportunists is Harvey's reflection on suffering *via* consciousness of *others'* suffering; suffering real but not
immediately personal. Harvey has comforts and no boils, yet he tells himself
(not Edward, by mail) that he experiences genuine pain in reflecting on Effie's
pain, *and* in disruption of his literary work, his critical discipline. The point is
that Harvey is not Job, but is a student of the Book of Job—and intellectual
detached involvement with the situation of another, especially when that
situation is universal, can become an emotional involvement. Intellectual emotion is real, and Spark would seem to be using Harvey (otherwise a rather bland
protagonist) to put before us her usual insistence that a wedge between human
experiences is unnatural. She gives us again "both . . . and," rather than "either
. . . or." The present study has taken note of the common complaint that
Spark's characters and narrators are unfeeling, and that she herself lacks the sort
of compassion expected of a serious—a major—novelist. That complaint, I
think, assumes not only that for many the nineteenth-century novel is the norm,
but that emotion of characters and narrator must be explicit. Neither of these

premises is valid. Moreover, I suggest that Harvey's introspection in the police station nicely weds intellect to emotion in his studious case and may very well suggest the situation of Muriel Spark, a most detached, satirical, shrewdly intelligent, seemingly uncaring author. She is acutely involved and concerned, I should say, even as Harvey is involved. "To study, to think, is to live and suffer painfully," whether or not the pain is obvious to others. [12]

We can now consider more profitably, I think, why *Problem* may be thought comic and why it belongs in the leaden rather than in the golden category. It is comic because it is almost exclusively social and because—like the Book of Job in a sense—it ends with the promise of new life (two children) to be sustained by Harvey's fortune. He reflects that (like Job) he will now "live another hundred and forty years" and "have three daughters" (p. 179). Society (family) has been at least minimally strengthened, although one would have to be blind to the society in question to consider Harvey's "latter end . . . more than his beginning" (Job 42:12).

Comic resolution is muted—as is Job's later life, despite children, health, and possessions—because Job's problem has obviously not been solved by Harvey's study. That problem has only been emphasized by Harvey's own experiences— his sense of pain at the loss and death of Effie. The comic ending is leaden, then, because the narrative stresses the fallen human condition, including the fallen human inattention to that condition—since God's permitting Job to be tested is tantamount to God's permitting Adam and Eve to be tempted, and to fall and take us with them. Harvey suspects that Job's "tragedy was that of the happy ending" (p. 176). That God's ways are not our ways is no resolution. What Spark gives us, then, is limited (i.e., social) resolution. The frenzied, worldly, role-playing chase continues largely out of human control, and—most importantly— there are here no characters like Jean Taylor or Henry Mortimer, and no narrator like the one who delivers *Memento Mori*, to offer us a gentler, more charitable, more hopeful, long-range view of human limitations attributable to the Fall and our own folly. *Problem* is not tragic, like *Driver's Seat*, but neither does it sympathetically rejoice in human inanity on its own terms, as *Memento Mori* does. Rather, it stares with a believer's grim amusement at our deregulated foolishness and hopes that we may come to see ourselves in this book.

That frightening foolishness obviously means something to Harvey as a believer which it could not mean to an unbeliever: he is an insider striving for an outsider's objectivity in his reading of Job (p. 30). Similarly, Muriel Spark consistently struggles to find and present a position that is at once inside and outside of her own belief. In the final chapter I want to consider in detail how she goes about fighting this battle. In the process of analyzing how four novels merge art and life, I will also have occasion to comment further, inevitably, on the common charge that Spark lacks feeling for her characters and by implied extension for her fellow creatures.

4

Taking and Making: The Page as Looking Glass

As we have seen, part of the comic texture of *The Takeover*—indeed of many Spark books—arises from the contrast between the magical and the mysterious. Magic is associated with fraudulence or misguidedness; mystery with either the finite and knowable or the infinite and unknowable. Magic is a snare, a temptation to what is delusory; and the basic trouble with magic is that it ironically employs matter to escape the claim, the reality, of matter. Mystery, by contrast, may be converted into the nonmysterious or known—if the mystery is the sort with which the police are finitely concerned. Or mystery may be that sort which is unknowable, the sort that induces awareness of infinite reality. This larger mystery must be believed, cannot be known. Understandably, Spark makes comic hay of the contrast between those characters who in good or bad faith will not acknowledge more than the finite kind of mystery and those characters who quite see the claims of the finite, but whose belief demands that these claims be accommodated with faith's firm reality. Spark's interest in the scope and manifestations of the real combines prominently with her concern for the creative act and has so combined from the beginning of her career. This in turn means that certain emphases upon balances between Being and beings, universal and particular, reality and realism, ubiquitous and here, eternal and now—that such emphases commonly tend to be shaped by the novelist's focus upon the mystery of making. My contention is that by violating (here as throughout) the chronology of Spark's development, and by stressing both early and later novels in the present chapter, I will be able to conclude this study in the demonstration that structural, generic, and textural interests are subsumed within Spark's role as creator, and that this role is most richly seen in her special theistic-aesthetic terms. We see this creative focus most plainly in *The Comforters, The Public Image, Not to Disturb,* and *Loitering with Intent.*

In retrospect *The Comforters* (1957),[1] Muriel Spark's first novel, can be seen to have established frames of mind and reference perennially hers in subsequent novels. On one level, for example, *The Comforters* is plotted as a finite mystery or detection story. Laurence Manders, his mother, Lady Manders, and his uncle

Ernest pursue a number of clues suggesting, accurately, that Laurence's seventy-eight-year-old grandmother, Louisa Jepp, is the leader of a jewel-smuggling ring. Details accumulate, the case builds as fascinating and funny, and eventually enough people learn about the proceedings to force Louisa and her crew to cease their activities. Incidentally, blackmail is important to this level of mystery, as in other Spark works. As might be supposed, money is a crucial motive, as in traditional comedy. Sex, too, counts as one force that makes things happen: heterosexual, homosexual, bigamous, frustrated, gently loving and remote, lustful and pain-making, even comically resolving. On this plane of social comedy and criminal detection, mannerism and social style count for much.

On the familiar second level, however, and of course simultaneously with events on the primary level, action and consequences are farther-reaching and by nature harder to discuss—whether by the characters or by the critic. Here we find Caroline Rose, who had lived with Laurence Manders for six years, but whose recent conversion to Catholicism has induced her to set up separate quarters. Caroline is an author, Laurence a sports commentator for the BBC. These two love each other, and Laurence's Catholicism, although lapsed, is sufficient for him to bear with Caroline's celibate demands. In any event, the important quality characteristic of this level of action is that Caroline hears voices and a typewriter, both untraceable. From these phenomena flow the more complicated mysteries of the book and of course the troubles Caroline experiences in trying to reconcile realms—for herself, to be sure, but also for Laurence and others with whom she lives her life.

Caroline is a novelist who is currently writing a study called *Form in the Modern Novel*. These two kinds of writing combine with her normal psychological perceptions as well as with her religious conversion, her altered relationship with Laurence, and Laurence's investigations into his grandmother's affairs to create an existence that is sometimes amusing, but just as likely to flirt with desperation and fear of insanity. What we can see in retrospect, after three decades, is that Spark was, even this early in her novel-writing career, contemplating narrative point of view in some depth—if one posits the psychological perspective of a believer in the larger reality.[2]

The book's omniscience sets up two plots. One is the plot line of Laurence's detecting game, the level at which, for instance, some characters in and readers of *Memento Mori* wrongly suppose the phone calls to originate. The second plot is not really a line at all, of course, but an intrusion of the realm of infinity, of the boundlessly real, that necessarily includes and influences and comments on the plot line which is Laurence's ratiocinative pursuit. Caroline can enter into the pleasures of Laurence's Holmesian adventure. But what no one can help her to handle, and what she sometimes doubts her own ability to live with, is her undeniable hearing of the voices and the typewriter. These phenomena are not recordable on tape (any more than those phone calls in *Memento Mori* are traceable by Scotland Yard), and of course she cannot tell anyone who is speaking or typing. She cannot supply scientific concrete evidence of what exists outside of the scientifically verifiable. This inability is attributable not to some mental derangement or some linguistic deficiency, but to the nature of the larger reality. Clues to the simultaneous temporal and extratemporal reality of these phenomena are present in two signs: what the voices say or chant and the typewriter records may be past or present or future, finished or prophetic; and the voices may narrate what concerns others elsewhere as well as Caroline herself. In other words, the voices are not confined temporally or spatially as they would be on Laurence's level of detection. For instance, the voices may say to Caroline what the narrator has just told us about Caroline's past activities, or the voices may project the future conduct of Caroline and others, or the voices may tell Caroline what the narrator has already told us of some characters other than Caroline. Caroline need not have been one of the book's characters to have experienced what she nonetheless learns from the voices. On the ratiocinative level there is no correlation between the tenses of the voices' narration and the inevitable presentness of Caroline's hearing that narration, regardless of whom it may concern, wherever or whenever. We note that, considerations of character-time and -place aside, the patches of Caroline's voice narrative given to us (always in italics) repeat verbatim the novel's own narrative language usually immediately preceding the italicized passage. In effect, Caroline overhears bits of the narrated fiction in which she, as overhearing character, appears before us readers.

Caroline is much occupied with the task of convincing herself and others that her mind is right. We have seen in other books something of her problem. Spark is fond of setting up the investigator of tangible evidence on one side, setting up an aficionado of the magical and superstitious on the other side, and placing between them a knower and believer, a rational skeptical insister upon evidence where evidence is to be expected for proof, but at the same time a firm insister upon the reality of his/her own experience despite the futility of expecting that concrete evidence exists to convince anyone else of that experience.[3] In other words, such a middle character typically signals Spark's norm. The middle way is explicit in Ronald Bridges's differences from Patrick Seton as well as from sheer skeptics; or again in the process by which Jean Taylor, Nicholas Farringdon, Sandy Stranger, January Marlow, and Barbara Vaughan bring together what senses know and what mind or spirit believes in. This middle way is only implicit, as we have seen, in such books as *The Driver's Seat, The Abbess of Crewe, The Takeover, Territorial Rights,* and *The Only Problem,* for in these fictions there is no character to straddle realms; emphases are on what is *not* available to the characters, with the result that the reader and the narrator have more of the heavy work to do.[4] In this earliest novel, however, the three attitudes are all discernible as characters. Laurence is the detective, Baron Willi Stock is the magic-fancier, and Caroline is the realm-straddler.

That she is the norm, however, is a function of the omniscient point of view—for she is certainly not viewed as normal by any of the other characters. Obviously, such a discrepancy is an indication of why Spark favors the third person, and indeed of why she requires levels of narration—notebooks, letters, newspapers, diaries, etc.—even in *Robinson* and *Loitering with Intent,* where the point of view is first-person. *The Comforters* shows Spark, from the start of her career as novelist, establishing her overall view by focusing upon aesthetic reality. Without an omniscient point of view in this instance we would apparently have no means by which to sort out the oppositions in the book and to make the judgment that Caroline's odd condition is perfectly in tune with the health of Jean Taylor, Ronald Bridges, and the others who exemplify Spark's moral and psychological center.[5]

Spark uses this book to explore and set out her own awareness of the wonders of any kind of creation. Typically, and understandably, Laurence's view supposes that reality is given, is objectively out there or in our heads, to be seen and explained, described, scientifically manifested. Far from incidentally, this is why he has ceased to practice his Catholicism: he cannot believe. He has come to rely solely on verifiable evidence. As a consequence, Laurence, for all his love for Caroline, is compelled to think that if her voices and typing cannot be recorded on tape, she must entertain the proposition that her mind is out of touch with reality. He expects a straightforward account of what she hears and a rational explanation of her doing so. Such is the finite limitation containing and controlling his view of mystery. Caroline, on the other hand, is perfectly ready to agree that she may well be mentally disturbed. But she also refuses to deny the reality of the voices and typing. She insists that what she hears is just as much a sensory experience or fact as anything that she and others may hear or touch or see together—despite the fact that in this case others cannot be made to share this experience. What her stance as norm also shows is that the main interest held by mystery of this other sort is not in solving it but in experiencing it as the reality in which one participates, willy-nilly, as maker. What establishes Caroline's normality is her assurance that, while she may be neurotic and somewhat awry from Laurence's point of view, she can admit to and live with that truth so long as she can find a way to include it within the larger point of view.

And point of view is the right term here, for this is a book that attempts with remarkable success to put together the facts of living with the facts of creating in words. Where Laurence would take the given or the findable and describable and make an ending of the story to which they add up, Caroline cannot so limit herself. She concentrates not upon taking but upon making; or, more accurately, she senses that what we do and are is not endable, finishable, but only seems to be temporally and spatially segmentable into beginnings, middles, ends. This point comes clear in a conversation between Caroline and Father Jerome—her mentor and, except for the homilist in *The Mandelbaum Gate,* the only sympathetically portrayed religious in Spark's fiction. He is assuring: "Neurotics never go mad." When she says that her condition is nonetheless "intolerable," he asks, rhetorically, "Doesn't it depend on how you take it?" (p. 68). It does indeed.

She keeps her sanity by positing the theory that her voices are evidence that she and her acquaintances are characters in a novel being narrated-written by unfindable voices-typists. On Laurence's level this conclusion makes a kind of sense because Caroline is a novelist interested in the form and workings of fiction, but for Caroline to be influenced in her life by such a theory is disturbing to Laurence. Omniscience, however, enables Spark to demonstrate that of course Caroline is right, because we are indeed reading the very fiction of which she overhears occasional echoes. In this way Spark omnisciently builds in the element of reliability just as she did in *Memento Mori*, for instance, by having Godfrey answer the phone and hear the voice's message not for himself but for his sister. Spark takes away from the reader, who is very likely to be of Laurence's frame of mind, the comforting possibility of supposing that he/she is all right and that obviously Caroline is crazy. Spark's narrator won't allow us to side with Laurence and prevents our disagreeing with Caroline's theory. The other characters may not be able to be shown the truth of that theory, but we as readers of this narrative cannot possibly do other than embrace it as the fact of the matter.

Such a theory implies much about the creative act. Where Laurence takes evidence and reaches conclusions from it, and stops there, Caroline takes evidence of Laurence's sort, makes the best she can of it, but goes beyond Laurence in believing that one must take some experience as evidence that something is being made of oneself and of everyone and everything else. Laurence takes the given (which is already limited sharply by the nature of what he will admit into the category of the given) and works to have done with it, to close the case—and the book. Caroline takes the given and makes of it what she can, in view of the fact that her given goes beyond what is sensibly perceivable. What she makes is the theory verifiable by us in the reading. For Caroline, the narrative art, like any kind of making, is not limited to the finitely positioned artist but is itself evidence that such a making artist is simultaneously being made, created by another force or artistic endeavor. Small wonder that, in the writing of her book on *Form in the Modern Novel*, she is "having difficulty with the chapter on realism" (p. 62).

"The evidence will be in the book itself" (p. 174), says Caroline in reply to Willi Stock's demanding proof of her theory that she and he are characters in a novel. And indeed the proof is Spark's book itself. But Spark doesn't stop here. It would be too simple and indeed destructive of Spark's whole sense of reality if we were allowed to settle for what is after all the relatively containable notion that we have here a character aware that she is a character. Indeed, Spark's narrator compels us to imagine beyond the finite and to become involved in discussion of inside and outside. The narrator reports that in the course of wondering about the truth of Laurence's theory that his grandmother is a smuggler, and of Stock's theory that Louisa Jepp's friend Mervyn Hogarth is a worker in black magic,

> Caroline found the true facts everywhere beclouded. She was aware that the book in which she was involved was still in progress. Now, when she speculated on the story, she did so privately, noting the facts as they accumulated. By now, she possessed a large number of notes, transcribed from the voices, and these she studied carefully. Her sense of being written into the novel was painful. Of her constant influence on its course she remained unaware and now she was impatient for the story to come to an end, knowing that the narrative could never become coherent to her until she was at last outside it, and at the same time consummately inside it. (Pp. 196–97)

By means of such passages as this, Spark's narrator makes clear that while *The Comforters* is in fact the story that proves Caroline right, Caroline is so very right about her being a character that we can see her inability to get completely outside of the book in which we encounter her, to enable herself to separate inside entirely from outside. Caroline is condemned to be aware of her characterhood and thereby condemned not to understand how the "she" of whom she is aware as also existent outside of that novel can be understood to influence the book in which she is sensible of being incorporated. We, on the other hand, as outsiders reading *The Comforters*, can see that Spark's novel and the novel taken down in notes by Caroline are not identical. Spark has made something more of Caroline than Caroline can make of herself, because Spark has made a narrator.

Two further points must be made about the aesthetic-philosophical value of Caroline's situation. For one thing, she is taking notes for a novel whenever she hears voices. That is, she is being inspired to creativity—the voices are her Muses. This in itself is mysterious, however commonplace in the remarking. For another thing, we as readers see that Caroline is like others in seeing clues that will enable her to wind things up and settle them, and we also see, when we have finished reading *The Comforters*, that Caroline cannot ever get "at last outside" her story to understand her role in it, her influencing its course, and her being made to influence its course. Nothing but a simultaneously sustained inside-outside role is possible to one of Caroline's sensibility. She is inspired to take notes that will become a novel created by herself, and in which she is the central and normal figure; but at the same time the even larger mystery is that she in her freely chosen creative act is also the center of Spark's narrative about her—which narrative Caroline cannot transcend and see as we see it. Only Caroline's faith finally distinguishes her from the tragic Lise in *The Driver's Seat*, who is likewise "impatient for the story to end" and to get herself "at last outside it." Because she lacks faith, Lise cannot achieve Caroline's eventual balance.

The importance of these two points—that Caroline must be seen as at once inspired writer and written artifact—becomes clearer on the book's (Spark's) last two pages. For if we had thought that Spark meant to limit her concerns to the mystery of Caroline's inside-outside status, we are here set straight. The achievement of these last passages requires and justifies, I believe, quotation at some length. At this stage, the smuggling has ceased, Louisa Jepp and her aged crony Mr. Webster have married, the villainess Mrs. Hogg has died, and Caroline, having finished her study of the novel, leaves London to write a novel.

A few weeks later the character called Laurence Manders was snooping around in Caroline Rose's flat. . . . to collect some books which she had asked to be sent to her.

He took his time. In fact, the books were the last things he looked for.

He thought, "What am I looking for?" . . .

He found the books that Caroline wanted, but before he left he sat down at Caroline's desk and wrote her a letter.

"I have spent 2 hours and 28 min. in your flat. . . . I have found those books for you, and had a look round. Why did you lock the right hand drawer in the wall cupboard? I had difficulty in getting it open, and then the hair curlers in one box and the scarves in another, and the white gloves were all I found. I can't lock it again. I have just found myself wondering what I was looking for.

"I found an enormous sheaf of your notes for your novel in the cupboard in that carton marked Keep in a Cool Place. Why did you leave them behind? What's the point of making notes if you don't use them while you are writing the book?

"Do you want me to send the notes to you?

"I wonder if you left them on purpose, so that I should read them?

"But I remember your once saying you always made a lot of notes for a book, then never referred to them. I feel very niggled.

"I will tell you what I think of your notes:

(1) You misrepresent all of us.

(2) Obviously you are the martyr-figure. "Martyrdom by misunderstanding." But actually you yourself understand nobody, for instance the Baron, my father, myself, we are martyred by your misunderstanding.

(3) I love you. I think you are hopelessly selfish.

(4) I dislike being a character in your novel. How is it all going to end?"

Laurence wrote a long letter, re-read it, then folded and sealed it. He put it in his pocket, stacked away Caroline's notes in their place in their carton in the cupboard.

The autumn afternoon was darkening as he turned into Hampstead Heath. Religion had so changed Caroline. At one time he thought it would make life easier for her, and indirectly for himself. "You have to be involved personally," Caroline had said on one occasion, infuriating him by the know-all assumption of the words. At least, he thought, I am honest; I misunderstand Caroline. His letter had failed to express his objections. He took it out of his pocket and tore it up into small pieces, scattering them over the Heath where the wind bore them away. He saw the bits of paper come to rest, some on the scrubby ground, some among the deep marsh weeds, and one piece on a thorn bush; and he did not then foresee his later wonder, with a curious rejoicing, how the letter had got into the book. (Pp. 220–21)

These final pages of *The Comforters* seem to me to recapitulate everything I have discussed to this point and to go well beyond recapitulation by incorporating Laurence, the nonbeliever, into the inside-outside relationship. A number of issues are raised, of course, including the query about where things will end. This is what Walburga asks in *The Abbess of Crewe*, as well as what is asked by any number of detective types throughout Spark's books, and as we surely know by now the question is one that cannot be made meaningful once the imagination ventures beyond what in fact is capable of ending (see, again, *Hothouse*). So there is a kind of irony in Laurence's asking yet again this characterizing question: for if he shared Caroline's sensibility (not necessarily her Christianity) he would not ask the question; and since he does not share that sensibility no answer will satisfy him. The asking marks his status as detective of the finite. Laurence's reading of Caroline is like many a critic's reading of Spark's novels. The critic-detective *takes* what is findable (what have we here?). But also the critic may fail to account for the extent to which he indeed *makes* meaning and moves from outside to inside of that meaning.

At the same time, we note on the other hand that Laurence is vaguely uneasy in this finite quest. Here he in fact asks himself and Caroline what he is looking for. He is known fondly as a snoop, a rifler of dresser drawers, so that we are hardly surprised to find him breaking into Caroline's cupboard and sifting through all her possessions. But we remember that earlier Caroline had thought thus to herself about Laurence's predilection: " 'He keeps trying to detect whatever it is he's looking for in life.' She admired his ability to start somewhere repeatedly; his courage" (p. 92). If Caroline has indeed deliberately planned on Laurence's finding and reading these notes (and this is likely, since all his intimates know of his habit and tolerate it), it is worth observing that she may thereby have intended to introduce him more directly to one problem in her psychoaesthetic bag: that of the difficulty of untangling objective, distanced creation from involved and actively influencing creation. That is, once he has read these notes Laurence is aware that he is a character in Caroline's novel (as she had felt all of them to be in the overheard novel); and once he absorbs and begins reacting to this knowledge, he is of course influencing events rather than participating fixedly according entirely to the wishes of his creator. Such a complication is decidedly high on the list of insights to which she has been working to introduce him, but to which, until this point, he has been obtuse. In any event, regardless of Caroline's intent, Laurence does become an active participant in the aesthetic process that has driven Caroline nearly crazy, and as a result he influences the fiction which draws to a close with the pages which we have here quoted.

This involvement is manifest as Spark's "character called Laurence Manders" reads of himself as a character in the notes of Caroline Rose that will eventually become her own novel. His first reaction—one kind of influencing—is to protest one-sidedness and distortion of himself and others. But his second reaction, the one on which the Spark narrative ends, is one of pleasure that Spark's narrator assures us he will feel in the future—when Spark's finite novel is over. This extraordinary operation is anything but cute or pixieish. In this narrative assurance Spark does several things that typify her art here and in subsequent fictions. For one thing she plays up what an orthodox realist might work to conceal: that Laurence's letter can be said to have been written, can be known by us readers, can be said to be destroyed, and can be salvaged for creation elsewhere and later. For another thing, Laurence is said to survive the book in which we meet him and to become aware (when? where? how?) of the letter in published form, as we are aware of bits of it. In short, Laurence becomes aware that he is inside Caroline's notes and is apparently to be inside the fiction she is now writing, and he assuredly, sometime, is to learn that his letter, here destroyed, survives in print. Laurence will rejoice in this wonder. He exists thus inside and outside his role as Caroline's character, for he is Spark's character as well, and he and his letter cannot cease to be once they have been made—for to be made is necessarily to begin influencing without end—as the reader finds in reading *Hothouse*. Everything and everyone needs an initial push, but once creation happens it goes on happening, partly from outside and partly with our own volitional participation.

What Spark demonstrates by creating a Laurence who may be intentionally thus directed by Caroline is how Caroline's notes of her voices make Laurence feel she feels about him, herself, and others. This skein is a fair microcosm of the simultaneous need and impossibility of "getting it right" in *any* version. Nobody can get it all down right. Perhaps the sanest view (and this is what makes Caroline Spark's norm) is to remember the nature of fiction and therefore to abandon, with anti-Faustian humility, the attempt to stand in for uppercase God. Caroline's sanity (which appears to her fellow characters as craziness) is manifest in her talking back to her voices: "And if anyone's listening, let them take note" (p. 75). Spark's narrator shows us the same brand of clearheadedness in another passage: "At this point in the narrative, it might be as well to state that the characters in this novel are all fictitious, and do not refer to any living persons whatsoever" (p. 75). Caroline's interacting with her Muses and Spark's narrator's issuing the formulaic disclaimer *in medias res* both light up a number of clichés that ought to convey much meaning: artists are inspired but not entirely controlled from outside themselves; characters do take over once they have been inspirationally set in motion; it may indeed be impossible to discern where the author leads and where the characters do so; *anything done* is a fiction, so that by nature the makers of art are themselves already created or made agents. Thus, anyone who shares Caroline's and Spark's sensibility finds (believes) it eminently

rational to speak of causes influentially inner and outer and also finds it redun-
dant (except for purposes of the fiction that is civil law) to assert fictitious status
for characters in a novel—since to call them characters or to speak of a work as a
novel is to say that already, even as speaking of "historical persons" in a
biography or document would be to posit fictitiousness. As we argued in chapter
1, the distinction between expressed fact and fiction is a fiction. The only
possible distinction in these aesthetic and philosophical matters is between
experience and the (re)presentation of experience: sanity and essential humility
begin in the realization that the artifact, the fiction, can never be the experience.

Spark's narrator thus demonstrates that Laurence's reading of Caroline's notes
effects that always miraculous relationship between the artifact and the experiencing of that finished and apparently objective thing. Objectively speaking, the
work is set and unchanging; subjectively, it is alive as its experiencer goes on
creating it anew. Caroline's notes have the effect of involving Laurence "personally," in getting him to take an action that he and we find cannot be retracted
and which goes on aesthetically affecting (and effecting) not only himself but
anyone who reads Spark's book. The experiencing of the artifact continues
cooperating with the experiencer in a creative act. "The words of a dead man /
Are modified in the guts of the living." Of course this static-dynamic simultaneity is paradoxical and miraculous, and of course it necessitates misunderstanding by implication, since no one's experience *is* the work of art and since
anyone's perception of the work is unique. Laurence is right, then, about
Caroline's misunderstanding what he understands, and he just as inevitably
shows us that Caroline is right in addressing the need "to be involved personally."

All of these intricate matters could, moreover, take a theistic cast, since Spark
arranges for Laurence to attribute Caroline's frame of mind to her religious
conversion. But I think that the psychology precedes the theology, and that
Spark's narrative assurance of how Laurence will react beyond the back cover of
The Comforters signifies that Laurence will share Caroline's psychology regardless
of his lack of religious conviction and commitment. Surely Spark's book comments indirectly on her own blending of religion and psychology in her aesthetic
practice, but one cannot assume or predict that any theistic commitment will
follow upon psychological conversion. Indeed, the religious conversion would
seem to be yet another miracle, as is suggested by the narrator's allusion here to
the parable of the sowing of mustard seed: some of the seed may "take," and
much of it will not. We and Laurence seem to have as little to do with causing
religious conversion as Laurence has to do with his letter's appearing in print.
Agency is real and undeniable (to the once-converted); yet, while that agency
works through persons it cannot be seen as synonymous with the individual will,
and it does require our assuming the element of grace, of the gratuitous. The
agency is miraculous, but what keeps it from the morass of the magical is its

necessary operation within the tangible realm. Magic denies the need for concrete fertile ground at all and posits the magician's efficacy, whereas Spark's and Caroline's paradoxical sensibility offers as perhaps the crucial mark of its own authenticity the fact of its being rooted in the here-and-now of personal inadequacy. The seed may not "take," but if it is to do so it surely requires terra firma, not ethereal transcendence.

What will assuredly happen to Laurence, and what has happened to bring about Caroline's conversion, are alike beyond their own doing—to some extent. This is an important matter not only when we enter into Spark's aesthetic immediately, as in the present instance, but also when we observe throughout her books a regular insistence upon privacy and individualism. In *The Comforters*, for example, snooping is tolerated but seen as something Laurence ought to get over eventually. Lady Manders, when she finds herself seeing her brother-in-law, Ernest Manders, through what the narrator tells us are Caroline's eyes, finds herself feeling for him in his homosexuality and respecting him in his person, a part of which is that homosexuality. Similarly, Father Jerome is not disturbed or annoyed by Caroline's hearing voices: "He seemed to assume simply that she was as she was" (p. 67). When Lady Manders is gaining confidence in the struggle to balance self and others, charity and moral cowardice, the narrator lets us know about her conversion: "[Lady Manders] thought, 'How exhilarating it is to be myself,' and the whole advantage of her personality flashed into her thoughts as if they were someone else's. . . . She felt her strength; a fine disregard, freedom to take sides . . . if necessary" (p. 165). The other side of this strength-gathering freedom is, of course, the expectation that others shall conform to what we would have them be. This is always shown to be undesirable or evil. Thus, Caroline is far from perfect: "What irritated Caroline now about her old friend [Eleanor Hogarth] was the fact that she had seemed not to change essentially in the years since . . . Cambridge . . . and was apparently quite happy with herself as she was. Now Laurence was another like that. But Caroline could like in Laurence many characteristics which in others she could not tolerate. And she was aware of the irrationality and prejudice of all these feelings, without being able to stop feeling them" (pp. 90–91). It would be good for Caroline to shed these prejudices as it was good for Lady Manders to value Ernest Manders for himself. The best negative support for this moral position is Georgina Hogg, who is seen by several other characters actually to disappear and said by the narrator to have no private life at all: the degree of her malice is measurable by this fact of her existing *entirely* to spy on and blackmail and spread rumors about others. This is quite different from Laurence's brand of snooping, and Laurence plainly does value others' individuality: *that* is not what he tampers with.

The point here is that religious morality overlaps aesthetic-philosophical premises. One must respect, even as sacred, another's status as unique person. Change, preferably for the better, is desirable—but that is only very limitedly anyone else's business. Artistically, this uniqueness is obviously a source of any writer's strength. Attention to individual traits of appearance, of speech, of gesture makes for caricature and character alike. And these personal traits prevail for reasons often misunderstood. In the realm of religious morality we are to keep hands off violating others' persons, in the realization that they, like ourselves, are what they are gratuitously in large part. Aesthetically, the parallel point is that characters and caricatures, like persons, both require a creator's start and then are largely on their own to change as their cooperation with their creating author's "grace" permits.[6] Persons and characters must not be confused, of course. But what they do have in common is their manifesting of both determinism and choice, fixedness and changeability. This kind of mixedness may sound like flummery to many of Spark's readers as to many of Caroline's fellow characters. Indeed, she suggests her own sympathy with others' perplexity and impatience: "Caroline thought, 'The demands of the Christian religion are exorbitant, they are outrageous. Christians who don't realize that from the start are not faithful. They are dishonest; their teachers are talking in their sleep. "Love one another . . . brethren, beloved . . . your brother, neighbours, love, love love"—do they know what they are saying?' " (p. 43). She can feel for the nonbeliever's troubles in accepting or comprehending her own beliefs, precisely because she cannot herself *understand* how to live her faith. All she knows is that she believes and must therefore work to live her belief. In the same way, one cannot begin to untangle the artistic paradox suggested in this book, but one sees that the terms of the paradox are operative and vital forces in reality. And to carry the analogy between paradoxes a bit farther, we may note that Caroline's or Spark's or anyone's awe before the undeniable and undiscussible signs of reality's interworkings is what breeds humility. This humility, and not merely some arbitrary touchiness, gives rise to Spark's stress upon the interest and sanctity of the individual human person. Persons are not ours to force; characters are not their authors' to compel. Influence and direction are appropriate and good to a point, but beyond that point person or character must be honored in its self. In practice, this means that just as Laurence is tested as to whether he can allow for the differences that are Caroline, whom he loves, so we are tested as to whether we can imaginatively entertain, uncondescendingly, Muriel Spark's typical abstract concreteness, clocked eternity.

Part of the test is coping with the danger often referred to in Spark's books. We saw this in Nicholas's awareness in *The Girls of Slender Means*, and it is present in every Spark work. For instance, this test and its dangers show up in Lise's plight as she fails to accommodate choice and determinism, in Sandy's need to betray Jean Brodie in order to hold onto her vision of both realms and of individual dignity, in Jean Taylor's less painful choosing to betray Charmian for Godfrey's benefit, and implicitly in the narrator's tacitly asking us how we might do the reconciling of realities in the *Abbess*, *The Takeover*, *Territorial Rights*, and *The Only Problem*. But since awareness of the double reality is the home truth of

Spark's world, anyone who shares that awareness must react to the immense difficulty as Nicholas responds to Selina: "Nowhere is safe." This is in fact what Caroline replies to Laurence when he, as one trained in Catholic doctrine, plays devil's advocate in asking her whether she isn't running spiritual risks in engaging her voices. Her reply is perfectly to the point: "There are spiritual dangers in everything. From the Catholic point of view the chief danger about a conviction is the temptation to deny it" (p. 104). This home truth could well be extended beyond Catholicism, obviously, to any way of thinking that demands loyalty to one's convictions of personal experience. "Everything's risky," she reminds Laurence elsewhere (p. 189), and the point is variously made in all Spark's books.

In view of these dangers, and of the limitations of reason, and of the inevitable impossibility of communication regardless of beliefs, and of the possibility of growing spiritually hubristic and reclusive (not cloistered—which is not itself a frame of mind)—given these dangers and obstacles, what can the title *(The Comforters)* possibly mean? It seems to me that Caroline can sanely—not complacently or self-righteously—take comfort in that she has not sold out, not let others talk her out of what she has experienced, not gone mad, not given up on the just claims of reason, and not betrayed her conviction of reality beyond reason's grasp. Her would-be comforters are, like Job's, no help. Affirmatively, her voices are comforting exactly because they do persist and thereby aid her resistance against those who would have her believe otherwise or believe not at all. She is coping with, is living, what her reason alone tells her cannot be lived—what Christianity demands of her. Or rather she is trying to do so: and her religion may remind her that the Holy Spirit, the Paraclete, is a "Comforter" in that effort (John 14:16, 26). The voices are an indication not that she is a lunatic, but that what she believes is real.[7] As *The Comforters* shows in various ways, you take what is given, including yourself, and you make of it what you can in the light of what you believe should be made. Impossible as this may seem, it must be attempted. And only the reality of the voices enables Caroline to keep making something of what is given—whether she regards that as given religiously or aesthetically. As Spark's book finishes up, I don't for a minute think that Laurence Manders accepts this view; but Spark's narrator omnisciently takes control to assert reliably that what Laurence knows on the book's last page is not a limitation on what will come to be. Change, conversion, is ongoing, and the narrator concludes the book with a look at a rejoicing Laurence to whom Laurence as character is not yet privy. I note these last pages, then, not as analogous to the *Messiah's* finale, but only to stress that Spark's ending is typically an implied or a promised change of view with which Laurence will have had something, but not everything, to do. That assurance, for us readers, may be tragic in *The Driver's Seat*, but here and more usually in Spark's work—as in Fleur's "rejoicing" in *Loitering with Intent*—it is comic or ironic.

An instance of the more harrowing sort of Spark comedy is *The Public Image*

(1968),[8] which steers a course between the tragic *Driver's Seat* and the comedies of resolution such as we have seen up through *The Mandelbaum Gate*. *The Public Image* shares the grimness of Spark's more recent work and can indeed be seen in retrospect to foreshadow the terrors of *The Driver's Seat*, written two years later. As the title suggests, Spark uses the film career of the protagonist, Annabel Christopher, as a means of entering once again heavily and deeply into life-art relationships such as those encountered in *The Comforters*.

The Public Image, Spark's ninth novel, is another third-person narrative and is limited, for all intents and purposes, to Annabel's perspective. The book's time present occupies the period from Friday to Monday during a bright Roman spring. After a few opening pages in the present, the rest of chapter 1 and all of chapter 2 are given to retrospection; thereafter, the book finishes with a chrono-logical rendering of time present. We are told that Annabel married Frederick Christopher twelve years ago, when she was twenty and the two of them were fledglings in British drama and film circles. Her career has gone forward remark-ably well in film while Frederick's has been disappointing: he no longer acts but writes screenplays occasionally. His friend Billy O'Brien has tagged along from England to Italy with the couple as Frederick's semicareer and Annabel's rise as actress have brought them both under the directing wing of Luigi Leopardi. Billy has always been a parasite upon the Christophers and was for a bored afternoon or two, years ago, Annabel's bed-partner. Annabel's infant son, Carl, is the most important person in her life. Frederick has an Italian mistress, Marina, and he does not know that Annabel both knows of Marina and apparently welcomes her taking this bored and quarreling husband off his wife's hands. For Annabel's principal concern, after Carl, is to maintain her "public image." We also learn that much public relations effort, generated by Luigi Leopardi, has gone into creating the image of Annabel as the "English Lady-Tiger." Annabel is pho-tographed everywhere in Rome during the day with her equally cool and Britishly cultivated husband, but she is understood to turn into an irresistible feline by night. She and Frederick are reputed thus to have the perfect marriage.

So much for retrospection. The book's present is concerned with Annabel's efforts to preserve her image and protect her son when Frederick commits suicide and leaves behind a number of letters that will inevitably destroy his wife's reputation if they are discovered. The opportunity for blackmailing is thus once more ripe in a Spark fiction, and Billy O'Brien is the agent of the present attempt. What the book shows is that Annabel and the baby eventually leave Rome and presumably her career, and that Billy fails to gain his end. But of course to say this is to settle nothing that matters finally; it is instead to raise once more the questions about how things get to this pass and about what agencies are responsible for such an outcome, and about what Spark is hereby saying on the subjects of the book's title and one's existence inside and outside of roles.

Perhaps the single most important narrative observation in the book is that "stupidity . . . thrives on the absence of a looking-glass" (p. 6). This remark refers in context to the younger Annabel, who, the narrator goes on to say, gradually got over this stupidity. The language here can be taken in Spark's many ways. It suggests, for example, that a mirror can help us see what we already see in our minds' eyes. It also holds out the possibility that we may see what we are striving to make others see in us. More interestingly and widely, the language may alert us to what others see in us *and therefore* have caused us to see in ourselves. Mirrors can give us back an image—can reflect—or they can enable us to go through or beyond them to something truer. Mirrors are often spoken of as both reflectors and the means of separating image from true self. These meanings and values are all at work in *The Public Image*, for indeed the foundational tension here arises from Annabel's struggle to decide for herself (i.e., without benefit of public relations staff) who she is in her own right and what part she plays in establishing that self. These same questions are of course suggested by the telephonic voices of *Memento Mori*, by the green world elsewhere in *The Ballad of Peckham Rye*, by the "accidental" outcome of *The Bachelors*, and by any number of other dualities examined in this study. Lise's response, for example, is one very credible reaction to the frustrated effort to answer these questions satisfactorily—or life-sustainingly. But for several reasons I think of the mirror's function in the present book as similar to the function of voices and typewriter in *The Comforters*, and I therefore find it useful to emphasize the aesthetic values of the questions.

"What's wrong with a public image?" (p. 22) Annabel asks Frederick in the midst of a quarrel, when he mocks her efforts to keep up appearances for the public. She has to arrive at an answer to this question—and we have to grasp the connection between that answer and her departure from Rome—before the book can round to its conclusion.

For one thing, a public image (which is not the tautology it may at first seem to be) is inevitable: granted the existence of everyone as other than alone, such an image must be. The real question, then, is not that of the rightness or wrongness of one's image, but rather that of the ends to which such an image may be used. We all must make suppositions about the characters and motives of others, even of those closest to us. Spark's book asks us to exercise the imagination required to see our own images in a metaphorical mirror; and to take the risks of such self-examination. Stupidity means lack of self-awareness, lack of understanding of what it may mean to come across in this or that way in others' eyes. To begin to shed stupidity means to take the chances of living a more fully human life. This chance-taking is dangerous for Annabel as it is dangerous for Caroline or Sandy or Barbara or anyone else whose quest for reality may well activate inquiries into whether one is in charge or is a victim; into whether —in Caroline's terms—one is inside or outside the story. Thus when Annabel reads her late husband's carefully planted suicide letters—to his mother (already two years dead herself), his son, his friend Billy, his mistress, his wife—she remarks that "I didn't realise that he was dangerous" (p. 103), and she eventually announces publicly that he was "insane" (p. 151).

Such judgments, however, are only instigators of the reader's own puzzlement and further inquiry. As we realize that the handwriting likely is authentic and that Frederick almost certainly did plan his own death in such a way as to ruin his wife's image (or at least his image of her image), we have to wonder what, other than insanity, could have prompted such behavior. Insanity can of course be very lucid, so that we avoid no difficulties by agreeing that he was mad. Presumably we come up with nothing like an answer, but we do arrive at the conclusion that such effects must have had proportionate causes: Frederick must have wanted so ardently to escape from his own image of his wife that he sought an end to his experiencing of that image and did everything possible to break what he saw her to be. For her to begin to glimpse her husband's sense of herself is for Annabel to sense that we are all constantly engaged in creating ourselves and thereby in creating the selves of all others who experience what they take to be the reality of us. Annabel may understandably call her husband mad, but we can very nearly observe the stupidity's melting away as we sense her eventual discovery that he, too, was brought to be who he was, and that she was as much a fashioner of him and of her public as ever the studio professionals were fashioners of herself. What is dangerous about the dissolution of stupidity is the fearful realization of one's own responsibility for events and for other persons. We see, and she will see, that Annabel made Frederick, in some degree, as Luigi has made Annabel. Her moral imagination dawns.

What is wrong with Annabel's public image—an image apparent to her in those incriminating letters which serve to give her back an altogether new sense of herself—is that she has presumed to live as if separate in reality from it. Spark continually and variously shows us that this kind of wedge between real self and imaged self cannot be driven. And of course this realization evokes once more Caroline's difficulties. Who's in charge here? Am I writing my life or am I written into "my" life by an ungraspable if necessary author? And furthermore, how am I perhaps involved in the authorship of another's reality (as Annabel of Frederick's)? While stupidity lasts, Annabel tries blithely if sometimes vexedly to keep her marriage, her motherhood, and her career in distinct compartments. Trouble—danger—begins in her sudden need to reconcile claims on her identity. She passes the test in one sense—that is, she defeats the bad guy, Billy the blackmailer—and willingly faces personal obscurity rather than give in to him and raise her son in Billy's shadow. But the danger posed by Billy is only a start. What she requires now is to read her experience as we are attempting to do.

Annabel is puzzled as the book ends. She has beaten Billy, she has escaped with her son, but she does not really know what to make of Frederick's conduct. As she leaves Rome, unrecognized, she feels "neither free nor unfree" (p. 152); or, as the narrator significantly alters the expression, "both free and unfree" (p. 153). This pair of expressions echoes much else that we have noted in Spark's paradoxes and dilemmas and matchings of realism against reality. Annabel feels joy and relief in having told the truth about the existence of the letters, but what she feels as her voluntary behavior is coated or indeed permeated with the equally strong conviction that she has been forced into taking this decision. Neither conviction is deniable, and neither is independent of the other. Annabel is in fact seeable both as the "beautiful shell . . . empty, devoid of the life it once held" (p. 112) that Frederick's public letter to her specifies and as "the empty shell" (p. 153) seen by the narrator in the book's last words. She is projected, that is, and depending upon who is doing the reading at what time, as one who no longer conforms to the image of a wife that Frederick wants or that he wants the public to think he wants; and she is also projected as one whose identity has to be acquired "after" the book ends (cf. *Hothouse* and *Comforters*)— one whose self must hereafter be rediscovered and recreated by her own efforts and by whatever else accounts for the authoring of selves. She is free of Billy but only beginning her indentured servitude to that two-way mirror. Annabel is permanently changed; whatever others may do to fill her self-shell, she will now have a hand—consciously—in that endeavor.

We may recall that Lady Manders says, in *The Comforters*, "How exhilarating it is to be myself." She does not say that she knows or understands or fully accounts for herself: she is happy in the knowledge that she *is* herself. This remark connects with Caroline's central role and with Annabel's as well—with the literary art as with the cinematic—in that it draws attention once again to the intrinsic value regularly assigned in Spark's fiction to the sacredness of the mysteriously unique individual. Blackmailers are frequently encountered in Spark's books, and they are always evil because they invade privacy. Blackmailing is wrong because it is an effort at coercive authoring of another person. It attempts to create or make another against the grain of another's will to enter as freely as possible into the self-creating process. Blackmailers violate privacy and personhood. Just as it is less than fully human—it is stupid—to remain unaware of one's freedom within reality's given pattern, so it is antihuman to twist the arm of another's will, so to speak. Annabel won't do as fragmented pseudoself; but Georgina Hogg and Billy O'Brien play knaves to her kind of fool and are thus much worse than she. The trick is to avoid foolishness and knavery alike; to get into balance one's own volition and one's being fictionized within the larger scheme of things. The difficulty is set forth in *The Comforters*, wherein the narrator sets Laurence the agent against Laurence the acted-upon and entertains as well times present and future for the "two" Laurences. Pulling off this trick— or failing to do so—is in a sense Spark's idea of the human condition. Lise fails at it; Ronald and Jean Taylor succeed at it; Annabel has a chance to succeed now that she is alert to what is involved.

All that Spark ever holds out is the possibility of partial involvement in one's own determination. She never makes so bold as to suggest that anyone can succeed or that a certain course will lead to happy conclusions. Grace and the gratuitous matter a great deal in other Spark books, and such is the present case despite this novel's complete secularity. Indeed it is this possibility of freely entering into the making of one's life and self that tags a Spark book definitively. Someone like Lise is tragically enabled to choose her destiny. In *The Public Image* some script-writing of herself is available to Annabel, once she is willing to pay the price. She thwarts Billy's and Frederick's and Luigi's image-making efforts and achieves a potentially comic ending for herself and Carl. She dodges the typecasting of herself by others. But at the same time she raises for her identity the questions that have been humorously if inadvertently raised earlier in the book by reference to *The Turn of the Screw* and *Pygmalion*. How many points of view must be comprehended, how many mirrors gone through, before the fullness of reality can be envisioned? And how do we break into that whirl which is Pygmalion's and Galatea's intercreating?

Annabel has no answers to such questions. She is not Jean Taylor or Ronald Bridges. She knows that she must give up the careless and dimly conscious practice of passively allowing others to decide who she is and seems to be and must instead take a hand in settling such matters for herself. She can opt for either Tom Wells or January Marlow. Small wonder that she should feel "neither free nor unfree," and that both Annabel and the reader should feel her new and unfamiliar danger. Annabel feels hedged about with a sense of what is lost in the gaining, as Sandy feels. Both Sandy and Annabel determine to put a stop to something and someone; and each woman loses something thereby. Sandy destroys her friend in ending her friend's conduct, while Annabel loses her career in stopping Billy's. Pain may well attend upon the decision to participate humanly in one's becoming. One may choose to enter knowingly into maker-made self-involvement; to endorse and live with inevitable if clouded awareness of being simultaneously inside and outside of (hi)story and the experiencing of one's life. Annabel chooses truth where the Abbess Alexandra and Luigi Leopardi choose mythology meant to deceive.

This experiencing of one's life is economically set in the midst of traditional realistic trappings. In Italy, Annabel, Frederick, Billy, and Luigi play out Annabel's book in the whirl of that contemporary Roman chaos and materialistic aimlessness and dissipation with which we are familiar from Italian films, and to which Spark reverts in *The Takeover* and *Territorial Rights*. Moreover, Spark uses the paraphernalia of Roman cinematic fever to play up her title and thus do with film what *The Comforters* does with literature. Frederick writes scripts for his wife and possibly for himself. Luigi's staff build a magazine image of Annabel and Frederick for the fans of the world. Billy relies upon Annabel's concern for illusion when he makes his blackmailing move. Frederick writes his five suicide letters to different persons, but always with an eye to the effect that any or all of the letters will have upon Annabel's image if the letters get to her fans. Newspaper reporters and television crews are everywhere, and cameras constantly click into action as images are made, unmade, altered. Annabel herself is conditioned to stage her appearance at the morgue and at her subsequent press conference with her neighbors as friendly support in her grief. In this way Spark makes credible Annabel's eventual awareness of the foundation to be torn up either by Billy's revelations of the letters or by her own prior revelation of them. In the end, she may well experience what Nicholas Farringdon meant by writing in his *Sabbath Notebooks* that "a vision of evil" is perhaps as forceful as a means of effecting change as is "a vision of good," or what Dougal Douglas implied about beating the devil by the good act of resisting temptation to evil. Annabel is driven to choose to leave behind a way of life as Nicholas, Sandy, and Lise are so driven. The truth, full reality, the name of goodness may be obscure, but the falseness of "scenes" and of the staging of her life is often plain. Annabel comes to know what she is against, and she knows that Carl is foremost in whatever life she may come to articulate and act out subsequently.

The operative point here is that she feels at last that she is in control of her own actions, up to a point. Just as Caroline defied others' views of her sanity in order to insist upon the reality of her voices and to cooperate with them in the writing of her novel as well as of her critical study, so Annabel overcomes all the forces (her "comforters") making her a creature of and for the media, in order to take at least some part in the Annabel-image that will reach her tomorrow as it begins to reach us. This is no small accomplishment, for the book is full of invitations to her to think of life as entirely fate. We note, for example, this discussion between Luigi and Annabel:

> "They told you . . . [asks Luigi] what had happened to Frederick . . . ?"
> "The doctor told me what he had done. It wasn't something that happened to him. Suicide was something he did."
> "Well, it's the same thing."
> "No, it isn't." (P. 121)

This conversation is typical of efforts to avoid blaming or accepting blame. Such efforts Annabel eventually overcomes. In another instance, a young woman who nearly dies of an overdose is said to have undergone psychiatric treatment of late, and thus to be unblamable. Frederick "blamed life for his life" (p. 135). Billy's wrongness is signaled in part by his superstitiousness and by his automatic insistence upon the force of "luck" (pp. 105–6, 143–44). Evildoers and superstitious persons—often the same persons—tip their hands in Spark's books partly by their planning the meanest of deeds for the harm of others and by unconsciously pleading fortune or the breaks or antivoluntarism in the next breath. Spark's protagonists, on the other hand, may not always win and most assuredly leave some loose ends, but they invariably acknowledge in some way their own willed participation in their lives. To plot and then plead helplessness is suspect in Spark's eyes; to plot and to feel compelled and also to embrace responsibility are the signs of characters after Spark's own heart. As telephone calls test the old people in *Memento Mori* and show us who they are, and as voices perform the same function in *The Girls of Slender Means* and *The Comforters*, so Frederick's suicide letters push Annabel to decide who she is: Frederick's version or some version of herself ongoing, inchoate, but definitively other. In leaving Rome, she proves to herself that she remains to some extent free. As usual, intriguing mysteries are planted not to be explained to the public or to the reader, but to test the protagonist and determine what she is capable of becoming. Someone like Jean Taylor knows who she is; Lise's successful struggle to choose fate convinces at least Lise that she knows what she wants, apart from who she may be. Annabel's status is locatable between these two: she knows what she wants to escape from, she certainly wants to go on living, but she has no very clear sense of what she will make of herself. Jean Taylor appears lucidly sane; Lise seems lucidly insane; Annabel has for now escaped a sure kind of madness. Annabel has grasped her new role as author, but, unlike Caroline, she doesn't yet know what she will write.

This confused condition was that of Caroline Rose in the midst of a large congregation at mass in the Brompton Oratory. The narrator says: "She could not immediately cope with this huge full-blown environment, for it antagonized the diligence with which Caroline coped with things, bit by bit" (*Comforters*, p. 110). Annabel on the last page is a lot like this Caroline of midbook, and also like the Abbess Alexandra on her last page: Annabel prepares, that is, to take and to make things as they come. For an even more complex treatment of Spark's handling of the all-at-once with the bit-by-bit, however, I should like to look now at *Not to Disturb*, which seems to me to convey quite brilliantly Spark's perception of life as work of art, or of art as act of living.

Switzerland impressionistically evokes international or extranational neutrality, Calvinistic theology, precision timekeeping. Switzerland is Byronically, romantically, otherwhere, to some, but also as concretely here-and-now as are chocolate, toys, and numbered bank accounts. In some ways it suggests escape and relief from temporal Western concerns; in other ways it epitomizes all those concerns in protected microcosm. These are at least some of the reasons why *Not to Disturb* is appropriately placed on the shores of Lake Geneva; or why a book deeply involved with the problem of creating is so placed.

Not to Disturb (1971)[9] happens one night "sixty-four shopping days [before] Christmas" (p. 36)—to speak, as one must in recounting plots, in the familiar temporal style. The servants at the Château Klopstock are the central characters, and their chief is Lister, the butler. During this stormy night the Baron and the Baroness Klopstock are locked in their library with a secretary, Victor Passerat, and have given orders not to be disturbed. Omniscient narration takes us into the communal servants' quarters, into the private quarters of this or that servant, into the porter's lodge, over a bit of the grounds, but not into the library. The book includes seven house servants, the porter and his wife, the heir apparent to the estate ("him in the attic") together with his keeper, the not-to-be-disturbed trio, "the Reverend," two public relations men, another local nobleman, and finally some police, newsmen, and other walk-ons. From late afternoon, when the "upstairs" characters seal themselves off from the "down-stairs" characters, until the next morning, when the library is unsealed and the three bodies are carried to the morgue (and when the book ends), Spark sees to it that her double view of the real interlocks with her double view of artistic creation.

More specifically, the servants speak consistently in terms that keep before us Spark's duality. On the one hand the servants—like us in our recounting of plots or other events—observe past, present, future distinctions. But on the other hand the servants speak not only of temporal segmenting, foregone conclusions, and inevitable consequences, but also of tenselessness, all-nowness, eternity. Even before (?) the narrative begins, these servants were making plans based on assurance that the library trio would (will?) meet on this night and be dead in the morning. Moreover, the servants have based nearly finished memoirs, journalistic accounts, and movie scripts on what seems their foreknowledge of library events and have made arrangements to deliver their story to selected reporters in the morning.

This foreknowledge inevitably raises Spark's kind of problem. Perhaps the first thing we ask of such characters is how they can possibly know what is to happen: but no sooner do we ask than we realize that Spark books urge us to ask such questions only to assure us that we're asking along the wrong track. A more rewarding track of inquiry may, however, emerge in our observing that while nearly everything foreseen by the servants does happen, the servants sometimes make mistakes or overlook details. This fact may be puzzling in view of appar-ently preternatural insight, but on the other hand it puts the servants in our own league—that is, it restores them to the realm of realistic fiction, where fore-knowledge is out of place and where characters (like us) must rely on predicting according to their experience of themselves and their fellows. The servants, we may be inclined to say, are "only human," for they can make errors, and they, like us, have a difficult time trying to communicate their own awareness of the atemporal.

What Spark is after, of course, is not a readership able to breathe easily because we're dealing with "normal" realism in spite of a few tricks. On the predictable contrary, Spark wants to keep us off balance; to make us juggle the realistic with whatever we come to call this larger reality. Indeed, the servants' difficulties in trying to balance this dual awareness account for much of the humor in this book. For instance, Clovis, the chef, who is polishing his memoirs early in the book, says, "To put is squarely . . . the eternal triangle has come full circle" (p. 29). This sentence has the wonderful ability to suggest both the inherent lunacy and the potential harmony of a three-figured merger, while it also raises the issue of tense: how can "has come" be reconciled with "is" or "comes"? Similarly, Lister refers to "vulgar chronology" (p. 49) as if one could avoid the subject and in the same spirit says, "Let us not split hairs . . . between the past, present and future tenses" (p. 4). On the other hand, however, he knows that this means not shifting to the eternal but combining temporal and eternal. Considering the sums taken by the servants as bribes, Lister remarks, for example, "Small change . . . compared with what is to come, or has already come, according as one's philosophy is temporal or eternal. To all intents and purposes they're already dead although as a matter of banal fact, the night's business has yet to accomplish itself" (p. 12). He performs the same two-step in commenting that "none of them [expected any trouble]. . . . They were not prepared for it. They have placed themselves, unfortunately, within the realm of predestination" (p. 45)—all the while he is listening to the three voices quarreling in the locked library, from which the commonsense reader would have the servants rescue them. But common sense is merely realistic, so that Lister can ignore such inquiry or expectation and can instead say, "What is to emerge must emerge" (p. 54).

Sometimes this sort of determinedly resigned attitude may annoy some readers, but sometimes, too, the time issue is likely to be found amusing—as when Lister complains that persons calling from the United States to Switzerland confuse their yesterday with ours: "They think that because they are five hours back we also are five hours back" (p. 79), an issue in this instance temporally relativistic rather than temporal-eternal. A final example will perhaps incorporate amusingly and profoundly the shape taken by Spark's time sense in *Not to Disturb*. Early in the book (it is impossible, of course, not to speak temporally—a matter of which more must be said), before the three victims arrive at the Château Klopstock, this wondrous dialogue occurs:

"Suppose the Baron wants his dinner?"
"Of course he expected his dinner," Lister says. "But as things turned out he didn't live to eat it. He'll be arriving soon."
"There might be an unexpected turn of events," says Eleanor.
"There was sure to be something unexpected," says Lister. "But what's done is about to be done and the future has come to pass. My memoirs up to the funeral are . . . more or less complete. At all events, it's out of our hands. I place the event at about three A.M. so prepare to stay awake."
"I would say six o'clock tomorrow morning. . . ." says Heloise.
"You might well be right," says Lister. "Women in your condition [pregnant] are unusually intuitive." (P. 8)

Of note in this passage are a number of things concerned with time. For one, the narrator records the doings and sayings of these characters in the present tense—ongoingly, now, in the fashion of Henry Green. Thus, to speak from the outside in, the outermost layer of narrative event impinges upon us presently, so that we are almost unobtrusively conditioned to think emphatically of what *is* (whether simply or progressively) and we are quietly conditioned away from past and future, however often causes and consequences may become issues. This method enables Spark to impress us with some sense of eternity even as her characters in many respects occupy the land of realism.

A second noteworthy feature of this passage is the serious but amusing attempts of the servants to get time straight for themselves. Thus, as we move from the narrative present into the characters' own experience of time, we find them past-present-futuring with realistic regularity like our own—and at the same time trying to fit their tense-shifting to a foresight and awareness of the inevitable that seem not ours, not realistic. Their conviction of what will happen is therefore so sure that they effect an aura of preternatural fore-knowledge which becomes only more prominent (and less realistic) when what they predict comes to pass. The future is as certain here as in *The Driver's Seat*.

Are they supposed to be gods? No, because a third point is that after all they can and do make some mistakes, and they don't exactly know when the triple killing will occur, and even their apparent leader, Lister, acknowledges that Heloise's intuition may be more reliable than whatever means the rest of them employ in order to know. Furthermore, gods would not have to estimate the time of an occurrence. These do not seem to be gods in servants' garments, then, but novelistic characters somehow instilled with most unrealistic vision. Up to a point, no doubt, we can say that these are simply servants who, like many servants, know the upstairs residents so well that it is not at all unusual for them to call some shots (so to speak) and to see some outcomes as inevitable: married couples of certain appetites and incomes and morals may (perhaps even will) almost certainly come to ends of a specifiable sort. But if we cannot think of these servants as deities, neither can we consider their psychology explainable on flat-out realistic terms. These characters are more than realistic and less than allegorically divine. Spark keeps us just where she wants us—walking the usual tightrope: by gods, nothing could be unexpected; by humans, so much could hardly be accurately expected. Moreover, in other respects the timing of these characters is eminently realistic. They know of their employers' past, they plan for their own future, they continually refer to clocks and watches in order to regulate their behavior in line with their foreknowledge, their completed scripts.

Such temporal-eternal complications would seem inevitably to raise an old theological debate; situation and psychology suggest the familiar conflict between God's foreknowledge and God's predestining. That is, the book poses the question of human choice, of free will. And in this matter, too, ambivalence prevails. Thus Lister can state both that the trio were unprepared for their trouble and that "they have placed themselves, unfortunately, within the realm of predestination" (p. 45). This multipurpose sentence, like Clovis's about squaring circular triangles, humorously struggles to embrace the ideas of freedom and nonfreedom. Lister here indicates that things happen and fortune runs its course, but he also indicates the idea of persons' placing themselves voluntarily in a position for fortune to work itself out. If, then, the Geneva setting suggests Calvinistic predestinational thoughts, it also evokes an atmosphere of neutrality or standoff, wherein seeming irreconcilables may not avoid each other. What Lister seems to be asserting is that fortune has had nothing to do (i.e., "unfortunately" here suggests "without positing fortune's intervention") with persons' bringing about their own ends. His words (I do not mean his intention) imply a usual response to those who would evoke Calvin as inevitably the last spokesman on predestination (we recall Sandy Stranger's encounter with Knox). Lister's words acknowledge Calvinistic awareness, but they likewise separate foreknowing from precausing. More importantly, the words implicitly accommodate eternal now and temporal sequence: eternally, God cannot not know what is; temporally, what is now to God was, is, will be to the rest of us. If this is kept in mind (I do not say understood), a reader can perhaps see more readily that no conflict need exist between, say, the baron's being spoken of as dead (where "dead" means more than "as good as dead") and his being spoken of in the next sentence as about to arrive at his home. Ideally, what is wanted is a means of expressing the *simultaneity* of humans' acting out choices sequentially and God's withdrawn permitting of this choosing toward what, eternally speaking, *is* (not *will be*). Language cannot, obviously, say these two thoughts as one, for the quite sufficient reason that language is a human medium and must proceed word-by-word, sentence-by-sentence, sequentially. God's "I am who am" may approximate the desired simultaneity, but even this expression is in language, human words, and must therefore work upon us from left to right or from right to left—not all-at-once. All of this means, in short, that God's knowing *how* we will choose to cooperate in achieving our own destiny is compatible with the genuineness of our freedom to choose. This basic tenet governs the present book and all Spark books, two prominent instances being *Driver's Seat* and *Hothouse*.

Lister refers again to this problem upon discovering that the servants' records (memoirs, scripts, tapes, etc.) are based on an erroneous assumption about the identity of the baron's heir. Lister says, "Fortunately [that key ambivalence again] we left room for error, and having discovered it in time [another key term], here we are. There is a vast difference between events that arise from and those that merely follow after each other. Those that arise are preferable. And Clovis amends his script" (p. 85). What Lister means is that Clovis will have an opportunity to revise his movie script (cf. the "scenarios" of *Abbess*) and to supply motives and explanations, and that the script would be implausible were such realistic causality not clear. More heavily, Lister suggests that it is better to be in charge and to cause things to happen than simply to register their happening one after another—a preference comically, ironically, or tragically evident in all Spark protagonists. No intuition, reasoning, or external source of information had apprised the servants, until now, that "him in the attic" is the rightful heir (so that Lister's "There was sure to be something unexpected" is borne out), but Lister is grateful that the opportunity remains to make what

(temporally speaking) accidentally happened to come to their attention fit
easily, unquestionably, into the eventual accounts to appear before the world. In
this way the point is once again made that these are meant to be both normal
fallible humans, like the rest of us revisers, and humans with a foreknowledge
surpassing our own as well as with a stake in minimizing mere sequentiality and
maximizing causality. The trick seems to be that of adjusting the unexpected to
look planned, understood, or taken for granted. "One foresees the unforeseen"
(p. 83), as Lister remarks, still in this accidental inevitable paradox. If, as
Eleanor speculates, "[to] say a thing is not impossible . . . isn't quite as if to say
it's possible" (p. 3), Lister brings her and us back to where we are accustomed to
live—in the realistic realm—by impatiently assuring her that they are concerned
with "facts. This is not the time for inconsequential talk" (p. 3). Always he
strives to pull matters into the region of *time* and (con)*sequence,* and to keep
away from speculation about the possible. We take his point, of course—as
January took Robinson's, and appreciate his level-headedness; but we know that
Spark demands more of our capacity for admiration.

What she requires of us in the present instance is that we take careful note of
life as art in our efforts to discern and to impose the pattern and thus the
meaning of this book. Indeed, *Not to Disturb* is not only concerned thematically
with the possibility and wonder of art; the book is more explicitly concerned to
embody or somehow to concretize the interwindings of art's origins, its processes, its realization, its being experienced as artifact. Spark is concerned to
address, by implication, such questions as: what is art? where is art? whose is art?
is art a quality of the artist? an achievement of the artist? or can it be seen as
both? In other words, she is concerned with particularizing the ways in which
artist, work, and receiver of the work are engaged.[10]

Another way to approach this complex subject of the nature and value of art is
to observe that this book is discussible as an entanglement of effects, of the
caused. Having made this seemingly obvious point, we may proceed to note
further that effects here and elsewhere range between those that may be understood as brought about by agents supposedly knowable and those brought about
by agents or agencies unknown and perhaps of no particular moment until
attention is drawn to them. In the overlapping and confusion caused when these
two categories of effect meet is Spark's inspiration.

For example, on the one hand we find a number of effects that look explainable enough. Several of the servants write accounts of what is playing itself out
in the book's time present, and these servants may be spoken of as authors of
books, scripts, tapes, etc. The servants are artists and makers, then, and they
understandably want their accounts to agree (p. 5). In the same vein, Lister
speaks of kings and popes as desiring stage props (like door knobs and parquet
flooring) for their acting out of public parts (pp. 33–34); the porter and his wife
talk about the baroness's "playing the game" vs. her choosing to "go natural" (p.
42); Lister can decide on the tone and manner to adopt for his taped account of

his past (pp. 50–55); photographs can be posed for, with an eye to making this or that illusion (pp. 61–65); events can be rehearsed and timed (pp. 66, 67, 80–81, 104). All such observations as the foregoing are meant to reinforce the hand taken by the servants in making things come out, or the awareness on the servants' part that they and others can and do stage effects; can and do make events emerge according to preconception; can and do organize chaos (p. 55).

Thus far we are talking about reason and the area within which realism functions as a convention. It is well and good to note that various persons write, tape, and film, and that such persons are what we mean by the realistic causes of certain artifacts. But to deal with intriguingly proffered murk, we have to go one step deeper into Spark's fiction.

Heloise's pregnancy may be a means of taking this next step. Nobody, not even Heloise, is certain of the fetus's father. This fact is a source of some predictable merriment and amusing speculation. The cause and the consequences of the pregnancy are, in being unknown, both demonstrative evidence of the servants' human status and occasion for the servants' working with temporally revealed facts of life. The pregnancy both imposes mystery and undercuts it, for while nobody knows who is paternally responsible for the fetus, every reader is familiar with maidservants' turning up pregnant, and everyone can admire the opportunistic use to which Lister and his crew put the pregnancy in their quick decision to attribute the deed to "him in the attic" and thereby marry Heloise and themselves into inheriting the estate.

The interest of this point lies, for me, in the wedge it drives between foreknowing and predestining, between the way things will (must) turn out and the human need to choose in order to make them turn out thus in spite of human inability to foresee all. What will be will be, but it nonetheless requires human enablers. This so-called commonsense effort to reconcile general and particular, divine and human, cosmic and individual, is obviously less tidy than a sheer Calvinistic position, but that is clearly its strength and its reason for being. The characters of *Not to Disturb* are created so as to demonstrate (secularly) both the eternal inevitability of how things are and the temporal determining, by human choice, of that same inevitability.

The effort to express this orthodox view, this untidy conviction, leaves some loose ends—in this book they are curious and amusing. Thus Lister instructs his fellows to deny entrance to the house to the two companions of Victor Passerat, since "they don't come into the story" (p. 38). He means, presumably, that these two do not have places in the versions prepared already by the servants, and that therefore these two are to be excluded from the house and the night's working-out of the inevitable—excluded as untidy or uneconomical to works of art.[11] But here the murk intrudes, for however little Lister may wish to insert these two into achieved fictions, they cannot be excluded. They are there despite his choosing, and the narrator keeps coming back to them in their repeated futile efforts to get into the house or to inquire after Passerat's welfare. Finally, the narrator mentions almost in passing that, having taken refuge from the storm under a tree on the grounds, the two are instantly and painlessly destroyed by a bolt of lightning (pp. 108, 109). To a reader, the presence of these two in Spark's book would appear unnecessary: they are shown as probable accomplices with Passerat in a blackmail attempt against the baron and the baroness, but one can readily agree with Lister that they are hardly needed, realistically speaking. Spark, however, speaks with two tongues. She doesn't need these characters for her rendering of the servants' version, but she does need them precisely because her own version of reality is larger than the servants'. Where the servants would wrap things up and organize chaos definitively, divinely, the narrator of *Not to Disturb* (which is the text larger than the servants' texts and may therefore be thought of as a kind of overtext) delivers a bigger book, a less tidily explainable book, with different ground rules (Spark's usual rules). The narrator leaves untied enough to suggest Spark's usual respect for the unknown, for mystery. No one has more respect for reason and for detection, but the obverse of this respect is her typical awareness of reason's margins. Therefore, some details get away from her characters, from her readers, from her narrators: those two walk-on characters are holes in the realistic girdle. They are intrinsic to that view of reality wherein what is left over and humanly unexplainable is eminently real. To paraphrase Lister, we must always expect the unexpected if we would empathize with Spark.

Muriel Spark would appear to have asked herself many times how to accommodate the unexpected. In the present case, she has written a hilarious episode showing the servants doing just that (pp. 83–103) in arranging for a dottily sincere minister to officiate on the spur of the moment at the nuptials of Heloise and the demented heir to the Klopstock fortune. The scene is very funny, but Spark gets more than humor out of what is after all one-sixth of this book. The episode happily pulls together what the servants can control and a suggestion of what escapes their clutches.

On the one hand, they have time to revise their book, so to speak. Thus, where they have packed and planned to depart upon the morning's discovery of the three corpses and the delivering of their own stories to various media for fat sums of money, their discovery that the heir is not the brother in Latin America but the brother in the attic causes them to bring together not only the couple in question, but themselves and the Klopstock wealth. To this extent, they can take charge of what ensues and can unpack their bags and rewrite their books. Moreover, everything about the marriage ceremony, however patched together it is in its hasty arrangements and slapdash execution, plays up its staged, if oddly ritualistic, reality (we remember the script-writing of *The Public Image* and *The Abbess of Crewe*). The cameraman is active, the bobbins of the tape recorder are in motion throughout, the traditions of music, of giving away the bride, of placing ring upon finger, of saying some kind of traditional words—all of these are made parts of the staging, not only because the Reverend is not privy to the servants' motives and must be allowed to take the marriage seriously, but because the event will have consequences for the servants' future in that it will figure as part of their revised books and even as part of the movie and tapes being prepared.

For all the opportunistic manipulating of this occasion, however, the reader is likely to have a feeling that things are probably somehow unforeseeably out of hand in ways to become apparent after the book ends (so to speak). That is, just as Passerat's two companions come to figure in the overtext where they had not at all mattered to the servants' text, so it is quite likely that the seeming neatness and convenience of this wedding will not preclude the unexpected. All the staging in the world cannot prepare one for the unexpected, and that is no less true for the servants' human limitations than for the blindness of the trio in the library. Whereas the servants know what they want and would say they know what they're doing in this marriage scheme, and although the Reverend is thoroughly ignorant of any motive save that of doing right by a pregnant woman and a potentially illegitimate child, and although the bridegroom is a lunatic unable to participate in the ceremony except as one desiring to throw himself upon any woman in the vicinity, all three of these sets of motives coincide in fulfilling the master plan, in writing the ultimate book. Such is the Spark view. Human choices are inevitable, as it were, and they also vary even though they tend to what may seem the same end. And what seems the single end—in this case matrimony—is likely to play its own part in the realization of a larger scheme of things.

As if to insist on this inscrutable element amidst rational unravelings, the book concludes with the juxtaposing of predictable and unpredictable. The novel's finale (pp. 106–21) shows us, on the one hand, that the servants' big moment has arrived. They stage the discovery of the corpses, call the police and ambulance, deliver their formal revised versions to selected newsmen, and tell the local reporters anything that comes to their minds, however little relevant to the trio supposedly in question, and preferably spicy or sentimental in nature. That is, they enact their scenario, bring their plans to fruition for the time being (a clause in itself implying the idea of the finished as the ongoing), and seemingly realize their plans to retire from service and to become even wealthier than they had assumed possible a few hours earlier.

But the partial nature of the servants' accomplishment and the fog in which that accomplishment is immersed, despite its discernibly clear reality, are beautifully implicit in the Brazilian servants' telephonic information that their own master, Count Rudolph Klopstock, cannot be told of the Swiss trio's deaths at the moment because the servants have been given strict orders not to disturb him while he is locked in his study with some friends (pp. 117–18). For me this piece of information sets the whole book to rights and clarifies the author's conviction of the unclarifiable. I think the moment means not so much that history repeats itself as that the ultimate book gets worked out variously or even almost identically, regardless of time and place and—more crucially—regardless of illusions that you or I, we or they, may be in charge. Temporally speaking, the trio in Switzerland doubtless made choices that constituted a life and brought them to their end; their servants also made choices and emerge from the book in a sense winners by virtue of those choices. The count and his friends in Brazil, and perhaps his servants as well, are likewise no doubt choosers, being human. But the juxtaposing of humanly planned outcome and thoroughly unforeseen event (their striking similarity is perhaps not crucial) imposes Spark's familiar view that anyone is idiotic to suppose he has foolproof outcomes figured out, and that profounder idiocy lies in supposing that since we cannot make sure plans, no sure plans can be. Lister's final assurance, "We've made our plans" (p. 119), is both a reminder of his freedom and a parting tip to the reader that plans are devised to impose one's will *and* to accomplish what will be (is) in any event.

The difficulty of expressing this artistic problem sometimes produces amusement. Spark's younger characters—Heloise, Pablo, and Hadrian—speak, for instance a brand of colloquialism that primarily marks them as Anglo-American (whatever their names may suggest) and that also signals their youth. But such terminology has the additional value of drawing attention to Spark's tightrope act.[12] Where Clovis will ask, in British idiom, "What's her trend?" (p. 66), Hadrian will remark a bit more to the present point, "There's such a thing as a trend" (pp. 68, 69). In this way even the throwaway conversation turns out to fit the problem of adjusting choices to a fixed plan. But the dominant instance of colloquially valuable language occurs in relaxed conversation among the three young people; more precisely, in their efforts to express approval or disapproval of some of their acquaintances upstairs and downstairs. Whether the expression in a given case is positive or negative, it is always an attempt to convey an idea of putting together. "I don't relate?" Heloise inquires indignantly of Hadrian (p. 68). Whatever Passerat's character, "it didn't correspond" (p. 69); "he didn't coordinate" (p. 70). Mr. Samuel, the photographer, on the other hand, is all right: "His perspectives coalesce" (p. 71). Lister is best at whatever these three are working to express, for Lister "can adjust whatever it is"; he "never disparates, he symmetrises." He's "got equibalance . . . and what's more, he pertains" (p. 73). In slightly different contexts, but still in an effort to combine various qualities colloquially, Pablo remarks that some "types" "don't connect" (p. 82), and Heloise says that "him in the attic" "doesn't cognate" (p. 85). Again, "Mr. Samuel energises" and the tapes and films of the wedding must "compass" (p. 87). Finally, the lunatic Klopstock "doesn't level, you can't really construe with him" (p. 95). All of this misusage seems very funny to me, as well as very clear in spite of its basic illiterate premises, but we cannot afford to patronize it: such language is closer to an adequate expression of complex merging of two levels than is anything else we might more literately devise; or, even if we should prefer different language on grounds of its familiarity and broader acceptability, we should be pressed hard, I believe, to convince ourselves of such language's superiority in pulling together the Spark levels or realms—for the problem is in the expression of simultaneity, and for this we seem to have no words.

This book, as I have said, is rooted in the need to try for adequate expression in various media and is intensely tied up with large questions about the nature of art. Whether we are noting Heloise's fear that "him in the attic" "might create or take one of his turns" (p. 8) or are observing Lister's comment that the same character "is full of style this evening" (p. 20) or are registering the experience of the servants in making home movies (pp. 71–72) that will assist them when they contract to play their own script professionally for Hollywood, we can hardly miss the concentration on artistic expression, on making. To revert to earlier questions raised in this chapter, we are compelled, I think, to challenge certain assumptions about the relations among artist, work, and audience; compelled to question our likely assumptions that while these three are temporally, consecutively, complexly conjoined, still their conjunction is a segmental sequence. Moreover, we may be inclined to regard the three steps as being eventually completed, and thus to way that after working hard we've got him or her (the artist) or we've got it (the work). In this way we assume a process moving from giver to receiver, a process completed (like a forward pass) when the thrown is caught. By giving some attention to prevalent aesthetic assumptions we can, I think, discover Spark's implicit attitudes to them, and we can thereby learn much about her imagination and the quality of her books.

To begin with, it seems obvious that Spark thinks of art not as the work completed, the artifact, but as an attribute in the mind of the perpetrator. In thinking this way she is of course in line with Aristotle: art is a virtue that inheres in the artist. Moreover, the virtue may inhere not only before the artifact is produced and while it is in progress, but after the work is completed. Nor, since a gap exists between the artist's conception and the work, is there anything to prevent the artist's idea of the work from changing once the achievement is approximated as artifact. Since criticism is directed to the artifact, and since the artifact is not to be confused with the producer's idea (originally or subsequently), and since the artifact cannot in any event *be* its producer's idea, one must not suppose that what the artist may say is bound to be a clue to an understanding of the work. Artistic intention should be sought for whatever it may provide, but intention imposes no obligation on the work to conform to it and no necessary limits on the reader's or viewer's imaginative capacities. Consulting the author's intention may be useful in an effort to write that author's biography, but a biography is not literary criticism.

Does the inevitable inability to check one's understanding against some idea matching of artist's mind and work leave one stuck with solipsism? Some, notably the practitioners and theorists of the *nouveau roman*, would seem to think so. Spark's works lead me to infer that she thinks not. Like any old-fashioned nonsolipsist, Spark shows in her books that one can use a work as a kind of guide or sighting device without taking that work for the artist's mind.

That is, works are clues to what she takes it on faith must be there, although she would seem reconciled to the fact that the work-clue will never uncover or fully account for what must be there. Another way of saying this is to posit that she would continue to inquire into the causes of real effects called works—and that the works are her means of inducing others to engage in their own inquiring. She has not given up on the fascinating practice of trying to grasp as much as one can in the way of clues to artistic causes, whereas the solipsist would seem to have concluded that, since the causes are ultimately unknowable and thus may as well not be, the only interesting intellectual endeavor amidst cosmic blank is that of spinning one's own reality. A solipsist is an interior monologist; Spark's faith can adopt any point of view, including the third-person omniscient.

Art, for Spark, is inherent in the artist since something has to be understood as having caused the artifact; or, to turn things around, the work serves the purpose of reminding us that something capable of performing this feat must have figured in the artist's reality. The clue-value of the work lies in its kinship with whatever inspired it (to use a term as good as another). But if art is a quality of the artist causing him or her to produce an artifact, and if the receiver's achieved understanding of that artifact is not equivalent to an identification with the artist's mind, what does the artist in fact communicate and what is the value of receiving (reading, viewing, hearing, touching, criticizing)? Granted that we do not have to accept solipsistic isolation and separation, what indeed does the work provide? Spark's books, and surely *Not to Disturb* in particular, without in the least dodging the fear and despair potential in one's having to read the world on one's own, nearly always make the receiving enjoyable and fulfilling because implicitly no work can avoid lighting up in some way the all-embracing reality posited by Spark's work—the reality that because it must be there to account for effects, she uses as foundation. In other words, by her works we obviously get to know her imagination's unique quality, and, in the same way and for the same reason, the value of any work is in the clue that it offers to its author's view of what is real—no matter that reality itself is irrecoverable.

Perhaps a shortcut to this conclusion is merely to say that critical readers, as they indirectly derive some notion of another's reality, are caused to become artists: art is inherent in them as they make for themselves a reality rooted in reaction to their reading of the work. Where is art, then? Art is in the maker of artifacts; and the maker is first the originating artist and second the receiving critic. Communication does happen, then, and my experience of Spark is of an imagination that posits a middle position between solipsistic mono-mind and the inaccurate if common idea that the artist communicates in some one-to-one fashion by means of giving us the work. Spark's way is slipperier than either of those, I believe, precisely because it tries to accommodate both of them as well as her own conviction—faith—that overall meaning exists.

I call Spark's books slippery in a most complimentary sense: I admire her extremely economical efforts to suggest what could hardly be a vaster view. In discussing *Not to Disturb*, for instance, I find it impossible not to think linearly and sequentially on some occasions, but I find it essential to think syn-chronically, organically, ubiquitously on others. Sometimes the classic manner is needed, sometimes the romantic. The main point after all is that Spark tries to give credit to all that goes to make up her view of the real. If, then, in the further discussion of *Not to Disturb* I should mix metaphors, the chances are that I will be aware of doing so—for figurative language will be needed and mixed figures may well be the only way to approach Spark's cross-purposed harmony.

Diachronically speaking, then, whether one thinks of a linear progression, or of Chinese boxes, or of a set of concentric spheres, cause-effect relations may be figured somewhat as follows—supposing that we move from smaller to larger on a line, or from inside to outside among boxes and circles. The servants' dry-run acting on film, their making of tapes and scripts and memoirs, their accounts offered to newspapers and television cameras—all of these are artifacts, and they are caused by approximations of human behavior that are based upon the servants' experience and intuition. Similarly, the effects discovered in the library would appear to bear out the extent and accuracy of the servants' predictions and would imply that a love triangle was the immediate cause of this bloody effect. At the next level, stage, or ring, we note that the servants themselves are effects—that is, they, not only their employers, are seen as effects within a scheme larger than their own scripts: the servants are fictional characters whose behavior must also be carefully, plausibly, rendered on the realistic level. And indeed, like their masters, they do perform according to type or stereotype, and we consequently derive that familiar sort of pleasure rooted in a combination of expectation and surprise. Still, however, there is something left over; some usual Spark sign that characters sometimes tend to escape the author's control and to become leaders rather than followers. For example, just as Lister and his friends have to adjust to the new knowledge of the rightful heir, so the reader has to adjust to what seems the useless presence of Passerat's two inadmissible compan-ions and to the seemingly functionless ominous dreams of the porter's wife. This awareness of the seemingly pointless draws attention to precisely those limits of realism which are Spark's trademark: planning and plausibility must coexist with the realistically implausible but no less real.

The novel itself, then, is another effect, another artifact, and its causes are not altogether traceable from its status as work. From here we can move from the fact of the book to the fact of the narrator as causer of the book but also as effect caused by the author. The persona called narrator tells a story in several respects unexplained, untidy. Next, we move to the author who made the choices (up to a point) to create this sort of limited (if illusorily omniscient) narrator, but which author has effected an illusion of mystery. Thereafter we move to the reader—or, rather, to any one reader—who, presented with an artifact that couples the realistic and the rest somewhat inconveniently if most neatly, must draw upon his or her own artistic capacity to make meaning of the whole series of cause-effect ties. For the reader, too, I contend, a (I do not say *the*) right reading will compel the making of a meaning with holes in it to accommodate the extras, the other rings and stages and boxes.

Finally, in this diachronic schema, after the fiction-making efforts of the reader-as-artist, we come to the place where a kind of ultimate or fundamental leap of faith must occur—a place of aesthetic and moral showdown, perhaps religious or theological, but certainly psychological. This is that place where Barthes and Robbe-Grillet see only empty nonexplanation, only the absence of any cause for all the cause-effect links mentioned thus far, and where these writers therefore pronounce the cosmos absurd and settle for the limitedly controllable, universally meaningless, lesser connections we have been describing. But this is also the place where Spark seems (at least to me as one maker of her made books) to find possible and necessary the traditional leap of faith, of belief in a cause beyond the individual reader to account for the artifact that is the reader's meaning. For reasons that can hardly be gone into, then, for faith is not reason, one kind of maker pushes a reader to make a book-world which posits that meaning stops at the outposts of human reason, while another kind of maker encourages us, by way of her artifact, to wonder seriously about what causes the effects that are ourselves in our causing of artifacts' meaning. That is, one kind of mind posits process, some modest attempt at cause-effect explanation, but ultimate and definitive discontinuity, while the other kind of mind is convinced of process, to be sure, but process wherein beginning circles back to fit into and become one with end, regardless of human reason's inability to comprehend such a state of affairs. One mind gives up on causal explanation, pushes for making happen what we punily can, starts from the premise that further speculation is futile and assured to lead to pain. The other mind goes about fictionizing its own awareness that reason is right to demand causes proportionate to effects, that causality prevails universally, and that human participation in the causal chain merely intensifies and deepens mystery. The first type despairs of the causal chase and is impatient with mystery; the second type sees no grounds for supposing that what is must be humanly reasonable before it can exist. One mind will not seek causes; the other mind cannot allow the inaccessibility of causes to shut out reason's insistence that they nonetheless must be.

If we change to a synchronic way of thinking, this whole process is even more mysterious and difficult to express. Synchronically, we have to think of the segmented line as circled back into itself and as flowing without beginning or end, and we have to conceive of the boxes and the circles, too, as porous and interconnected more than separated. The metaphorical difficulty is moreover made impossible to control when we note that these figures, however strenuously we try to make them serve as symbols of all-inclusiveness, still imply what is outside of any such metaphorical expression of reality; what must be outside in order to cause things to be, whether diachronically or synchronically. Theologically, what's wrong with pantheism is its supposing that what makes things to be is organically one with those things: nothing thus distinguishes ultimately between source and product, creator and creature. Psychologically and aesthetically the trouble would seem to be the same: we have to seek beyond the thing made for a fuller understanding of its cause. Spark's orthodox Christian psychology regularly presents us with antipantheistic situations; situations that manifestly share in being by virtue of their having been created by an author and by ourselves, but which implicitly take directions of their own, apart from the choices of the author or the expectations of us reader-makers. We cannot get handles on these situations, and we may therefore see them as caused by accident, until we reflect that accident is merely the name we assign to what our limitations do not extend to. Once again, in this manner, we arrive at the place where absurdists take one path, Spark another: "accident" means nothing but a combination of untraceable meaning and nonmeaning to the absurdist, while to Spark "accident" is merely a stopgap label pinned on what reason cannot explain but what faith insists must have a causal identity when understood from its own authorial overview.

All of this abstract discussion of cause-effect relationships is borne out by what may otherwise seem the odd behavior of the servants at times. Of course their discussion is limited, since their perspective is humanly limited; still, they occasionally drop suggestions of the long view that evoke Spark's familiar attitudes. Lister is usually the spokesman on this subject as on others. Not only does he quote the predictable "Sic transit gloria mundi" (p. 18) and some *carpe diem* lines from Marvell's "To His Coy Mistress" (pp. 77–78), but he repeats Ophelia's "Good night, sweet, sweet, ladies" (p. 13), and, getting closer to our point, cites Webster's lines from *The Duchess of Malfi:* "Their life," he says, "a general mist of error. Their death, a hideous storm of terror" (p. 3). This suggests that Lister's sensitivity shows up in his feeling the universality of this night's events. Thus he informs Heloise, without explanation, that the identity of the Klopstocks' guest in the library is irrelevant: "It might be anybody" (p. 62). Again, "Sex is not to be mentioned. . . . To do so would be to belittle their activities. On their sphere sex is nothing but an overdose of life. They will die of it, or rather, to all intents and purposes, have died. We treat of spontaneous combustion. One remove from sex, as in Henry James" (p. 14). These words evoke reflections on *Memento Mori* and *The Takeover.* They are also Lister's effort to see his employers at a distance, and this effort fits what we have been saying about the extension, the depth, the interinvolvement of causal relationships. Apart from his own clear temporal motives, then, Lister tries to adopt a sort of removed, Old Testament dignity in his considering of the Klopstocks' case: "What were they doing anyway, amongst us, on the crust of this tender earth?" (p. 36). Or, still in prophetic vein, he responds to Eleanor's comment that "they [in the library] couldn't have been all bad": "Oh, I agree. They did wrong well. And they were good for a purpose so long as they lasted. . . . As paper cups are suitable for occasions, you use them and throw them away" (p. 37). In several ways, then, Lister supports the idea that whatever one may be planning, bigger plans are in control of somehow inevitable outcomes: there are spheres and uses beyond, although cooperating with, our own. As Hadrian observes, "There's such a thing as a trend" (pp. 68, 69); and included in Spark's trend-making, as a means of evoking a moral stance, are some echoes of others' works (as we have seen).

One prominent author drawn upon indirectly is T. S. Eliot, as in this exchange between Theo, the porter, and his wife, Clara. "What's wrong with the relief men tonight?" Clara says. "Where's Conrad, where's Bernard, where's Jean-Albert, where's Stephen? Why don't they send Pablo, what's he doing with them up there at the house? My sleep is terrible, how can I sleep?" To this her husband responds, "I'm a simple man . . . and your dreams give me the jitters, but setting all that aside I smell a crisis" (p. 42). For me this exchange triggers recollections of *The Waste Land*, part 2, and of the Tallulah Bankhead-like neurotic woman whose "nerves are bad tonight" and who therefore pleads with her man to "stay with me." The same poet comes to mind when we read Spark's rendering of the interviews given by the servants to the local press. What is given us is a series of disconnected snippets collected from among the assorted servants, so that we feel the fragmentariness of human attempts to account for what in fact happened—in addition to appreciating the servants' deliberate efforts, of course, to rattle on to no point except that of filling the reporters' notebooks and getting these people out of the house. After these unintelligible "reports" (pp. 114–18), another local nobleman calls on the servants and announces, "The neighbours have been parked out on the road all morning. They didn't have the courage to come. Admiral Meleager, the Baronne de Ventadour, Mrs. Dix Silver, Emil de Vega, and all the rest" (p. 119). This string of names could well suggest Pope, Sheridan, Waugh, or any satirist, to be sure. However, coming as it does after the fragments of reportage, it more especially puts me in mind of Eliot's satirical names in *The Waste Land* and elsewhere.

Such an accumulation of literary allusions (of a particular kind), efforts to take the long view, dropping of nuggets—what all this suggests is the rightness of seeing another of Lister's seemingly throwaway thoughts as most central to Spark's book and her moral imagination. Lister, who would appear to have no special right to the sentiment and no particular reason to utter it, remarks, "How like . . . the death wish is to the life-urge! How urgently does an overwhelming obsession with life lead to suicide! Really, it's best to be half-awake and half-aware. That is the happiest stage" (p. 14). Like the other sobering thoughts expressed, and like the works wherein some of these thoughts originate, this wisdom carries the experience of the human race as that experience is re-collected in tranquility. Here would seem to be unqualifiedly accurate observation and good advice, sober to the point of platitudinous ho-hummery—a bit like Mr. Samuel's impotently firm advice to Passerat's companions: "You should always . . . avoid terrible places" (p. 106). Who would question the idea that extremes may be understood as the same thing from varying viewpoints, or that the middle way by definition avoids extremes—apart from the meaning of happiness and the desirability of half-conditions? The answer, it seems clear to me, is that Muriel Spark's books are her own probing of this truism (as in Sandy's conversion, Barbara's risk-taking, Nicholas's disillusionment, Lise's death wish, Annabel's acquisition of a looking glass).

Muriel Spark suggests the same attitude toward Lister's truism that we would expect her to take toward any reduction of reality's abundance. She shows us that obviously the truism wouldn't have attracted so much notice in human affairs had it not proven commendable after the fact for so long. But she also shows us that the facts of living range from the possibilities of comedy to those of tragedy, and that these possibilities are not to be thought of as intellectual or abstract, as we live, but as complexly emotional, obscurely motivated or multimotivated, variously deliberated or spontaneous, and otherwise beyond the reach of any platitude's extension. Her books show us in fact that what underlies her artistic enterprise is precisely (or imprecisely) the fascinating clash or harmony or in any case vicissitude effected by the encounter between received abstract wisdom such as Aristotle's and the minute-by-minute making of one's life. Aristotle is concerned with stating an idea of the *via media* so all-inclusively general that we will necessarily honor its accuracy for all people everywhere at all times. But just as obviously, one's temporal existence is not limited to honoring or even to implementing any ideal. What this in turn tells me as I read Spark is that she makes a career out of embodying this balancing act between what her mind or her common sense tells her and what it's like to live despite this capable intelligence. More particularly, this novel gives us—in what the characters construct, in what the narrator tells us, and in the book that is both of these, for our greater fiction-making pleasure—lots of paradoxes and ambivalences, among the most nearly central of which is this manifold expression of terrible or funny or puzzling or bemused interoperating general idea and particular experience.

Every author no doubt pits universal against particular in some way; but Spark's difference seems to lie in her implication that reality requires making it most plain that ultimate authorial resolution is hardly possible. Books must and do end; situations may be said in some sense to come out or to be resolved; but it is the realists on one side and the absurdists on the other—and not Muriel Spark—who would convey the illusion that such tidying up is consistent with what is—consistent, that is, with what we can imagine or suppose to be. Rather than start from nothing or build on nothing, Spark gives up on nothing (in two senses) and makes artifacts out of her need to take on and honor all the somethings, unintelligible as some of these may be. She does indeed occupy a middle ground, then, and is assuredly of moderate or conservative disposition in her honoring of traditional Western psychology and morality; but in no sense may her traditionalism be flattened out and adequately suggested by any platitude. On the contrary, Spark's complexity is in her disciplined ordering of her work to meet the world where it sees itself—which requires stretching her imagination to cover many views not her own—and to pit such other attitudes against her own. I do not suggest that she is engaged in a sort of moral gymnastics match in writing her books, but implicitly she indicates that the fact of hers being decidedly a minority view is all the more reason for testing it regularly. She means, I think, that others' views must be faced and sounded, and that one's own view is only as strong and valid as what emerges from one's serious effort not to beat down or ignore others' visions, but to accommodate these within what one regards as reality. Thus, if her books—like *Not to Disturb*—sometimes create the illusion of open-endedness (and I think they do), the reason for this is not Robbe-Grillet's (the premise of ultimate nonmeaning) but is instead her implied belief that universal meaning has to be, whether knowable or not. [13]

Not to Disturb, then, like Spark's other books especially concerned with aesthetics, is a work for a reader-critic to make by virtue of its implied faith in the reconcilability of opposites that seem contradictory: varying particulars and overall pattern. We are presented with standardized symptoms of mystery and ominous intrigue (banging shutters, remote setting, thunder and lightning, lunatic in the attic, suddenly discovered lineage, exotic residents, plotting servants, sexual luridness) and with (supposing a norm) *Waste Land*-ish deviations from regularity: curious foreknowledge, frightening dreams and prophecies, heavy blackmailing, directionless sexual experimentation, rootlessness of any apparent motive save colossal self-interest, strong implication that all of these signs are everywhere prevalent rather than confined to a particular context. But we are conversely presented with a noncommittal air not necessarily designed to promote comfort, whereby Spark implies the overview suggested by her title and by the Psalms, which admonish us to trust in God and to be not disturbed. It is as if what happens narratively and what the servants and other characters do and say were the particulars, while what is understood to be going on in the library were a microcosm of the inevitable: neither causable by the servants who seem to be causing things nor preventable by the servants. The goings-on in the library (about which we know because the servants report sounds occasionally and because the bodies are eventually hauled away—"Klopstock and barrel," as Lister remarks [p. 113]) microcosmically demonstrate the truth that what will be will be—that it is not disturbable; while all the rest of the book (what we might be tempted to call the realistic book) demonstrates choice-making and change-making and self-directing. Spark's point is, then, that the two realms are perfectly compatible and that the compatibility is demonstrably mysterious, not less so for its appearing low-keyed and usual. Spark's art is in her insistence upon the simultaneity of realistic choosing for change and mysteriously chosen changelessness. The fictions we make of her artifacts abide in our happy or uneasy or terrified awareness of such precarious balance.

To round out this study and particularly to conclude the present chapter on the oneness of art and life, I am delighted to have available for discussion Muriel Spark's *Loitering with Intent* (1981).[14] Except for *Robinson,* this is Spark's only first-person novel. It takes the form of the autobiography of Fleur Talbot, it is narrated about 1980, and it focuses on "the months between the autumn of 1949 and the summer of 1950" (p. 196), that period of gestation during which Fleur grew from aspiring if nearly destitute poet to successful novelist. This autobiography-as-novel doubtless bears some resemblance to the facts of Spark's own life. Interestingly, it also echoes events in the career of Caroline Rose, protagonist of Spark's first novel, *The Comforters.* Indeed, we might say that a Rose by a somewhat different name is Fleur. *Loitering* also evokes recollections of characters and occurrences in other Spark fictions, among these *The Ballad of Peckham Rye, The Bachelors, Memento Mori, The Driver's Seat, The Takeover,* and *Not to Disturb.* Fleur speaks as Caroline thought and as Spark has appeared to think throughout her career (and in the present study). Fleur speaks for all three women writers when she says of the persons in those nine months of her life that "they were morally outside of myself, they were objectified. I would write about them one day. In fact, under one form or another, whether I have liked it or not, I have written about them ever since, the straws from which I have made my bricks" (p. 196).

Readers of Spark will not be surprised to find a number of her favorite themes and motifs on display here. Blackmail figures heavily in the plot that is Fleur's life and Spark's story, and the blackmailing is wed to drug-induced manipulation and cultism. Catholicism also matters here, although Fleur's religion is much less pronounced than Caroline's. Both women embrace the faith rather than the faithful. Where Caroline had Mrs. Hogg to endure, Fleur's noisome coreligionist is Dottie Carpenter: "Years later when she made dramatic announcements that she had lost her faith I was rather relieved since I had always uneasily felt that if her faith was true then mine was false" (p. 64). Privacy is, as usual, a concern; the protagonist here is immediately and rightly suspicious when the blackmailing Sir Quentin Oliver pleads for "complete frankness." Another familiar note is Fleur's love for language traits, for idiom. She takes note of such expressions as "perfectly all right," "He thinks I'm ga-ga," "fluxive precipitations" (for incontinence), "It is with some trepidation that I take up my pen," "There are some universal phenomena about which it is not for us mortals to enquire," "the board's asunder" (the switchboard is under repair), "Fuck the general reader," "Dear Fleur (if I may)." As she says, "My ears have a good memory. . . . the aural images first and the visual second" (p. 19). We also note the reality of a world at once elsewhere and here: "When people say that nothing happens in their lives I believe them. But you must understand that everything happens to an artist; time is always redeemed, nothing is lost and wonders never cease" (p. 116). Small wonder, then, that the book opens with Fleur's sitting on a grave-stone in Kensington, trying to create a poem. We are reminded of the collapsing-ascending image with which *Girls of Slender Means* begins. Spark's—and Fleur's—very title takes a common police-docket charge and puns it into new meaning to convey the wonder and joy of making. She may be living a dying, but all the while she is striving to make new art-life. As *Girls* focuses on the few months between V-E Day and V-J Day but implies timelessness, so *Loitering* concentrates on these nine months "right in the middle of the twentieth century" (p. 197), even as it implies the unity of spirit and matter (pp. 94–96), of time and eternity (pp. 215, 217).

While *Loitering* features so many of Spark's traits, however, it is primarily taken up with how living, autobiographical writing, and the novel contribute to the making of one another. And this involvement suggests in turn the melding of times past, present, future. These are the overlappings and blendings—as in *Comforters*, *Public Image*, and *Not to Disturb*—that lead me to speak summarily of Spark's union of life and art. Fleur recalls having said to herself in 1949, "How wonderful it feels to be an artist and a woman in the twentieth century" (p. 26), and the thought recurs on several occasions. While her book records anger, fear, disgust, worry, it principally carries the note of conviction that she is and will remain an artist. This conviction and her pleasure in alertness to everything around her and within her are the main reasons that this work is so joyful—in contrast to the rest of Spark's later books. *Loitering* is like Caroline Rose's hypothetically remembering herself as she was twenty-five or thirty years earlier, and remembering for herself and us that she is still moved by the same love of living and making that drove her then. And we observe that the same is true of Spark, whatever the leaden tint may suggest to the contrary.

In time present, then, Fleur Talbot sets about writing her autobiography. Her models and inspirations in this genre are John Henry Newman and Benvenuto Cellini, Newman for his foot-on-the-ground insight into spirit, and Cellini for his concrete reflections on making. Played off against these ideals and ideal writers, in 1949, is Sir Quentin Oliver, founder of the Autobiographical Asso-ciation. Sir Quentin induces the members of his cult to write their lives "frankly." Fleur, his secretary, then alters some of the details in order to enliven what she sees to be ill-written and tediously image-serving versions of the truth. The initial writers in some cases balk at Fleur's additions, in other cases accept what Fleur has written as more interesting, and in yet other instances credit the alterations to prophetic or magical insight on Fleur's part. Fleur suspects that the befuddled writers may sometimes come to believe what never happened at all, just because it makes them look less drab. In any case, Fleur's intention has been harmless—that of an editor or of an author in search of some telling details. What Fleur suspects and then discovers to be true is that Sir Quentin subse-quently builds on her versions with an eye to creating eventually "lives" for his members that will enable him to blackmail them. In other words, we are back again to the distinctions made in *Robinson* among facts, innocent plausible conjecture, and malicious plausible conjecture.

This temporal and generic entanglement requires clarification. To be more precise, in 1949 Fleur had begun a novel entitled *Warrender Chase*. She then took the job with Sir Quentin, met the members of his group, read and touched up their early attempts at autobiography, and continued writing her novel. She comes to find that the characters and events in her fiction bear remarkable resemblance to some persons and events in those autobiographies, and she also finds that some of the similar passages in the novel were written before, and some after, her involvement with the cult and its writings. Sir Quentin, fearing that Fleur's novel is built on his group's autobiographies and that her novel will expose him and beat him out of his blackmailing plans, steals Fleur's manuscript, blocks publication, and destroys the publisher's proofs. She then steals his files on the members of the cult and reads enough of them to see that he has used her proofs to embellish those lives for his own purposes. Fleur then recovers her stolen typescript by stealth. Sir Quentin in turn steals back his files. The files are eventually destroyed, Fleur's novel is published as the first in her now (1980) extensive career, and she is left in time present to meditate autobiographically on what she has learned from this personal and generic struggle. What she has learned about the art-life mix is the essence of her autobiography, which is Spark's novel.

Predictably, the lessons embrace what the writer can control and what she cannot control. The tightest discipline has its limits, and reality continues to exert its influence beyond realism. Scattered throughout *Loitering* is frightening and funny evidence that one's experience becomes the stuff of one's fictions, of course, but that one's fictions will then reverse the process and keep the fact-fiction cycle unbroken. Whether one speaks in metaphors as I tried to do in analyzing *Not to Disturb*, or whether one tries for abstract exposition, the problem is that of expressing the mystery that somehow keeps experience and the manifestation of experience feeding each other. This mystery is accepted as such by Fleur and by Spark. Sometimes it brings grief—as in Lise's case—and sometimes it brings great joy—as in Fleur's career-launching and in her delighted relations with Solly Mendelsohn and Sir Quentin's aged mother, Lady Edwina. What appears to seal the study laid out to this point, and especially to support the art-life merger discussed in the present chapter, is the attitude that Fleur adopts toward her careful art and toward that which will inevitably surprise her best-laid plans. It is in this attitude that Fleur would appear closest to her own creator.

Fleur states that three vices are to be avoided in writing autobiography, and Spark's works make it clear that she thinks they are to be avoided in fictions as well. "One of them was nostalgia, another was paranoia, a third was a transparent craving . . . to appear likeable" (p. 31). The same attitude shows up in

Fleur's deliberate effort to remain seemingly detached. Of her *Warrender Chase*, for instance, she says, "I knew I wasn't helping the reader to know whose side . . . to be on. I simply felt compelled to go on with my story without indicating what the reader should think" (p. 73). Or again, "I wasn't writing poetry and prose so that the reader would think me a nice person, but in order that my sets of words should convey ideas of truth and wonder, as indeed they did to myself as I was composing them. I see no reason to keep silent about my enjoyment of the sound of my own voice as I work" (pp. 80–81). This statement appears to corroborate my contention in discussing *The Only Problem* that intellectual involvement breeds its own kind of emotional intensity. On the same lines, we note Fleur's comment that "I never described, in my book, what Warrender's motives were. I simply showed the effect of his words, his hints. . . . I didn't go in for motives, I never have" (pp. 82–83). Unlike Sir Quentin, Fleur is convinced "that complete frankness is not a quality that favours art" (p. 104). Unlike the critic (poor plodder), Fleur, like Spark, lays down a myth (pp. 139, 149) and then narrates her story, her plot, according to her experience, her intelligence, her voices, her sense of rhythm, and that instinct for which there is no accounting. In this course she is not surprised that sometimes her writing reflects what has happened outside her books and sometimes predicts what subsequently happens outside them. For as we have seen in book after book, the notion of inside and outside is a realistic one; it is precluded ultimately by Spark's all-encompassing view of the real.

That I have written here as though Spark and Fleur were interchangeable is inevitable, and decidedly intentional. *Loitering* is the autobiography of a writer and it implicitly and explicitly addresses those who would have this writer behave otherwise.[15] Spark is detached, but is no antinovelist. Spark is moved by concern for humans but requires us to uncover and share that concern for ourselves. She offers us, with economic generosity, one opportunity after another to share in the life that is her art. Fleur cites on several occasions (once in Cellini) words we find as well in *Pilgrim's Progress*, but first in Acts 8:39, after Philip baptizes the eunuch: "And when they were come up out of the water, the Spirit of the Lord caught away Philip, and the eunuch saw him no more: and he went on his way rejoicing." That final clause, recurring seven times in the book, admirably conveys the solitariness of the artist as well as the profound joy—in spite of everything leaden—in taking and making, perceiving and creating, reality.[16]

Notes

CHAPTER I. TRICK OR TRUTH? REALITY IN *ROBINSON*

1. I am aware that I touch here upon a controversial issue. One school of thinking holds or at least strongly suggests that the very existence (the reality) of an idea depends upon its being expressed. My own view, which I presume to call romantic, is that expression is not an implicit part of the definition of idea; that ideas and their expressions are distinct in nature and that expression at best dimly approximates the idea that gives rise to it.

2. This point may be clearer if we note two critical tendencies. Several critics, on the one hand, make limited comparisons between Muriel Spark and Jane Austen. Derek Stanford, "The Work of Muriel Spark: An Essay on Her Fictional Method," *The Month* 28 (August 1962): 92–99, notes that both writers are social commentators, both satirists, and both moralists of delicate touch. Charles Alva Hoyt, "Muriel Spark: The Surrealist Jane Austen," in *Contemporary British Novelists*, ed. Charles Shapiro (Carbondale and Edwardsville, 1965), pp. 125–43, comments that Spark "is ever the reasonable recorder of unreason: she is the Jane Austen of the surrealists." "The meticulous ironic intelligence of the Augustan observer presides over a world which has proceeded one step beyond reality [sic]." And Bernard Harrison, "Muriel Spark and Jane Austen," in *The Modern English Novel: The Reader, the Writer, and the Work*, ed. Gabriel Josipovici (London, 1976), pp. 225–51, superbly illustrates how Spark's similarities to Austen merely stress how different the two writers are, and how different their two worlds and world views are. These three critics all use the two authors for purposes of analogy, and all three stop to note contrasts without assuming that one or the other writer must be deemed better for doing things in a particular way.

On the other hand, and quite typically among Spark critics, we find those who acknowledge some good qualities in Spark's work, but who finally reject total acceptance of her writing because that writing is not what they would have it be. For example, V. M. K. Kelleher, "The Religious Artistry of Muriel Spark," *Critical Review* (Melbourne) 18 (1976): 79–92, is a fine reader of several novels, including *The Prime of Miss Jean Brodie, The Ballad of Peckham Rye,* and (especially) *The Girls of Slender Means,* but finally says that Spark would be a bigger, better writer if she were to confront specific temporal issues, problems, solutions. Kelleher clearly not only prefers realism but thinks it inherently superior to what Spark offers us. Again, Richard Mayne, "Fiery Particle: On Muriel Spark," *Encounter* 25 (December 1965): 61–68, likes Spark's wit and eccentric economy, but he is suspicious and quite resentful of her Catholicism. Unaccountably, he assumes that liking Spark's work enthusiastically will mean consenting to her religious beliefs. Moreover, he resents her "cocksure narrator, telling us what's funny and what only makes people laugh." This seems to mean that Mayne likes Spark so long as she stays within secular humanistic bounds, realistic limits. Finally, among these critics who know what they like, we may note Patrick Swinden, *Unofficial Selves: Character in the Novel*

177

from Dickens to the Present Day (London, 1973), pp. 221–30, 231, 256. Swinden professes to admire Spark's plots and shifting points of view, but, like Mayne, will not accept Spark on her own terms. "Mrs. Spark . . . does not appear to be much concerned with the moral life [*sic*]. Her Catholic beliefs, and the relationship with her fictions they have allowed her to create, have encouraged her to detach herself from the messy, unfinished and inelegant surface of a word [world?] without a destiny." Perhaps Mayne's, Kelleher's, and Swinden's problem (and it *is* theirs, not Spark's) is best summed up in these two sentences of Swinden's: "Pattern and reality are distinct. Reality, in fact, has no plot—unless, like Muriel Spark, the novelist can produce a God to supply one." These words may suggest something of the audience problem faced by Muriel Spark, and they certainly indicate the need in this chapter to distinguish between realism (Swinden's) and reality (Spark's).

3. It may be advisable at this point to place the ensuing comparison in the context of modern debate over *Robinson Crusoe*. On the one hand are those who see Crusoe predominantly in political and economic terms. These scholars are perhaps best represented by two works: Ian Watt's *The Rise of the Novel* (Berkeley and Los Angeles, 1957) and Maximillian Novak's *Economics and the Fiction of Daniel Defoe* (Berkeley and Los Angeles, 1962). On the other hand are two works that strive to offset Crusoe as *homo economicus* by demonstrating the place of *Robinson Crusoe* in the context of seventeenth- and eighteenth-century spiritual writings—biography, guide literature, sermon, autobiography, and the like. These two studies are G. A. Starr's *Defoe and Spiritual Autobiography* (Princeton, 1965) and J. Paul Hunter's *The Reluctant Pilgrim* (Baltimore, 1966). A third position, one that attempts to honor and profit from these two major tendencies and yet to stake out phenomenological claims independent of ideological commitment, is that of John J. Richetti's *Defoe's Narratives: Situations and Structures* (Oxford, 1975).

My hope in the comparison between Crusoe and January Marlow is obviously to compare and contrast attitudes, not to judge the characters morally. Like Richetti, I think it possible and only fair to accommodate Crusoe the colonial entrepreneur and Crusoe the convert to Puritan Christianity. At the same time, I am more persuaded by Watt and Novak than by Starr and Hunter, and my convictions will quite properly emerge. I should also state that I am primarily interested in the psychology of Crusoe rather than in the intentions of Defoe or the literary traditions so persuasively traced and laid out by Starr and Hunter. In my view, Crusoe's psychology must be understood as that of genuinely converted Puritan capitalist, and in my discussion this imbalance between *genus* and *differentiae* is quite conscious.

4. Muriel Spark, *Robinson* (New York: Avon, n.d.). All parenthical references are to this edition.

5. See Richetti, *Defoe's Narratives*, p. 31: "The real task of [Defoe's] kind of narrative seems to be not the development of a new self but the discovery or establishment of an environment where the self can emerge without blame as a response to reality rather than as the creator of it." Richetti is ambiguous here but seems to be talking of Defoe, more than of Crusoe, as presenter of a self in blameless response to a given reality. I should like to use Richetti's language to paraphrase an important point in the present study: January Marlow's narrative accentuates the new self who differs from the journal writer. That new self is a function of the play among January's preisland self, her journal notes, her present narrative, her involved responses (in each case) to reality, and her role (in each case) as creator of reality. These aspects of self will become clearer in chapter 4, below, but for the moment I hope it is clear that I find Crusoe relatively static, January consciously dynamic. And if it is asked how I can assert that Crusoe experiences religious conversion and yet remains essentially changeless, I must say that conversion might more accurately be called reversion to that for which he is destined: *we* see where he has been going, even

if he does not. He circles and goes back home to tell us what is over with, in the telling. January also returns home but never ceases to reflect on the ceaseless vicissitudes of her inner-outer experience.

6. Some clarification may be in order here. As I read these novels, both Crusoe and January are true believers. At the same time, it is obvious to me that Crusoe's faith and his earthly lot—his earthly success—never have occasion seriously to trouble each other but seem in fact to buttress each other. This is a happiness devoutly to be sought and in no way signifies hypocrisy; but without in the least questioning Crusoe's religious convictions, I am compelled to find them too easily acceded to, only superficially appraised. For this reason I find his material progress conveniently sanctified—rather than radically tested—by his faith. On the other hand, January constantly examines the implications of her belief and emerges perhaps more committed than ever, because of the steady series of trials she experiences. Both castaways are tried, but January's circumstances emphasize discrepancy between her capacities and the fullness of reality and therefore stress *obstacles* to, not support for, sustained belief. For a telling case in point, see Umberto Eco's recent novel, *The Name of the Rose*, trans. William Weaver (New York, London, San Diego, 1983). Eco's fourteenth-century sleuths are Holmes and Watson in monks' clothing. Because the mystery that they attempt to solve turns out to be unexplained by their theories, they eventually lose their religious faith. Whatever postmodernist thesis Eco may have in mind, what he shows us in the monks' testing is that their belief could not have been very deep or strong if its validity depended upon human ability to understand the unknown. These monks are in fact only realists. January's belief is strengthened, but hardly because she comes to *understand* mystery.

7. This matter is not easy, as may be seen in the array of extranovelistic efforts—Spark's and her critics'—to make it plainer. In Frank Kermode, "The House of Fiction: Interviews with Seven English Novelists," *Partisan Review* 30 (Spring 1963): 79–82, for example, Spark separates "my novels" from that "absolute truth" in which she is interested: "What I write is not true—it is a pack of lies"—but a pack of lies "out of which a kind of truth emerges." On another occasion she refers to "the nevertheless idea" that she sees at the heart of her sensibility—the idea that something more can and must be said, and that it only *appears* to be irreconcilable with that to which it is added ("Edinburgh-born," *The New Statesman*, 10 August 1962, 180). Then in an interview with Philip Toynbee in the *Observer*, 7 November 1971, 73–74, Spark again nudges the question of truth: "I might claim to be the opposite of C. P. Snow in every possible way. He thinks he's a realist: I think *I'm* a realist and he's a complete fantasist." Her critics have picked up on these leads. Thus, Peter Kemp opens his book, *Muriel Spark* (London, 1974), p. 7, with a long quotation from "Edinburgh-born" and writes a fine chapter on Spark's economy-in-abundance. Alan Kennedy, *The Protean Self: Dramatic Action in Contemporary Fiction* (New York, 1974), pp. 151–211, begins his essay on Spark by borrowing G. Gregory Smith's term "Caledonian antisyzygy": "An antisyzygy is a union of opposites. It is not to be conceived of as a fusion of contraries in which the two lose their identities and become one, but as an existing together of mutual exclusives." Francis Russell Hart, "Region, Character, and Identity in Recent Scottish Fiction," *Virginia Quarterly Review* 43 (Autumn 1967): 597–613, had cited the term "Caledonian antisyzygy" and had noted that the Scot "finds in himself an extraordinary jostling of distinct identities." David Lodge, "The Uses and Abuses of Omniscience: Method and Meaning in Muriel Spark's *The Prime of Miss Jean Brodie*," *Critical Quarterly* 12 (Autumn 1970): 235–57, addresses the same problem (and implicitly takes on Swinden et al.) in defending Spark against the charge that she is somehow operating in what Sartre calls "bad faith" when she adopts an omniscience to convey some notion of her own faith. Karl Malkoff, *Muriel Spark*, Columbia Essays on Modern Writers Series (New York and London, 1968), p. 3, likewise

begins his study with an attempt to capture Spark's awareness of one-with-many. Ann B. Dobie, "Muriel Spark's Definition of Reality," *Critique* 12 (1970): 20–27, sees the naturalistic and the supernatural in Spark, and that reality in her books is a mixed thing. Josephine Jacobsen, "A Catholic Quartet," *The Christian Scholar* 47 (Summer 1964): 139–54, notes the "determination never to attempt the lifting of the material into the realm of the spiritual which belongs to a day after life." Spark's effort instead is "to incorporate the spiritual into the body of humanity." Carol Murphy, "A Spark of the Supernatural," *Approach* 60 (Summer 1966): 26–30, speaks of the difficulty of "juggling the worldly and the otherwordly," since modern readers expect the latter either not to show up or to be readily explained away. George Greene, "A Reading of Muriel Spark," *Thought* 43 (Autumn 1968): 393–407, examines Spark's "effort to distinguish between diverse levels of reality. It is here that technique fuses most specifically with metaphysics." Samuel Hynes, "The Prime of Muriel Spark," *Commonweal*, 23 February 1962, 562–63, 567–68, observes that Spark "offers no comfortably secular explanation for . . . events; her stories are more likely to create mystery than to explicate it, and she is content to leave the supernatural that way—Mysterious. The world of human experience is complex, and not ultimately explicable . . . and reality is odder than you think." Irving Malin, "The Deceptions of Muriel Spark," in *The Vision Obscured: Perceptions of Some Twentieth-Century Catholic Novelists*, ed. Melvin J. Friedman (New York, 1970), pp. 95–107, says that Spark "believes that our 'precise' plans cannot account for the 'eccentric event' which simultaneously shows human limitation and divine complexity. We cannot fathom cosmic meaning, but this spiritual fact is the very center of the Plan. Mrs. Spark, however, can present such painful, vague paradoxes by presenting the 'impossible' and the 'unnatural' *as possible and natural.* She can teach us by deception." Nancy A. J. Potter, "Muriel Spark: Transformer of the Commonplace," *Renascence* 17 (Spring 1965): 115–20, singles out several Spark characters who experience a change of vision. John Hazard Wildman, "Translated by Muriel Spark," in *Nine Essays in Modern Literature*, ed. Donald E. Stanford (Baton Rouge, 1965), pp. 129–44, observes that Spark "translates" some "vast abstractions into crisp, containing modern terms, never losing the necessary qualities of suggestiveness and humility." Finally, two recent works are quite sympathetic to the sacred-secular mixedness informing Spark's psychology. See Allan Massie, *Muriel Spark* (Edinburgh, 1979), esp. pp. 14–18, and Ruth Whittaker, *The Faith and Fiction of Muriel Spark* (New York, 1982), esp. pp. 3–5, 11–12.

8. It is also more than a Freudian matter, in my opinion, despite the careful Freudian readings of Malkoff, *Muriel Spark*, pp. 11–16, and of Carol B. Ohmann, "Muriel Spark's *Robinson*," *Critique* 8 (1965): 70–84. At the same time, I obviously endorse one Ohmann generalization: "*[Robinson]* stands as a primer to Mrs. Spark's later novels; it spells out in a round, unmistakable hand the essential nature of Mrs. Spark's moral vision and the strategy by which she works to persuade us of it." Agreed; but I think Freudianism essential neither to Spark's vision nor to her strategy. Nor is it clear why Whittaker thinks *Robinson* an account of Spark's "illness, conversion and adjustment to Catholicism" (*Faith and Fiction of Muriel Spark*, p. 53).

9. These observations do not imply that Muriel Spark is a phenomenologist or that my reading is phenomenological. Otherwise, however, I think my comments here are basically in agreement with those of Wolfgang Iser, *The Implied Reader: Patterns of Communication in Prose Fiction from Bunyan to Beckett* (Baltimore and London, 1974). I allude especially to Iser's final chapter, "The Reading Process: A Phenomenological Approach," pp. 274–94.

10. In this connection, see especially George Levine's admirably concise point that "All fiction is fiction," in his "Realism Reconsidered," in *The Theory of the Novel: New Essays*, ed. John Halperin (New York, London, Toronto, 1974), pp. 233–56.

CHAPTER 2. REALITY'S GENERIC AND STRUCTURAL RANGE

1. "My Conversion," *Twentieth Century* 170 (Autumn 1961); 58–63: "The Catholic Church for me is just a formal declaration of what I believe in any case. It's something to measure from" (p. 60). I take my thematic cue from this sort of remark. Others approach Spark differently. For example, Francis Russell Hart, *The Scottish Novel: From Smollett to Spark* (Cambridge, Mass., 1978), is concerned to establish the distinctive characteristics of Scottish fiction. He studies the works of some two hundred authors to define the tradition in question. Pp. 294–310 discuss Spark's novels. Or, again, Nina Auerbach emphasizes *The Prime of Miss Jean Brodie* in her book, *Communities of Women: An Idea in Fiction* (Cambridge, Mass., 1978), pp. 167–83. Auerbach's feminist reading stresses the difference between Spark's twentieth-century "community of women" and "communities" given us by Jane Austen, Charlotte Brontë, and other earlier writers. Such emphases are both interesting and instructive but are marginally pertinent to my own—as is mine to those. On the other hand, Whittaker, as her title makes clear, puts religion at the foundation of Spark's enterprise. See *Faith and Fiction of Muriel Spark*, esp. pp. 37–63, 79–81. As I have noted in my Introduction, my disagreement with Whittaker in this regard is largely a matter of emphasis.

2. Muriel Spark, *Memento Mori* (Cleveland and New York: World Publishing Co., 1960). All parenthetical references are to this edition.

3. This is the type of psychology studied by William F. Lynch, *Christ and Apollo: The Dimensions of the Literary Imagination* (New York, 1960).

4. Muriel Spark, *The Bachelors* (New York: Dell, 1964). All parenthetical references are to this edition.

5. See, again, Spark, "My Conversion": "I never think of myself as a Catholic when I'm writing because it's so difficult to think of myself as anything else. It's all instinctive" (p. 60). On the same point, see "Keeping It Short—Muriel Spark Talks About Her Books to Ian Gillham," *The Listener*, 24 September 1970: "Why did you feel you had to become a Catholic?" "I couldn't believe anything else. It didn't particularly appeal to me: it still doesn't, but I'm still a Catholic. If I could believe anything else, I would" (p. 412). On this point Massie cites the confusion of Alec Warner, in *Memento Mori*, and attempts a distinction between "human values" and "truth" (*Muriel Spark*, p. 27). Massie's intention is clear, but his terminology ironically demonstrates the difficulty of negotiating this Blakean psychology.

6. See Greene, "Reading of Muriel Spark," pp. 394, 395.

7. Even the best of critics can underestimate Spark's notion of the real, I believe. John Updike, who has regularly reviewed her novels and who obviously relishes her spare art, nevertheless (as we may say) manifests of late a certain impatience, an uneasiness at her disinclination to finish off what to an extrarealist must appear humanly unfinishable. See, for example, Updike's otherwise sympathetic reviews of *The Abbess of Crewe* (and other Spark novels after *The Mandelbaum Gate*)—*The New Yorker*, 6 January 1975, 76–78—and of *The Takeover*—*The New Yorker*, 29 November 1976, 166–174.

8. Muriel Spark, *The Ballad of Peckham Rye* (New York: Dell, 1964). All parenthetical references are to this edition.

9. In short, Spark earns the right to her narrator's last words in *Ballad*: "[Humphrey] saw the children playing there and the women coming home from work with their shopping-bags, the Rye for an instant looking like a cloud of green and gold, the people seeming to ride upon it, as you might say there was another world than this" (pp. 159–60). See also Stanford, "Work of Muriel Spark": "Miss Spark remarked how literally 'economic' the Catholic cosmography struck her as being. The skies and the aether were

populated with legions of spirits—instead of being just so much waste space"; but she "is careful not to overwork the imagination of the miraculous" (pp. 95, 96).

10. Muriel Spark, *The Mandelbaum Gate* (New York: Fawcett Crest, 1967). All parenthetical references are to this edition.

11. As might be expected, Swinden likes this novel best of all Spark books, but it, too, fails for him in the end: "Even where the facts are wanting, the truth must subsist" (*Unofficial Selves*, p. 229). Similarly, Patricia Stubbs, *Muriel Spark*, Writers and Their Work Series (London, 1973), likes *Mandelbaum Gate* as Spark's "most successful novel" for its realism—something to be taken seriously; the book avoids excessive "fantasy and wit" in favor of "a central seriousness and a concern to portray the world and individuals as they are, not to pattern them into convolutions to suit and titillate their creator" (p. 26). Warner Berthoff, "Fortunes of the Novel: Muriel Spark and Iris Murdoch," *Massachusetts Review* 8 (1967): 301–32, also equates the serious with the realistic: "Despite the larger, fuller design of *The Mandelbaum Gate*, we fall back once more onto the simplifying ground of stacked parable and trumped-up morality play where everything is preconceived and self-illustrating and the risky options of actual life are never really entered into. . . . At the center, instead of a graspable action of love, faith, participation in destiny, Muriel Spark gives us her sharp, definite, restrictive ideas about these things and about the effect their presence or absence has upon individual men and women" (p. 313). The question begging buried in Berthoff's terms "actual life" and "restrictive ideas" is of course a prominent issue in the present study.

12. Whittaker is confused about this certificate *ex machina* (*Faith and Fiction of Muriel Spark*, p. 77). She takes it to be a forgery and supposes the irony to reside in the Church's disinclination to investigate, to take its rules seriously. In fact, the baptismal certificate is a copy of Clegg's genuine certificate. He was in fact baptized. The irony is, then, that Clegg—a Christian married to a non-Christian—is automatically eligible to appeal to "the Pauline Privilege," according to which his marriage is not recognized by the Church. Miss Rickward's ill will has led her to accomplish what she had meant to prevent. As Mortimer notes, in *Memento Mori*, "If you look for one thing . . . you frequently find another." Presumably such an outcome sours Swinden, Stubbs, and Berthoff, but it assuredly contributes to Spark's view that realms of agency work together to unpredictable ends, irrespective of human agents' intentions. See R. Kugelman, "Pauline Privilege," *New Catholic Encyclopedia*, 1967 ed.

13. This tendency to somberness and darkness is specified well in Velma Bourgeois Richmond, "The Darkening Vision of Muriel Spark," *Critique* 15 (1973): 71–85. Richmond focuses on *The Public Image*, *The Driver's Seat*, and *Not to Disturb*.

14. Muriel Spark, *The Girls of Slender Means* (New York: Avon, n.d.). All parenthetical references are to this edition.

15. Allan Casson, "Muriel Spark's *The Girls of Slender Means*," *Critique* 7 (Spring-Summer 1965): 94–96, not only writes a perceptive review of this novel but thoughtfully identifies most of the sources of Joanna's poetry recitations.

16. Anthony Burgess, *The Novel Now: A Student's Guide to Contemporary Fiction* (London, 1967), p. 131, lists Nicholas's notebook among the works of Muriel Spark.

17. On the sprinkling of voices throughout the narrative, as well as on the achieving of distance within a short and seemingly intimate work and on the adroit managing of repetition, see George Soule, "Must a Novelist Be an Artist?" *Carleton Miscellany* 5 (Spring 1964): 92–98.

18. Other critics have remarked on not so much a coldness as a noncommittal tendency to promote pensiveness in the reader. Thus, Updike, "Between a Wedding and a Funeral," *The New Yorker*, 14 September 1963, 192, says that Spark's novels, "like detective stories, . . . pose puzzles temporarily; like parables, they pose puzzles finally." Soule traces this effect to Spark's art of ironic distancing ("Must a Novelist Be an Artist?"

p. 97). Malin states that Spark "attempts to capture . . . those events which are so
extraordinary that they demonstrate the beautiful complexity of cosmic design. . . . She
is not content . . . to accept human relationships as clear or rational" ("Deceptions of
Muriel Spark," p. 95). Renata Adler, on the other hand, while she admires Spark's skill
in this novel, is, I believe, blind to the positive value of Nicholas's eventual choice.
Several times in her six pages, Adler speaks of Nicholas's "retreat"—as if his vocation
were an escape, an entirely negative event. See Adler, "Muriel Spark," in *On Contempo-*
rary Literature, ed. Richard Kostelanetz, expanded ed. (New York, 1969), pp. 591–96.
    19. Muriel Spark, *The Prime of Miss Jean Brodie* (New York: Dell, 1964). All paren-
thetical references are to this edition.
    20. Perhaps more criticism has been devoted to *The Prime of Miss Jean Brodie* than to
any other Spark novel; and most critics touch in some way upon this troubling ending and
its implications. Lodge, "Uses and Abuses of Omniscience," uses the omniscient point of
view in this book as his means of getting at Spark's duality. Kermode, "Muriel Spark," in
his *Modern Essays* (London, 1971), pp. 267–72, stresses Spark's "unremittingly Catholic"
sensibility but notes as well her delight in "mess." Hart speaks thus of Sandy's predicament: "She escapes, we might say, from a regional self not hers to a universal with which
she is evidently not at peace; or she flies from a false regional identity to a true one"
("Region, Character, and Identity," p. 608). And of course we recall Spark's "Edinburgh-
born" and Kemp's first chapter of *Muriel Spark* for their references to her "nevertheless
idea," as well as Kennedy's incisive adoption in *Protean Self* of the term "Caledonian
antisyzygy." Edinburgh as emblematic of split values is also important to Philip E. Ray,
"Jean Brodie and Edinburgh: Personality and Place in Murial [sic] Spark's *The Prime of*
Miss Jean Brodie," *Studies in Scottish Literature* 13 (1978): 24–31. Garry S. Laffin, "Muriel
Spark's Portrait of the Artist as a Young Girl," *Renascence* 24 (Summer 1972): 213–23,
also emphasizes that the artist judges Sandy as Sandy judges Jean, with the result that the
book is ambiguous and paradoxical at the bar-clutching end. Finally, Harrison, Greene,
and Jacobsen make considerable use of this book in establishing their own views of Spark's
duality. Greene, especially, is noteworthy in this regard: "In [Spark's] world the central
test is training oneself to accept and thereby to cope with . . . the ironies of God"
("Reading of Muriel Spark," p. 406). Massie is acute in discussing Sandy's leading part,
her antisolipsism, and her uneasy living with her choice (*Muriel Spark*, pp. 45–51).
    21. Muriel Spark, *The Driver's Seat* (New York: Knopf, 1970). All parenthetical
references are to this edition. In her "Keeping It Short" interview, Spark comments on
the mood of *The Driver's Seat*: "I frightened myself by writing it, but I just had to go on. I
gave myself a terrible fright with it. I had to go into hospital to finish it" (p. 413).
    22. Appropriate here are the remarks of Kermode, "Sheerer Spark," *The Listener*, 24
September 1970, 425: "Apart from a few swipes at heresy . . . there is nothing here to
remind one of the writer's religious plots. Nor . . . is there much to encourage those who
think of Mrs. Spark as a light comic novelist." Whittaker is excellent on the frightening,
severe detachment of the narrator in *Driver's Seat*; see *Faith and Fiction of Muriel Spark*,
esp. pp. 96–97, 117–19, 140–42.
    23. Kermode, "Sheerer Spark," separates Spark from postmodernism by noting that
she "has studied Robbe-Grillet with care and decided that his methods, considered in
isolation from the anti-metaphysical propositions he advances to support their general
validity, are useful if you want to present obsessed or manic states. But she herself has
always been obsessed by plot, and has devoted a great deal of original thought to it"
(p. 425). Spark's experimentalism as distinct from that of Robbe-Grillet as well as from
realistic practice is also the subject of my article "After Marabar: Reading Forster, Robbe-
Grillet, Spark," *Iowa Review* 5 (Winter 1974): 120–26.
    24. Muriel Spark, *The Hothouse by the East River* (New York: Viking, 1973). All
parenthetical references are to this edition. Burgess, *Novel Now*, p. 131, lists "The Hot

House on the East River. 1964" among Spark's books. Careless indexing rooted in knowledge of Spark's work in progress very likely accounts for this item.

25. See, for example, Derwent May, "Holy Outrage," *The Listener,* 1 March 1973, p. 284: "The pleasure of interpreting [the parable of Purgatory] survives only to the point where you think you've probably got it right. After all, one doesn't believe any of it: and that thought once entertained, one wishes as much as Paul does at the beginning that Elsa's shadow would go away. What we want from Miss Spark is her worldly wisdom." As we have seen, May is not alone in knowing and demanding what he wants.

26. Others have noted the Purgatory point. See, for example, May, "Holy Outrage," pp. 283–84; Kemp, *Muriel Spark,* pp. 142, 145–46; and Jonathan Raban, "On Losing the Rabbit," *Encounter* 40 (May 1973): 84.

27. "My Conversion," p. 60.

28. Kermode, "House of Fiction", pp. 80–81.

29. On the creative powers and human limits of the imagination, see also pp. 38, 111–12, 116, and 131–33, among other references in *Hothouse.*

CHAPTER 3. COMIC TEXTURE: ECHOES GOLDEN TO LEADEN

1. This observation has been made somewhat differently by Frank Baldanza, "Muriel Spark and the Occult," *Wisconsin Studies in Contemporary Literature* 6 (1965): 190–203. Speaking of Spark's first seven novels, Baldanza notes that while her characters cannot all be said to be religious, the supernatural plays large parts in five of these novels. But "the author's main interest does not lie so much in the solution as in the reactions of various characters to the mystery" or moral problem set up in the novels. Supernatural forces do not cause the moral problems; human failings are the causes (pp. 191–92).

2. Massie discusses perceptively the "betrayals" of Charmian by Jean Taylor (*Muriel Spark,* pp. 26–27) and of Jean Brodie by Sandy (pp. 50–51). His purpose is to distinguish religious motivation from worldly motivation. He rightly finds such tidy separation impossible.

3. I am well aware of the vagueness of reference in such terms as "one" and "one's" as I drop them here. In chapter 4 I will take a closer look at the tangle of author, narrator, character, and reader merely hinted at in the present passage.

4. In her admirable reading of *Memento Mori,* Whittaker (*Faith and Fiction of Muriel Spark,* pp. 53–58) finds this book "pessimistic" because the characters do not change but merely manifest who they were before the story began. While it is true that the characters do not change, I have tried to suggest how the long view qualifies such pessimistic response as would be appropriate to a strictly realistic text.

5. Muriel Spark, *The Abbess of Crewe* (New York: Viking, 1974). All parenthetical references are to this edition.

6. The values of mirrors and self-reflection will also be more extensively discussed in the next chapter. Spark is obviously intrigued by the motives, processes, and consequences of attempts at self-invention.

7. Muriel Spark, *The Takeover* (London: Macmillan, 1976). All parenthetical references are to this edition.

8. Muriel Spark, *Territorial Rights* (New York: Coward, McCann & Geoghegan, 1979). All parenthetical references are to this edition.

9. On Spark's interest in money and the moneyed, Whittaker is instructive in referring to "religious substitutes" (*Faith and Fiction of Muriel Spark,* p. 85) and to Spark's liking Alexandra and Maggie (p. 86). Massie refers to worshiping of "idols" in *The Takeover.* "Time substance is invisible. Earthly things will pass away . . . the new cults are false religion. When people cease to believe in God, they do not believe in nothing; they believe in anything. And this is our modern position" (*Muriel Spark,* p. 87).

10. This aura, which I see as comic texture decidedly reserved, Whittaker finds not pessimistic, unlike her reading of *Memento Mori* (see note 4 above). "Like Waugh's, hers is still a Christian perspective [despite the detachment in *Territorial Rights*], which, paradoxically, saves her from pessimism, since it would be more disturbing to her if a godless world were virtuous. This accounts for her light-hearted approach, for her resolute seizing on what is funny or beautiful or ripe for satire" (*Faith and Fiction of Muriel Spark*, p. 87.) I think Spark can appreciate, on their own terms, the children of darkness, but that her own dual vision qualifies that appreciation, which is more subdued in *Territorial Rights* than in *Memento Mori*.

11. Muriel Spark, *The Only Problem* (New York: G. P. Putnam's Sons, 1984). All parenthetical references are to this edition.

12. On this controversy, see the extensive notes to chapters 1 and 2, above. See also John Updike's review of *The Only Problem*: "A Romp with Job," *The New Yorker*, 23 July 1984, 104–7. Updike, as always, admires Spark's style and her concern with the creative act but thinks she makes only a sketchy start on the "good and profound novel [that] lies scattered among the inklings" of this book (p. 107). The same confusion underlies Massie's otherwise happy Johnsonian discussion of wit, for the purpose of finding Spark's minor place (*Muriel Spark*, pp. 90–96). Whittaker regards Spark's lack of overt emotion as a flaw (*Faith and Fiction of Muriel Spark*, esp. pp. 12–17), but at the same time Whittaker—rightly, in my opinion—undercuts her own objection: "Her comedy, while suggesting a superior attitude to the rest of mankind, is really a method of covering her fearful vision in which she, too, is on the wrong side of the abyss. Thus the novels are rich in comic distractions, and the sheer pleasure of Mrs. Spark's wit and humour often deflects the reader from their more serious implications" (p. 145). Exactly: one must work with such implications, which are not those of a "minor" writer or of an unfeeling one.

CHAPTER 4. TAKING AND MAKING: THE PAGE AS LOOKING GLASS

1. Muriel Spark, *The Comforters* (New York: Avon, 1965). All parenthetical references are to this edition.

2. Spark had doubts about writing fiction rather than poetry: "Before I could even write the novel, I had to write a novel about somebody writing a novel, to see if it was aesthetically valid, and if I could do it and live with myself—writing such a low thing as a novel" ("Keeping It Short," p. 412).

3. Baldanza puts the matter a bit differently. He sees the supernatural giving way to naturalism in Spark's development, but the two combined in such novels as *The Comforters*. In this novel, he notes, are "three obsessions: one based on mundane assumptions; one concerning supernatural intervention; the other, supposedly occult, is patently false" ("Muriel Spark and the Occult," p. 195).

4. On this controversial point of whether Spark's economy is artful or not, note the endorsement of her art by Malcolm Bradbury, "Muriel Spark's Fingernails," in *Possibilities: Essays on the State of the Novel* (London, Oxford, New York, 1973), pp. 247–55. He lays stress on what she deliberately chooses not to tell us and on what she does not wish to do. A contrary view is expressed by Updike, "Seeresses," *The New Yorker*, 29 November 1976, 166: "The generous . . . curve of her career raises the ungrateful question 'Is that all?' and her so conspicuous gifts open to the critic the tempting option of judicious disappointment. Her recent fiction has seemed curt and distracted, though in every sentence she brings us still a sense of art, of strict intention." Because Bradbury's view goes more readily with the given and is less inclined to make demands, I think Bradbury is more to the critical point. As the experience of Jean Taylor, Nicholas, and others makes clear, Spark has trouble communicating on her own terms.

5. On omniscience, see again Lodge, "Uses and Abuses of Omniscience," pp. 237–38.

6. In an interview with Mary Holland—"The Prime of Muriel Spark," *Observer* (Color Supplement), 17 October 1965, 10—Spark would seem to deny this point. She insists that she always knows her characters are fictions and she says that they don't take over, as some writers say of their characters. I am sure that she is always in charge and is aware of her work as fiction, but I stand by my contention that characters come to cooperate with their creators.

7. Ann B. Dobie and Carl Wooton, "Spark and Waugh: Similarities by Coincidence," *The Midwest Quarterly* 13 (July 1972): 423, make an interesting comparison between *The Comforters* and Evelyn Waugh's *The Ordeal of Gilbert Pinfold:* "Both novels have a novelist as protagonist, and both novelists hear disembodied voices which have some relationship to characters in a novel not yet written. The plots of both novels deal extensively with the mystery of the source and the occasions of the voices and, ultimately, with their meaning and their proper disposition. . . . Both [authors] seem coincidentally at approximately the same time [1957] to have been concerned with the problems caused by an artistic imagination which encounters the possibility of a reality that seems neither contained nor defined by any conventional conception of the objective real."

8. Muriel Spark, *The Public Image* (New York: Ballantine Books, n.d.). All parenthetical references are to this edition.

9. Muriel Spark, *Not to Disturb* (New York: Viking, 1972). All parenthetical references are to this edition.

10. See, on this issue, Kermode, "Foreseeing the Unforeseen," *The Listener,* 11 November 1971, 657: "The conceit [in *Not to Disturb*] is founded on the proposition that since the end of a fable is known, in its essence if not in its accidents, from the beginning of the telling, it follows that the telling of it in a manner which admits this fact will help to explain the nature of fictions, the kind of relation we may expect them to have to truth."

11. Whittaker's analysis of *Not to Disturb* as "plot" is exemplary (*Faith and Fiction of Muriel Spark*, pp. 119–21). She also provides insight into the topic of Spark's "economy" (pp. 126–27, 137–45).

12. On the value of language in this novel, see Kemp, *Muriel Spark*, pp. 139–40.

13. In her *Observer* interview with Toynbee, Spark says that she seeks "compression and obliqueness." She admires "Robbe-Grillet, certainly, though I don't in the least accept the theory of the anti-novel. His novels have a special kind of drama—perhaps the drama of exact observation" (p. 73). On this Robbe-Grillet matter, see also my "After Marabar," pp. 120–26, as well as Massie, *Muriel Spark*, p. 69, and Whittaker, *Faith and Fiction of Muriel Spark*, pp. 6–11. Spark's books suggest that "absurd" for her means "lacking sense" rather than "operating in a void." On this point, see Whittaker, p. 81.

14. Muriel Spark, *Loitering with Intent* (New York: Coward, McCann & Geoghegan, 1981). All parenthetical references are to this edition.

15. As we have seen, many critics want Spark to write a different kind of book. Whittaker likes *Loitering* where she finds it warmer and more overtly emotional than much recent Spark fiction (*Faith and Fiction of Muriel Spark*, 121–25), and indeed Whittaker expresses regularly a lack of sympathy for that very coolness which Fleur advocates and Spark practices; see esp. pp. 77–79, 128–29, 133, 150–51. In striving to express her preferences, Whittaker is sometimes led into an illogical distinction between "moral" and "religious," "moral" and "divine" (pp. 106, 110, 115, 116). Updike, "Fresh from the Forties," *The New Yorker,* 8 June 1981, 149, likewise both relishes *Loitering* for its "new verve and expansiveness" compared to Spark's books since *Jean Brodie* and hopes that she will open up in the future. I have stated throughout this study that I should like to encourage more readers to see and appreciate what Spark succeeds in writing inten-

tionally, and to refrain from applying to her books the realistic grid that does not apply to them.

16. Spark is quite modest about her work. "I decided that I was writing minor novels deliberately, and not major novels. An awful lot of people are telling me [this in 1963] to write big long novels—Mrs. Tolstoy, you know—and I decided it is no good filling a little glass with a pint of beer" (Kermode, "House of Fiction," p. 80). Kermode has continued to wed this throwaway attitude with Spark's importance: "Muriel Spark, perhaps the most accomplished and ambitious novelist we have, is successful in every way but one: people will not take her seriously. . . . Mrs. Spark is serious in a manner that recognises and requires frivolity, and where we see frivolity we feel we are excused from seriousness. She is frivolous about death, about normal chronology, the ordinary routines of narrative and plot. There is, on the one hand, the gay contingency of ordinary language and behaviour, and on the other the dogmatic simplicity of the divine facts of life which that language and behaviour distort" ("God's Plots," *The Listener,* 7 December 1967, 759). Finally, Spark herself, in her Blashfield Foundation address, sums up her novelistic endeavor both in its traditional ties and in its break with tradition: "I only say that the art and literature of sentiment and emotion, however beautiful in itself, however striking in its depiction of actuality, has to go. It cheats us into a sense of involvement with life and society, but in reality it is a segregated activity. In its place I advocate the arts of satire and of ridicule. And I see no other living art form for the future. . . . I would like to see in all forms of arts and letters . . . a less impulsive generosity, a less indignant representation of social injustice, and a more deliberate cunning, a more decisive undermining of what is wrong. I would like to see less emotion and more intelligence in these efforts to impress our hearts and minds" ("The Desegregation of Art," *Proceedings of the American Academy of Arts and Letters and the National Institute of Arts and Letters,* 2d ser., no. 21 [1971]: 24, 25). She may decline the part of "Mrs. Tolstoy," but we would be plainly foolish to underrate either her economical moral intent or the effectiveness of her acerbic art.

Select Bibliography

This Bibliography is virtually limited to works cited in the present study. For nearly all reviews, other Spark writings—stories, poems, essays—and other interviews, and criticism, including doctoral dissertations, see Thomas T. Tominaga and Wilma Schneidermeyer, *Iris Murdoch and Muriel Spark: A Bibliography*. The Scarecrow Author Bibliographies, No. 27 (Metuchen, N.J.: The Scarecrow Press, Inc., 1976).

MURIEL SPARK'S NOVELS

In England Muriel Spark's novels through *Territorial Rights* were published in cloth by Macmillan in London. *Loitering with Intent* and *The Only Problem* have been published by the Bodley Head Press. In the United States chronological clothbound publication (New York) is as follows: *The Comforters, Robinson, Memento Mori, The Ballad of Peckham Rye, The Bachelors,* and *The Prime of Miss Jean Brodie* were published by Lippincott. *The Girls of Slender Means, The Mandelbaum Gate, The Public Image,* and *The Driver's Seat* were published by Knopf. *Not to Disturb, The Hothouse by the East River, The Abbess of Crewe,* and *The Takeover* were published by Viking. *Territorial Rights* and *Loitering with Intent* were published by Coward, McCann & Geoghegan. *The Only Problem* was published by G. P. Putnam's Sons. Penguin is currently publishing paperback editions in England and the United States. Other United States paperback editions are those by Avon, Ballantine, Bantam, Dell, Fawcett Crest, and Meridian (World). The following alphabetical list includes for each novel both the date of first publication and the date of the edition used in the present study.

The Abbess of Crewe (1974). New York: Viking, 1974.

The Bachelors (1960). New York: Dell, 1964.

The Ballad of Peckham Rye (1960). New York: Dell, 1964.

The Comforters (1957). New York: Avon, 1965.

The Driver's Seat (1970). New York: Knopf, 1970.

The Girls of Slender Means (1963). New York: Avon, n.d.

The Hothouse by the East River (1973), New York: Viking, 1973.

Loitering with Intent (1981). New York: Coward, McCann & Geoghegan, 1981.

The Mandelbaum Gate (1965), New York: Fawcett Crest, 1967.

Memento Mori (1959). Cleveland and New York: World Publishing Co., 1960.

Not to Disturb (1971). New York: Viking, 1972.

The Only Problem (1984). New York: G. P. Putnam's Sons, 1984.

The Prime of Miss Jean Brodie (1961), New York: Dell, 1964.

The Public Image (1968). New York: Ballantine Books, n.d.

Robinson (1958). New York: Avon, n.d.

The Takeover (1976). London: Macmillan, 1976.

Territorial Rights (1979). New York: Coward, McCann & Geoghegan, 1979.

ADDITIONAL SPARK WRITINGS CITED

"The Desegregation of Art." The Annual Blashfield Foundation Address. *Proceedings of the American Academy of Arts and Letters and the National Institute of Arts and Letters.* 2d ser., no. 21, pp. 21–27, New York: Spiral Press, 1971.

"Edinburgh-born." *New Statesman* 64 (10 August 1962): 180.

"My Conversion." *Twentieth Century* 170 (Autumn 1961): 58–63.

INTERVIEWS WITH MURIEL SPARK

Gillham, Ian. "Keeping It Short—Muriel Spark Talks About Her Books to Ian Gillham." *The Listener,* 84 (24 September 1970): 411–13.

Holland, Mary. "The Prime of Muriel Spark." *Observer* (Color Supplement), 17 October 1965, pp. 8–10.

Kermode, Frank. "The House of Fiction: Interviews with Seven English Novelists." *Partisan Review* 30 (Spring 1963): 61–82. The Spark interview occupies pp. 79–82.

Toynbee, Philip. [Conversation with Muriel Spark]. *Observer* (Color Supplement), 7 November 1971, pp. 73–74.

RELEVANT BOOKS AND ARTICLES ON SPARK

Adler, Renata. "Muriel Spark." *On Contemporary Literature.* Expanded ed. Edited by Richard Kostelanetz. New York: Avon Books, 1969.

Auerbach, Nina. *Communities of Women: An Idea in Fiction.* Cambridge: Harvard University Press, 1978.

Baldanza, Frank. "Muriel Spark and the Occult." *Wisconsin Studies in Contemporary Literature* 6 (1965): 190–203.

Berthoff, Warner. "Fortunes of the Novel: Muriel Spark and Iris Murdoch." *Massachusetts Review* 8 (1967): 301–32.

Blodgett, Harriet. "Desegregated Art by Muriel Spark." *International Fiction Review* 3 (January 1976): 25–29.

Bradbury, Malcolm. "Muriel Spark's Fingernails." *Critical Quarterly* 14 (1972): 241–50. Reprinted in Bradbury's *Possibilities: Essays on the State of the Novel,* pp. 247–55. London, Oxford, New York: Oxford University Press, 1973.

Burgess, Anthony. *The Novel Now: A Student's Guide to Contemporary Fiction.* London: Faber & Faber, 1967.

Casson, Allan. "Muriel Spark's *The Girls of Slender Means.*" *Critique* 7 (Spring–Summer 1965): 94–96.

Dobie, Ann B. "Muriel Spark's Definition of Reality." *Critique* 12 (1970): 20–27.

———. "*The Prime of Miss Jean Brodie:* Muriel Spark Bridges the Credibility Gap." *Arizona Quarterly* 25 (Autumn 1969): 217–28.

———, and Carl Wooton. "Spark and Waugh: Similarities by Coincidence." *Midwest Quarterly* 13 (July 1972): 423–34.

Eco, Umberto. *The Name of the Rose.* Translated by William Weaver. New York, London, San Diego: Harcourt, Brace, Jovanovich, 1983.

Enright, D. J. "Public Doctrine and Private Judging." *New Statesman.* 15 October 1965, pp. 563, 566.

Feinstein, Elaine. "Loneliness Is Cold." *London Magazine.* n.s. 11 (February–March 1972): 177–80.

Gable, Sister Mariella. "Prose Satire and the Modern Christian Temper." *American Benedictine Review* 11 (March–June 1960): 29–30, 33.

Gifford, Douglas. "Modern Scottish Fiction." *Studies in Scottish Literature* 13 (1978): 250–73.

Greene, George. "A Reading of Muriel Spark." *Thought* 43 (1968): 393–407.

Grosskurth, Phyllis. "The World of Muriel Spark: Spirits or Spooks?" *Tamarack Review* 39 (Spring 1966): 62–67.

Grumbach, Doris. Review of *The Mandelbaum Gate,* by Muriel Spark. *America* 113 (23 October 1965): 474–78.

Harrison, Bernard. "Muriel Spark and Jane Austen." In *The Modern English Novel: The Reader, the Writer, and the Work,* edited by Gabriel Josipovici, pp. 225–51. London: Open Books; New York: Barnes & Noble, 1976.

Hart, Francis Russell. "Region, Character, and Identity in Recent Scottish Fiction." *Virginia Quarterly Review* 43 (1967): 597–613.

———. *The Scottish Novel: From Smollett to Spark.* Cambridge: Harvard University Press, 1978.

Holloway, John. "Narrative Structure and Text Structure: Isherwood's *A Meeting by the River* and Muriel Spark's *The Prime of Miss Jean Brodie.*" *Critical Inquiry* 1 (March 1975): 581–604.

Hoyt, Charles Alva. "Muriel Spark: The Surrealist Jane Austen." In *Contemporary British Novelists,* edited by Charles Shapiro, pp. 125–43. Carbondale and Edwardsville: Southern Illinois University Press, 1965.

Hunter, J. Paul. *The Reluctant Pilgrim: Defoe's Emblematic Method and Quest for Form in* Robinson Crusoe. Baltimore: The Johns Hopkins Press, 1966.

Hynes, Joseph. "After Marabar: Reading Forster, Robbe-Grillet, Spark." *Iowa Review* 5 (Winter 1974): 120–26.

Hynes, Samuel. "The Prime of Muriel Spark." *Commonweal* 75 (23 February 1962): 562–63, 567–68.

Iser, Wolfgang. *The Implied Reader: Patterns of Communication in Prose Fiction from Bunyan to Beckett.* Baltimore and London: The Johns Hopkins University Press, 1974.

Jacobsen, Josephine. "A Catholic Quartet." *Christian Scholar* 47 (1964): 139–54.

Karl, Frederick R. *A Reader's Guide to the Contemporary English Novel.* Rev. ed. New York: Farrar, Straus & Giroux, 1972.

Kelleher, V. M. K. "The Religious Artistry of Muriel Spark." *Critical Review* (Melbourne) 18 (1976): 79–82.

Kemp, Peter. *Muriel Spark.* Novelists and Their World Series. London: Paul Elek, 1974.

Kennedy, Alan. *The Protean Self: Dramatic Action in Contemporary Fiction.* New York: Columbia University Press, 1974. To the point of the present study is chapter 4: "Cannibals, Okapis, and Self-Slaughter in the Fiction of Muriel Spark." pp. 151–211.

Kermode, Frank. "The British Novel Lives." *Atlantic Monthly* 230 (July 1972): 85–88.

———. *Continuities.* London: Routledge & Kegan Paul, 1968. Reprints two reviews under the titles of "To *The Girls of Slender Means*" and "Muriel Spark's *Mandelbaum Gate,*" pp. 202–16.

———. "Diana of the Crossroads." *New Statesman* 91 (4 June 1976): 746–47.

———. "Foreseeing the Unforeseen." *The Listener* 86 (11 November 1971): 657–58.

———. "God's Plots." *The Listener* 78 (7 December 1967): 759–60.

———. "Judgement in Venice." *The Listener* 101 (26 April 1979): 584–85.

———. *Modern Essays.* London: Collins Fontana Books, 1971. Reprints the two reviews in *Continuities* (above) and a review of *The Public Image,* pp. 267–83.

————. "Sheerer Spark." *The Listener* 84 (24 September 1970); 425, 427.

Keyser, Barbara Y. "Muriel Spark, Watergate, and the Mass Media." *Arizona Quarterly* 32 (1976): 146–53.

Kugelman, R. "Pauline Privilege." *New Catholic Encyclopedia.* 1976 ed.

Laffin, Garry S. "Muriel Spark's Portrait of the Artist as a Young Girl." *Renascence* 24 (Summer 1972): 213–23.

Levine, George. "Realism Reconsidered." In *The Theory of the Novel: New Essays,* edited by John Halperin, pp. 233–256. New York, London, Toronto: Oxford University Press, 1974.

Lodge, David. "The Uses and Abuses of Omniscience: Method and Meaning in Muriel Spark's *The Prime of Miss Jean Brodie.*" *Critical Quarterly* 12 (1970): 235–57. Reprinted in Lodge's *The Novelist at the Crossroads and Other Essays on Fiction and Criticism,* pp. 119–44. London: Routledge & Kegan Paul, 1971.

Lynch, William F. *Christ and Apollo: The Dimensions of the Literary Imagination.* New York: Sheed and Ward, 1960.

Malin, Irving. "The Deceptions of Muriel Spark." In *The Vision Obscured: Perceptions of Some Twentieth-Century Catholic Novelists,* edited by Melvin J. Friedman, pp. 95–107. New York: Fordham University Press, 1970.

Malkoff, Karl. *Muriel Spark.* Columbia Essays on Modern Writers Series. New York and London: Columbia University Press, 1968.

Massie, Allan. *Muriel Spark.* Edinburgh: Ramsay Head Press, 1979.

May, Derwent. "Holy Outrage." *The Listener* 89 (1 March 1973): 283–84.

Mayne, Richard. "Fiery Particle: On Muriel Spark." *Encounter* 25 (December 1965): 61–68.

McBrien, William. "Muriel Spark: The Novelist as Dandy." In *Twentieth-Century Women Novelists,* edited by Thomas F. Staley, pp. 153–78. Totowa, N.J.: Barnes & Noble Books, 1982.

Murphy, Carol. "A Spark of the Supernatural." *Approach* 60 (Summer 1966): 26–30.

Novak, Maximillian. *Economics and the Fiction of Daniel Defoe.* Berkeley and Los Angeles: University of California Press, 1962.

Ohmann, Carol B. "Muriel Spark's *Robinson.*" *Critique* 8 (1965): 70–84.

Potter, Nancy A. J. "Muriel Spark: Transformer of the Commonplace." *Renascence* 17 (1965): 115–20.

Quinton, Anthony. Review of *The Ballad of Peckham Rye,* by Muriel Spark. *London Magazine* 7 (May 1960): 78–81.

————. Review of *Memento Mori,* by Muriel Spark. *London Magazine* 6 (September 1959): 84–88.

Raban, Jonathan. "On Losing the Rabbit." *Encounter* 40 (May 1973): 80–85.

————. "Vague Scriptures." *New Statesman* 82 (12 November 1971): 657–58.

Raven, Simon. "Heavens Below." *Spectator,* 20 September 1963, p. 354.

Ray, Philip E. "Jean Brodie and Edinburgh: Personality and Place in Murial [sic] Spark's *The Prime of Miss Jean Brodie.*" *Studies in Scottish Literature* 13 (1978): 24–31.

Richetti, John J. *Defoe's Narratives: Situations and Structures.* Oxford: The Clarendon Press, 1975.

Richmond, Velma Bourgeois. "The Darkening Vision of Muriel Spark." *Critique* 15 (1973): 71–85.

Schneider, Harold W. "A Writer in Her Prime: The Fiction of Muriel Spark." *Critique* 5 (1962): 28–45.

Sears, Sallie. "Too Many Voices." *Partisan Review* 31 (Summer 1964): 471, 473–75.

Soule, George. "Must a Novelist Be an Artist?" *Carleton Miscellany* 5 (Spring 1964): 92–98.

Stanford, Derek. *Muriel Spark: A Biographical and Critical Study* (includes a bibliography by Bernard Stone). Fontwell: Centaur Press, 1963.

———. "The Work of Muriel Spark: An Essay on Her Fictional Method." *Month* 28 (1962): 92–99. Reprinted in slightly altered form in Stanford's *Muriel Spark* (above).

Starr, G. A. *Defoe and Spiritual Autobiography.* Princeton: Princeton University Press, 1965.

Stubbs, Patricia. *Muriel Spark.* Writers and Their Work Series. Harlow: Longman for the British Council, 1973.

———. "Two Contemporary Views on Fiction: Iris Murdoch and Muriel Spark." *English* 23 (1974): 102–10.

Swinden, Patrick. *Unofficial Selves: Character in the Novel from Dickens to the Present Day.* London: Macmillan, 1973.

Thomas, Edward. Review of *The Driver's Seat,* by Muriel Spark. *London Magazine,* n.s. 10 (October 1970): 95–98.

Updike, John. "Between a Wedding and a Funeral." *The New Yorker* 39 (14 September 1963): 192–94.

———. "Creatures of the Air." *The New Yorker* 37 (30 September 1961): 161–67.

———. "Fresh from the Forties." *The New Yorker* 57 (8 June 1981): 148–56.

———. "A Romp with Job." *The New Yorker* 60 (23 July 1984): 104–7.

———. "Seeresses." *The New Yorker* 52 (29 November 1976): 164–74.

———. "Topnotch Witcheries." *The New Yorker* 50 (6 January 1975): 76–78.

Watt, Ian. *The Rise of the Novel: Studies in Defoe, Richardson and Fielding.* Berkeley and Los Angeles: University of California Press, 1957.

Whittaker, Ruth. *The Faith and Fiction of Muriel Spark*. New York: St. Martin's Press, 1982. This work incorporates Whittaker's essay, " 'Angels Dining at the Ritz': The Faith and Fiction of Muriel Spark." In *The Contemporary English Novel*, edited by Malcolm Bradbury and David Palmer, pp. 157–79. Stratford-upon-Avon Studies 18. New York: Holmes & Meier Publishers, Inc., 1980.

Wildman, John Hazard. "Translated by Muriel Spark." In *Nine Essays in Modern Literature*, edited by Donald E. Stanford, pp. 129–44. Baton Rouge: Louisiana State University Press, 1965.

Index

195